THE TENACIOUS SPY

The Story of
Major William Morris Jones

By

Karen Rempel Arthur

Walnut Hill Books

1

Rempel Arthur, Karen

The Tenacious Spy: The Story of Major William Morris Jones

ISBN-13: 978-1469966755

ISBN-10: 1469966751

1. War. 2. History. 3. Biography. 4. Adventure. 5. William Morris Jones. 6. War Hero. 7. Spy. 8. Military.

Contact: Walnut Hill Books
         walnuthillbooks@gmail.com

Cover photo courtesy of Bill Jones Jr.

CONTENTS

Prologue 6

Chapter 1 – In the Beginning 7
Chapter 2 – The Roots of War 9
Chapter 3 – Learning the Ropes................................. 12
Chapter 4 – Introduction to Battle............................. 16
Chapter 5 – An Canadian Embarrassment 23
Chapter 6 – Back in Full Swing 29
Chapter 7 – Hill 70.. 33
Chapter 8 – Bloody Passchendaele 36
Chapter 9 – Finishing the Job 39
Chapter 10 – Reconstituting....................................... 45
Chapter 11 – A Work Interlude................................... 49
Chapter 12 – Jones the Businessman 52
Chapter 13 – Sweetheart Appears.............................. 55
Chapter 14 – Elbow Flexing 62
Chapter 15 – With Nine Dollars in His Pocket........... 68
Chapter 16 – There's Always a Hitch........................ 81
Chapter 17 – Convolutions of Bureaucracy 85
Chapter 18 – Finally! 101
Chapter 19 – Into the Wild Blue 110
Chapter 20 – Orders to the Middle East.................... 112
Chapter 21 – The Middle East 117
Chapter 22 – Some Very Unusual Training.............. 121
Chapter 23 – The Country and the Players 125
Chapter 24 – Zdravo! 133
Chapter 25 - Amazing... 139
Chapter 26 – Let's get the Show on the Road........... 144
Chapter 27 – Checking out a Village 152
Chapter 28 – ZAVNOH 156

Chapter 29 – An Invitation 161
Chapter 30 – A Dicey Trip to Slovenia 163
Chapter 31 – Baza 20...170
Chapter 32 – Spy or Mole?..177
Chapter 33 – Churchill Speaks 179
Chapter 34 – The Battle of Zuzemberk 180
Chapter 35 – The Bridges at Zidani Most 186
Chapter 36 – Major William Jones vs General
                          Guido Cerruti 188
Chapter 37 – Plans...194
Chapter 38 – The British Problem 198
Chapter 39 – Autumn in Slovenia 200
Chapter 40 – The Battle Heats Up 203
Chapter 41 – The Month of Christmas 209
Chapter 42 – John Denvir...213
Chapter 43 – The Cat is out of the Bag 216
Chapter 44 – Bleak Winter, Empty Cupboards 225
Chapter 45 – A Very Long Walk................................240
Chapter 46 – Ten Days With Tito...............................247
Chapter 47 – Back to England 252
Chapter 48 – Home at Last!.......................................257
Chapter 49 – Jones the Farmer 261
Chapter 50 – Besides Farming....................................268
Chapter 51 – The Grand Garden Parties....................273
Chapter 52 – A Remarkable Invitation......................276
Chapter 53 – A Most Unforgettable Man 283

Epilogue...288

For Bill Jones Jr. who had a most remarkable father.

PROLOGUE

This is the story of a man, a Nova Scotian by birth, not very tall, but physically and mentally built of steel. After surviving the horrors of World War I, he met and married the charming Helen, ran his own real estate business, bamboozled his way into the RAF during World War II and made a monumental impact reporting to Britain's MO4 about his profoundly hush-hush activities.

The farm beside the meandering Welland River came later and the most satisfying achievement of his life, the birth of a son.

A man of charisma and presence, a keen interest in people and the world around him, he could do just about anything he set his hand to including a practical joke. He loved peace, but when pushed, took the bull by the horns, set his own personal safety aside and did what had to be done. He was tenacious and fearless. Absolutely fearless.

Regrettably he passed away before divulging the whole story but with the help of interviews, papers, letters and conjecture, here is a reconstruction of that amazing life.

Presenting Major William Morris Jones, a.k.a. 'Jonesy', 'Will', 'Bill', 'Billy', by his wife, Helen, as 'Nurts' and "Sweetheart," and "Dad" by his son Bill Jr.

CHAPTER 1 – IN THE BEGINNING

Digby, Nova Scotia residents, Frank and Margaret Jones, begat William Morris on August 12, 1895, an in-between child, sandwiched among Douglas, Helen and Cecil.

Frank, K.C. was a brilliant lawyer who graduated from Dalhousie University with the highest marks (97%) ever achieved in Canadian law to that date. With his tremendous memory, he knew the law inside out. His ability to quote every word written by Shakespeare made him a popular parlor entertainer. On the downside, he was domineering and greedy, a combination that drove him to financial success.

There was the family farm at Joggins Bridge, where little Billy flourished, and after his Bear River Hotel burned to the ground, he acquired another hotel in Digby.

An excellent lawyer and later a judge, Frank had no regard for human rights in the world sense. He understood individual rights as prescribed by law but had little comprehension of the rights of a people or nation, particularly the beleaguered, and this became a bone of contention between Frank and young Bill. They never understood each other.

Bill's mother, Margaret (Douglas) Milligan of Stanley, New Brunswick was a widow with three children, Jessie May, Margaret and Francis, when she and Frank married and produced the additional brood above.

When young Bill was old enough to roam alone, the local native Mi'kmaq children became his playmates. In fact, he romped through several ethnic groups including the dusky descendants of slaves who had fled north after the American Revolution. It was a happy mingling but he loved his solitude as much he enjoyed their company. Though a peaceful child, he was a born leader and organizer. He loved sports and always insisted on fair play, an outstanding characteristic that served him well.

Life was not all a frolic through the woods. His parents ensured that he attended school from 1901 to 1913 and Bill matriculated with a teacher's diploma at the ripe old age of 18. He taught school for a year (1913-14) at Masstown in north central Nova Scotia, then took a course at the Summer School of Science in Truro.

Teaching was an interim career. Bill's Presbyterian background, fueled by stories of Dr. Albert Schweitzer who gave up a brilliant music career to become and doctor and eventually set up a hospital in Lambaréné, French Equatorial Africa (now Gabon), inspired him to humanitarian service.

A second man Bill admired greatly was James Endicott. After graduating from the University of Manitoba's Wesley College in 1893, Endicott joined a new Methodist mission in Szechuan, China and served there until 1910.

Bill digested every nuance of their lives thus fertilizing his own concern for people dying of curable diseases, starving in far-off countries and lacking education and resources that he felt richer countries should provide. Bill Jones' dream was to become a medical missionary in Africa.

Frank Jones could not comprehend this strange son's dream. There was no money in it.

The village of Bear River from an old postcard. Bill Jones Jr. Collection.

CHAPTER 2 – THE ROOTS OF WAR

Bill Jones soon discovered there was no guarantee his dreams would be fulfilled. Suddenly, old events across the cold Atlantic came to nasty fruition. This is how it happened.

A settlement following the Franco-Prussian war (1870-1871) left France bothered over losing Alsace-Lorraine to Germany and anxious to regain their territory.

In 1879, Germany and Austria-Hungary entered The Dual Alliance as protection against Imperial Russia busy stock-piling armaments, then Austria-Hungary allied itself with Serbia to prevent Russia from gaining control of Serbia. Next Germany and Austria-Hungary allied themselves with Italy to prevent Italy from taking sides with Russia. In retaliation (1894), Russia allied itself with France leaving Europe straight-jacketed in treaty knots.

In 1904, the Entente Cordiale between France and Britain brought Britain into the debate. New lines formed. The Anglo-Russian Entente (1907) allied Britain and Russia, an arrangement influenced by Russia's Tsar Nicholas II, the first cousin of Britain's George V, marrying Princess Alix (Alexandra) of Hessedarmstadt, the great grand-daughter of Queen Victoria.

In 1907, Russia, France and Britain signed The Triple Entente to counter a growing German threat.

By 1900, Britain had holdings on five continents. France controlled large areas of Africa and elsewhere. Industrialized nations needed new markets and these became their colonies. Germany, however, late to enter the race, only managed to acquire a few small areas in Africa. They wanted more.

Widening European divisions and the realignment of allies produced an arms race which threatened armed conflict. Between 1870 and 1914, France and Germany, doubled their armed strength.

In 1906, Britain launched the mighty battleship *HMCS Dreadnought*. Germany countered by launching an equally great battleship. The boys were showing off their toys.

9

Germany's only solution to the saber-rattling was war.

While chief of Germany's general staff (1891-1905), Alfred Von Schlieffen drew up his great plan in anticipation of a European conflict. Based on defeating the British and French, they would concentrate 90 percent of their forces in the west for a lightning invasion of France via Belgium. They would smother France into submission. Next they would rush troops east and trounce the Russians. The plan moldered for a decade.

In 1904, Britain presented Morocco to France, but Morocco wanted self-rule. Germany replied by supporting Moroccan independence. At a hasty conference, the parties declared that France would retain Morocco. In 1911 Germany protested again and was placated with a chunk of French Congo.

The Bosnian Crisis arose in 1908 when Austria-Hungary assumed ownership of the once Turkish Bosnia. Angry Serbs insisted the province was theirs. Serbia threatened Austria-Hungary with war, a serious enough threat that Russia allied itself with Serbia. Then Germany allied itself with Austria-Hungary, and began sharpening their sabers to threaten Russia. War was avoided when Russia backed down. Next, Austria-Hungary dove into the fracas forcing Serbia to cede recent acquisitions. The tension between Serbia and Austria-Hungary was electric.

The whole European atmosphere was volatile with jittery nations tottering on the brink of war. Only constant negotiation staved off conflict.

In 1908, Austria-Hungary appropriated Bosnia and Herzegovina. The antagonized Serbs formed the Black Hand Secret Society (*Ujedinjenje ili Smrt* or Union or Death) in May, 1911, "To realize the national idea, the unification of all Serbs. This organization prefers terrorist action to cultural activities; it will therefore remain secret."

Archduke Ferdinand, heir to the Austria-Hungary throne, outraged the Serbs by travelling to Sarajevo, the capital of Bosnia and Herzegovina, to direct maneuvers of two army corps stationed there as a national presence.

On June 28, 1914, Gavrilo Princip, a member of the Society, drew his revolver, assassinated Ferdinand and those gunshots

10

thundered across the western world.

On Tuesday, July 28, 1914, Austria declared war on Serbia blaming them for Ferdinand's death. Russia, as Serbia's ally, began mobilizing and since they were allied with France, the French were obliged to respond.

Germany declared war on Russia on August 1, 1914, and two days later on France. They dusted off the von Schleiffen Plan and poured troops into Belgium aimed headlong for that country. Sir Edward Grey, British foreign secretary, ineffectively demanded that Germany instantly withdraw from neutral Belgium.

The Germans were not intimidated. On Tuesday, August 4, 1914, Britain declared war on Germany, and Canada, though still only a British colony, was automatically at war.

With only a small army, barely 3,110 men, plus a tiny navy still wet behind the ears, Canada was not ready to enter a world conflict, though no one dreamed it would escalate to those proportions.

Even so, Canada proposed raising The Canadian Expeditionary Force to aid its parent and Britain accepted the offer of 25,000 trained men. Over 31,000 departed in the first contingent.

Canadians generally greeted the outbreak of war enthusiastically and volunteered in droves as William Morris Jones wrote:

"They heard the Voice
Though knew not where
The path of Freedom lay;
But in their hearts they vowed to stand
And Truth should point the way.

They heard the Voice,
And followed on,
Through blood and toil and pain;
And from the hill where Truth did lead,
Found Freedom in the plain.".

11

CHAPTER 3 – LEARNING THE ROPES

Ten days after war was declared by Britain, Bill Jones mothballed his dreams and enlisted as a private with the 17th Nova Scotia Battalion.

He was sent to St. Gabriel de Valcartier some 18 miles north of Quebec City. Much of the town had been transformed into a military training camp known as Valcartier Camp. It was here that the First Canadian Expeditionary Force was trained.

Jones marched into this hastily constructed camp under the leadership of Colonel Struan Robertson. He signed his Attestation Paper for the Canadian Over-Seas Expeditionary Force on September 27, 1914 declaring he was born on August 23, 1893, thus making him 21 years of age though actually only nineteen. He stated he was a teacher and minister, single, willing to be vaccinated and knew what he was doing. He agreed to be attached to any arm of the service for one year, or during the hostilities between Great Britain and Germany, should they last longer, plus another six months afterwards if his services were required. The form noted that he was 5'7", dark complexioned, brown eyes, black hair and Presbyterian. The Medical officer declared William Morris Jones physically fit, then he was inspected and approved by the commanding officer.

The camp was organized in neat rows of conical, white canvas tents. A cook's tent dished out meals for thousands. There were no showers but a nearby swimming hole served the purpose. Sports provided physical conditioning and promoted cooperation and teamwork and Jones reveled in that emphasis.

Daily training and exercises were given to soldiers depending whether they were to become riflemen, scouts, bombers or runners. Everyone was inoculated against typhoid. Regiments were shuffled and re-shuffled into battalions and battalions were shuffled into brigades.

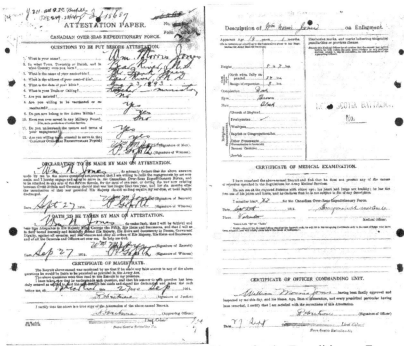

Bill Jones' Attestation Papers signing him up for the Expeditionary Force on September 27, 1914.

In October, 1914, with barely two months' training, Private Bill Jones said goodbye to family and friends and was shipped to England in the largest convoy ever to cross the Atlantic.

His destination was Salisbury Plain, famous for Stonehenge, and if Jones and the others thought Valcartier was a Boy Scout camp, they soon detested the long, miserably cold, drizzly winter at Salisbury Plain. It would only get much worse.

After training at Tidworth Barracks, Jones was sent on to Risboro Lines Barracks at Shorncliffe in Kent.

His 17th Nova Scotian Battalion was reassigned to other units. Jones' good fortune on April 15, 1915, was being drafted as a reinforcement private into the already prestigious 13th Battalion Royal Highlanders of Canada (Black Watch) where he served in "D" Company under Major W.E. Macfarlane.

A digression here looks at this regiment that would strike terror into the souls of the German enemy, such that they nicknamed them *"Die Damen aus der Hölle"* or "The Ladies from Hell."

Based in Montreal, the Black Watch (Royal Highland Regiment) of Canada was formed in 1862. Its regimental motto *Nemo me impune lacessit* (No man provokes me with impunity), was firmly embraced and they first earned distinction in the South African Boer War (1899-1902). Their opportunity to shine again had arrived.

During all this troop training, the war carried on.

In August, 1914, Russia marched into Prussia but miscalculated the difference in railway gauges making it difficult to move troops and supplies. Germany quickly used its own railway system and surrounded the Russians' Second Army at Tannenberg (Stebark), East Prussia before the poor Russians realized what was happening. Thousands died and 125,000 were taken prisoner. It was a costly German victory, leaving 13,000 crack soldiers dead and many more injured.

In September, having trounced the Russian Second Army, the Germans took on the Russian First army at Masurian Lakes in East Prussia. The Germans lost but still took 100,000 Russian prisoners.

On October 29, 1914, Turkey assisted in a German naval bombardment of Russia. Days later, Russia declared war on Turkey and on November 5th, Britain and France both declared war on Turkey.

In late 1914, the Germans reached France via Belgium, though less smoothly than anticipated. Supposedly neutral Belgians blew up railway lines hindering transportation of German supplies and French counter-attacks at Ardennes, Belgium, slowed the Axis march into France. The Allies brought the German machine to a grinding halt at the River Marne. British troops moved from the northern coast of France into Mons, Belgium, initially held off the Germans, but then retreated. The British suffered enormous losses at the first battle of Ypres and by Christmas no hope remained for a

14

speedy end to this conflict.

By February, 1915, the Canadian troop training was finished and they graduated to the front lines. The 13th Black Watch Battalion was placed in the 3rd Brigade of the 1st Division, along with the 14th, 15th and 16th Battalions. On February 16th, excited, razor-keen and invincible, 19-year-old Private Bill Jones headed to France to do a grown man's job. He wore a khaki cloth cap for head protection–the steel Brodie shrapnel helmet was not developed until the following year–and he carried the bane of Canadian soldiers, his well-maintained, but defective Ross rifle. This was going to be exciting and glorious and there was nothing like a good, honest fight. How could a teenager know he was descending into a hell on earth that would be his for the next three and a half years. He found out. They all found out.

CHAPTER 4 – INTRODUCTION TO BATTLE

"My father never talked much about the First World War." -
- Bill Jones Jr.

We see The Great War in faded sepia photographs, silent, frozen in time, but it was really blinding technicolor, mud and khaki and black smoke, flaming oranges and yellows, the red of spilled blood, a moving collage filled with deafening surround-sound and the smell of death. And this carnage will be followed through the whereabouts of Bill Jones and the engagements of his beloved 13th Black Watch.

He learned the real ropes in France. No more practice. The ammunition was real. After acclimatizing at Hazebrouck in northern France, Jones' 1st Division was ordered to the Fleurbaix sector in northern France where they took command of 6,400 yards of front line trenches on the left flank of Britain's First British Army. Here young Bill was inducted into the heinous invention of trench warfare.

By April of 1915, Jones' 13th Battalion was used to reinforce British and Canadian lines in Flanders, Belgium and Ypres and were proving themselves worthy and skilful.

The Trenches

The complicated network of trenches characterized much of the fighting on the Western Front.

Laid in front of the trenches facing the enemy, were high tangled rows of barbed wire. Periodic breaks allowed soldiers to creep through into "No Man's Land" to monitor enemy activity. Opposing enemy trenches were often so close they could overhear their plans.

They were dug with regular jogs called traverses. Should the enemy penetrate a trench, they could not fire at troops up and down the line. The top edges were lined with sandbags; the floors covered with duck boards over a shallow sump designed to keep the trench from becoming waterlogged when it rained. Two to three feet above, ran a platform called the fire step which raised the soldiers high enough to see over the earth wall and sandbags to fire at the enemy.

Immediately behind the front line were regularly spaced machine gun nests manned by two or three soldiers who blazed at the enemy over the heads of the front line troops.

Behind the machine guns were underground bunkers for stores: food, weapons, artillery and ammunition. The command centers with telephone links for reporting and receiving instructions were located here in the one roofed area protected from the elements and incoming shells.

Behind this another trench housing first aid stations and kitchens provided a second line of defense should the front line be taken.

Perpendicular to the first and second lines of defense, regularly spaced communication trenches allowed men to go back and forth to move supplies and transport the injured to field hospitals.

And finally, positioned between the communication trenches was the artillery line of big long-range field guns. They fired above the heads of everyone below and the noise was deafening and earth shaking. Their mainstay field gun was the reliable British 18 pounder Mark 11. Needing up to 12 men to operate, they had a range of 5,966 meters and delivered devastating blows with 4.6 kg. to 8.4 kg. shells that detonated on impact.

An hour before day break, soldiers were awakened with their first "stand to" and sent to the fire step. Bayonets were fixed for close combat just in case the enemy planned an early "over the top" raid.

As the sun crawled above the horizon, machineguns, artillery shells and even handguns were fired toward enemy trenches, supposedly to test them, but also to warn off a dawn raid. Soldiers hated this noisy wake up. Sometimes there was a raid, or they were ordered over the top to conduct one–straight into enemy fire. Backed by machinegun and artillery fire, the advancing Canadian soldiers had no personal protection except their next-to-useless Ross rifles. They simply kept moving forward or dropped in their tracks, a senseless way to die before breakfast.

Breakfast was hot oatmeal, bread with jam and tea, and this time was unofficially respected by both sides.

Next came inspection by the commanding officer followed by daily chores like draining water-logged trenches, cleaning latrines, refilling sandbags, repairing damaged trench walls.

Days were endlessly long and tense. Either nothing was happening or everything at once. Snipers on both sides constantly fired at anything that moved, but soldiers could write letters or sleep while the officers planned strategies in the command centre.

At dusk, the second "stand to" was ordered and soldiers returned to the fire step in the deepening darkness, a dangerous time for surprise attacks, but also the time when men were sent for supplies. Every two hours, sentries on the fire step were replaced lest they be overcome with sleep–a punishable, inexcusable occurrence. Barbed wire was repaired. Patrols were sent into "No Man's Land" and if they met enemy patrols, they would hurry on their separate ways rather than engage in hand-to-hand fighting. Nobody wanted to die.

In Jones' Black Watch Regiment, the regimental piper, kilted in Royal Stewart blue and green, customarily lead the troops over the top. His job was ferociously dangerous because he stood in full view of the enemy. The 13th's wild bagpipe skirling so terrorized the Germans that they often dropped their rifles and fled.

Pipers, accompanying patrols, played the Regimental March, *Highland Laddie*, before diving back into the safety of their own trenches: "Where ha' ye been a' the day? Bonnie laddie, Hielan' laddie. Where ha' ye been. . . ."

Cut and dried in theory, in the heat of battle, it was a melee of thundering artillery, shouts, cries, machine guns, dirt, mud, the dying, the useless Ross rifle backfiring into some poor private's face, fresh troops stumbling forward over the bodies of dead comrades amid the swirling smoke to take their places on the fire

18

step. It was madness.

Then it was over. Everything stopped. Everyone slumped in their tracks against the trench walls, perhaps staring at the sightless eyes of the man with whom they'd shared breakfast. It was such a small hole in his forehead, yet he was dead!

It might be days before this happened again, or it might happen tomorrow but meanwhile the dead were removed and the injured taken to first aid stations.

This was Private Jones' world.

The Gas

Trench warfare achieved few gains and horrendous losses.

The Germans began experimenting. In October, 1914, at Neuve Chapelle, they fired shells at the French containing an irritant that caused violent fits of sneezing–ineffective and almost laughable. On January 13, 1915, they tried tear gas on the Russians at Bolimor. The cold weather prevented the tear gas liquid from vaporizing. They tried an improved tear gas concoction at Nieuport against the French in 1915.

The Battle of Gravenstafel Ridge on April 22, 1915, was the first battle of the Second Battle of Ypres. The 13th Black Watch was positioned along the Ypres Salient with the 15th Battalion and reported odd pipes protruding above the German parapets.

This British, Canadian and French-held Salient was 10 miles long and bulged ominously into German territory. The British and Canadians defended the central portion. Immediately to their right and directly behind the 1st Canadian Division, the little village of St. Julien, enjoyed their temporary protection. Bill Jones was in the thick of things.

That morning, German guns bombarded the area around Ypres, then fell unnaturally silent. What was up? Around five o'clock, they began again as a dinner-time distraction.

A new bombardment hid the Germans opening valves on the canisters of their new weapon of death. Chlorine gas flowed through a series of lead pipes laid over the low walls of their front line fire trench. A low yellowish-green haze rolled relentlessly

19

forward dancing in the light easterly breeze.

French and Algerian lookouts spotted the odd cloud drifting their way and assumed it masked a German infantry advance. Men were ordered to the fire step. Too late. The bilious cloud was upon them and they began dropping from asphyxiation. Within seconds of inhaling, a victim's respiratory organs failed bringing on choking, then death.

Panic-stricken survivors fled willy-nilly leaving a four-mile unguarded gap in the Salient. The Germans had not foreseen this possibility and failed to take advantage of the situation.

Troops quickly learned to stay on the fire step rather than running, as the gas would pass by. Those who suffered the worst were those who lay down in the trenches. Troops were ordered to place wet handkerchiefs or cloths over their faces in future gas assaults and this proved helpful.

Suffering from the attack, the rear of the 13th Black Watch Battalion was dangerously exposed, but quickly formed a flank with French troops to protect the left wing of the British sector. Their flimsy trenches, unprotected by traverses, were being blown to bits leaving only inches of cover but they fought on.

After the Gravenstafel gas attack, little St. Julien became the front line.

The troops stubbornly defended the St. Julien-Poelcappelle Road, hindering the German left wing, but on the 24th, the Germans released another cloud of poison gas. It rolled toward the reformed Canadian lines west of the village. Horrified soldiers watched helplessly.

Bill Jones Jr. recalls: *"My father saw a cloud of gas creeping along the ground. It was heavier than air and quickly settled into the trenches. I'm guessing that he was affected by it but with his knowledge and military training, he realized that men were falling and dying in the trenches and they needed to get into clear air.*

"He started pulling troops out of the trenches. I remember him saying how totally exhausted he was after working all night getting men to safety–hauling out all that unconscious dead weight. Who knows how many lives he saved. It was unbelievably hard work

but that night's work won him the Distinguished Conduct Medal."

Sergeant William Jones' Distinguished Conduct Medal, created for army ranks below commissioned officers, was the second highest award for gallantry in action, second only to the Victoria Cross. It was awarded to him specifically for his leadership, initiative, skill and judgment in patrolling and reconnaissance in the heat of battle, one of only 2,132 Canadians to receive the award.

The Germans took St. Julien after that gas attack and held it for the next two years.

During four days in May, 1915, British, Canadian and Indian troops heavily bombarded the Germans in France's Artois. Four hundred heavy guns launched over 100,000 shells to soften the enemy. Attacks between May 20-24 captured Festubert and the Allies held that town until the spring of 1918. This victory cost 16,000 casualties and the Allies advanced less than a kilometer.

As the 13th Black Watch was involved in the Battle of Festubert, it is presumed that Sergeant Bill Jones did his part.

A small note reported in the Casualty Records of the 13th Battalion of the Royal Highlanders of Canada stated that #46282 Sergeant W. Jones was slightly wounded on August 5, 1915. This record claims he was a prisoner at Roulers, a front-line German garrison town in Belgium, but a further notation claims he was not a prisoner as per Red Cross letter dated August 12, 1916. Was he a prisoner or wasn't he? Perhaps he was only briefly misplaced.

Seething from the gas attack at Gravenstafel Ridge, the British quickly prepared a suitable response. Under Lieutenant-Colonel Charles Foulkes, they formed Special Gas Companies. The word "gas" was taboo and the actual canisters were labeled "accessories." Military doublespeak was already in use. By the evening of September 24, 1915, the Companies had 400 chlorine gas emplacements along the British front line around Loos, Belgium. After the gas was released, the wind unfortunately shifted and the clouds were blown back into sections of the British trenches. The

21

British may have suffered more casualties than the Germans that morning, a retaliation deliberately forgotten.

CHAPTER 5 – A CANADIAN EMBARRASSMENT

The Great War progressed in fits and starts.

In April, 1915, gas-filled German Zeppelins attacked London but Allied planes shot down the slow-moving balloons.

The Battle of Jutland (Denmark), the only full-scale naval battle of World War I, began on May 31, 1916. The British had blockaded the German forces in port. The annoyed Germans tried Horatio Nelson's Trafalgar tactics. They steamed out of port planning to split the British fleet in two and sink their warships one by one, however British Admiral Beatty recognized the maneuver. A smaller force lured the German vessels into range of Admiral Jellicoe's main fleet, and following a brief exchange, the Germans scuttled back to port.

Next day the Germans tried again and damaged the British fleet considerably before dashing to safety. The engagement was deemed a draw.

Though the British sustained more losses than the Germans, Kaiser Wilhelm and Admiral Scheer were alarmed and decided to keep their fleet in port thereafter.

The time was ripe for the 13th Battalion's "Ladies from Hell" to make their next legendary appearance.

St. Eloi, Belgium, five kilometres south of Ypres, lay on a corner of the Allied Salient, already the scene of vicious skirmishes because of a desirable elevated area called the "Mound." Whoever was "king of the castle" could see for miles around.

Sappers secretly dug an elaborate underground trench system beneath enemy positions, then planted 30,000 tons of explosives in three shafts or mines 50 to 90 feet beneath the German-held "Mound."

At 0415 hours on March 27, 1916, the British simultaneously fired guns and artillery and detonated the explosives. The enormous blast was even heard in Folkestone, Kent, England. It wiped out all the battlefield landmarks, collapsed trenches and resulted in seven large craters pock-marking the "Mound."

The British 9th Brigade swarmed over the German lines capturing their objective. The 4th Royal Fusiliers, busy in Craters 5 and 6, less successfully struggled through mud up to their armpits and left a gap through which the Germans flowed and occupied those craters. A week of bloody hand-to-hand combat finally drove out the Germans.

Next the Canadian 2nd Division received its initiation. Replacing exhausted British soldiers and wearing their new steel Brodie helmets, they had their first awful taste of battle. Early on, Division Commander Malcolm Mercer was killed and one of his brigadiers was captured, leaving the troops nearly leaderless. The ravaged trenches offered scant protection, and as daylight broke they were met with the ghastly sight of dismembered body parts protruding from the mud and bloated corpses floating in the craters. After 13 days of dismal guidance and confusion over possession of seven water-filled craters, the Canadians suffered 1,373 casualties, an utter embarrassment ignored by future historians.

The 3rd Canadian Division's initiation was even more horrendous. The Germans attacked at Mount Sorrel just south of the Ypres-Menin Road, the fiercest bombardment experienced by Canadian troops. Entire trench sections were obliterated. Explosions hurled human bodies and trees skyward. There was nowhere to hide. Unbelievably, the enemy advance was actually checked though the Allies lost important ground–Mount Sorrel and Hill 62.

A Canadian counter-attack the following morning failed. More ground was lost—a severe lesson in mismanagement and an ill-conceived sacrifice of 8,430 Canadians.

Lieutenant-General Sir Julian Byng, newly appointed Commander of the Canadian Corps (formerly the Expeditionary Force), was determined to clean up the mess. He laid a careful plan to be carried out by the seasoned 1st Canadian Division, the home of Jones' 13th Battalion. The strike would be supported by artillery under the command of Major-General Arthur Currie.

Popularly called "Guts and Gaiters" by Canadian troops, Currie was born in Napperton, Ontario in 1875. In Victoria, B.C., he briefly taught school, then sold real estate, but his real interest was the military. He enlisted and was fast tracked to the rank of Lieutenant-Colonel of Artillery. When the war erupted, Canada had a first-rate leader waiting in the wings. His successful leadership soon got him appointed General of the Canadian army, and at his insistence, Canadian troops always fought as a unit so they could take pride in working together as Canadians.

He took part in every major Canadian action on the Western Front and his brilliant tactics literally won the war for the Allies.

On June 13, 1916, at 1:30 a.m., in wind and rain, the Canadian infantry attacked the sleeping Germans.

William Jones had the "plan of attack" memorized as did every soldier. He knew where the roads were, the German lines, where his own lines were just southeast of the village of Zillebeke, Belgium.

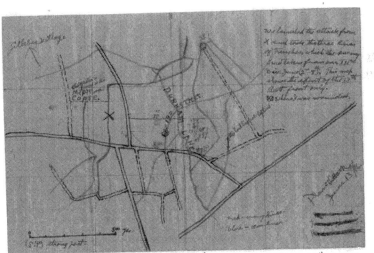

This Plan of Attack, as it applied to the 13th Battalion on June 13th, 1916, was hand drawn on a scrap of green paper by Jones just shortly after the event.
Bill Jones Jr. Collection

25

The 1ˢᵗ Canadian Division was positioned facing the German lines, some 400 yards away. The barrage began as the lines moved forward. The "X" on the map indicates Jones' starting position. Dodging, ducking, zigzagging, he covered 350 yards before being seriously injured in the leg by flying shrapnel. His day ended at the first German line they encountered.

His comrades finished the mop-up and Jones happily noted: "We launched the attack from X and took the three lines of trenches, which the enemy had taken from our III Div. June (2ⁿᵈ – 8ᵗʰ). This map shows the extent of the 13ᵗʰ Batt. front only." His map jubilantly notes "the last line we captured" at the furthest German line. The 13ᵗʰ's "Ladies from Hell" did their job admirably and recovered ground once lost to the Germans.

On a sad note, a tiny notation on the drawing beside the 'Maple Copse' states: "Otis Meister is buried in this woods."

Otis, a good friend of Jones, came from New Ross, Lunenburg County, Nova Scotia. A farmer by trade, he also trained at Valcartier. "Wm. M. Jones" witnessed Otis' Attestation Paper dated September 26, 1914 and both were assigned to the 13ᵗʰ Black Watch Battalion. Otis was shot in the head and died instantly.

On June 13ᵗʰ, 1916, William Jones was transported to England to recover from his leg wounds and they never could remove all the shrapnel. Friendly and personable, Sergeant Jones made numerous long-lasting friends at the military hospital.

While impatiently convalescing, he heard about enemy air raids on London. War by air was a development being fast-tracked on both sides. These were Red Baron days with aerial dog fights between little airplanes and a bored Jones caught the excitement of flying, an excitement to be rekindled decades later.

To his chagrin, he missed his battalion's efforts at the terrible Battle of the Somme in Northern France where the Canadians fought in local offensives along the southern part of the Ypres Salient. They successfully prevented the Germans from doing mischief elsewhere while the Armageddon of Verdun raged between the Germans and French.

The first Battle of the Somme was preceded by eight days of heavy bombardment, the plan being to kill as many Germans as possible and destroy their barbed wire barricades. On July 1, 1916, at 7:28 a.m. the British exploded mines they had tunneled under the German dugouts. Two minutes later, their men went "over the top", ordered to walk in a straight line across "No Man's Land" having no idea their bombardment had failed. Artillery shells intended to penetrate German dugouts fell short and the shrapnel meant to destroy the barbed wire, only tangled it worse. Enemy fire mowed down the advancing troops by the hundreds. No ground was gained and this battle lasted until November of 1916.

That first day of the Somme conflict exacted a terrible British toll of 19,240 lives and 38,230 injured and words cannot describe the carnage and bad planning.

Meanwhile, Jones' 13th Battalion was involved in engagements related to the major Somme event. The Battle of Pozieres Ridge in France took place between July 2nd and August 7, 1916. Primarily an Australian undertaking, it proved an ordeal costing thousands of lives, however the fortified village of Pozieres was critical to German defenses. After that struggle ended, the Canadians relieved the fatigued Australians, took that sector in September and held it until the end of the war. This became the starting line for the Battle of Flers-Courcelette.

This was Canada's first major involvement in the Battle of the Somme and the first time soldiers of the 1st Division wore a red patch, two inches by three inches on both sleeves of their uniforms and painted the emblem on their helmets as identification. Canadians were developing an identity and reputation.

At the Battle of Flers-Courcelette in September, 1916, the British brought 49 tracked tanks to the scene. With a top speed of half a mile per hour, the ungainly 28-ton creatures never reached the actual battlefield, however the picture of warfare was repainted. German High Command laughed, said the tank would be defeated though they initially had a devastating effect on German morale. Aided by the 2nd Canadian Division, the Germans were expelled from Courcelette on the first day of battle aided by just one tank but these would eventually contribute greatly towards ending the terrible trench warfare.

During the Battle of the Somme, British attacks had been to the right. Now General Haig turned his attention to the left, to the River Ancre. The job of clearing the Germans from Thiepval Ridge, a high spur of land running northwest from Courcelette fell to the Canadian Corps under Lieutenant General J.H.G. Byng. Part of four divisions along a 6,000 yard front, the Canadian Corps captured this spur on the first attack. Haig then attacked from both sides of the river squeezing off a German salient in the process. The British reached their objective on September 30th but failed to clear out two German redoubts at Stuff and Schwaben.

Poor Bill was crawling out of his skin. He was missing important events.

The Battle of Ancre Heights raged in France from October 1st to November 11th. The British Army Reserve attacked, advanced east for five miles and four miles behind the German front line. The Canadian Corps, situated north of Courcelette attacked on their right flank, advanced 400 yards east of Courcelette, but made no progress, however the two German redoubts of Stuff and Schwaben, missed earlier, were taken.

After a day or two of plan revisions, the final phase of the first battle of the Somme, known as the Battle of Ancre, began November 13th. The German front line, where it crossed the Ancre River, was captured despite heavy resistance.

In the final attack on November 18th-19th Beaumont was captured, though the rest of the assault ended chaotically in driving sleet and snow. Their goal was met but at the mind-boggling cost of 1.5 million casualties.

Winter temporarily ended the carnage. The Germans hunkered down and constructed their new Hindenberg Line across northern France. The Allies maintained control of their acquisitions. Lloyd George became Prime Minister of Britain in December and met daily with his highly successful war cabinet.

CHAPTER 6 – BACK IN FULL SWING

Finally, after a snail-slow eight-month recovery, Jonesy left the care of his nurse, Betty Dunham (nee Ashley), at the military hospital in Birmingham, England. He would keep in touch with her over the years along with other new acquaintances.

In February, 1917, he returned to the continent to his 13th Battalion. Newly promoted to Sergeant-Major and Acting Regimental Sergeant Major, at 22, Bill Jones was a seasoned soldier.

Winter was waning and there was much planning and re-equipping being done.

Trench lines were impenetrable by current arms and tactics, battle lines see-sawed back and forth with massive loss of life and negligible gains. Soldiers lived in dirt, cold, mud and misery. A seemingly decent diet became dreary and monotonous—corned beef, hard biscuits, flavorless jam. Fleas and lice infected the soldiers with low-grade "trench fever." Their constantly wet feet led to a condition soon named "trench foot." Soldiers were instructed to change to dry socks at least three times daily and to rub their feet with whale oil. Untreated foot infections often led to gangrene and amputations. A meager pleasure was the regular tot of rum, though some officers saved it for just prior to an attack.

Sergeant-Major Jones eagerly returned to this nasty world for the spring offensive.

Looking over the Douai Plain, Vimy Ridge runs at a slight angle from north to south 10 kilometers north of Arras in northern France. It was here the Germans built the Hindenburg Line with three layers of deep trenches, concrete pillboxes, endless barbed wire and deep tunnels. It met the main German trench lines leading north from Hill 70 near Arras, France. The Ridge rises a mere 150 meters above sea level, yet commands a significant view of the surrounding lowlands. No one could approach unseen and it lay defiantly between French and British held areas. The 1917 Allied spring offensive would begin there.

The trench warfare stalemate had to be broken and Field Marshal Sir Douglas Haig ordered the Canadian Corps: "Take that ridge," a nearly impossible task.

Lieutenant-General Julian Byng commanded the Canadians. Well liked, unassuming, professional and no slacker when it came to planning and fighting, an outlook he shared with his chief lieutenant, Major-General Arthur Currie. Preparation, planning, practice, and then some more.

They laid out a full-sized plan of Vimy Ridge with all its landmarks. Soldiers were placed in the positions they would assume. They were indoctrinated with every gun emplacement, trench locations and tunnels. They could find their way in the black of night. Every man knew his job and was equipped with a map. They practiced and drilled, then did it over again.

Meanwhile, the engineers or sappers, built 40 kilometers of roads and 30 kilometers of railway. They laid 70 kilometers of water pipe and more than 150 kilometers of signal wire. Seven kilometers of tunnels were dug connecting front lines with safe areas at the rear. These would protect troops until the very last moment. Up to 1,000 men could be secreted in each tunnel, and it all happened right under the unsuspecting German noses.

Past methods of engagement were scrapped. Machine guns were no longer defensive weapons. The idea of "indirect firing" was created meaning they would constantly fire machine guns into enemy positions, day and night, making life impossible.

The Germans assumed that when the artillery bombardment ended, the Allies would make their move and they were ready. Instead, Canadian artillery would keep exact pace in front of their troops as they dashed across "No Man's Land". The troops practiced this rolling barrage. They moved at a swift pace of 100 yards every three minutes toward enemy trenches. Artillery fire landing ahead of them would provide cover and keep German machine gunners cowering at their posts. What a surprise! The shocked enemy would find our troops already on their doorstep when the artillery fire ended.

For three weeks, Canadian machine guns and 600 lighter gauge field guns hammered German positions. Information from airplanes and balloons allowed them to map German machine-gun and artillery positions to be specifically targeted. Microphones hidden throughout "No Man's Land" helped triangulate enemy fire. Daily, 2,500 shells rained down. German trench lines, transportation and communication positions were destroyed. They could not bring in food, ammunition and fresh troops, and all the while, feeding Canadian guns, was the railway network constructed by the engineers. The enemy lived on cold rations with 85 percent of their batteries silenced by the deadly firing.

The Germans called the week preceding the attack "*die woche das leidens*", "the week of suffering," as a million shells rained down on Vimy Ridge. It was pure hell for them.

Never had plans been so carefully and thoroughly conceived. Everything was ready. One hundred thousand Canadians were about to make their mark in history. Jones was primed to lead his contingent into history.

The men of the Canadian Corps were lined up by divisions from north to south. The 4th Canadian Division was the most northerly. To their south was the 3rd, then the 2nd and finally the 1st Canadian Division. This is where Sergeant Major Bill Jones was stationed. These last two divisions were the most experienced and had the most ground to cover.

It was Easter Monday, 4 a.m., April 9th. The men of the Canadian Corps swiftly moved to their "ready" positions, each man fortified with a hot meal and shot of rum. Esprit de corps ran high. No one doubted their success.

The weather was foul with driving snow and sleet blowing into German faces as if this too had been requisitioned from the Almighty.

At 5:30 a.m., still black night, 983 guns suddenly erupted with orange fire and smoke, accompanied by 150 blazing machine guns. It was a staggering awakening for the enemy.

Sticking closely to the scheduled 100 yards every three

31

minutes with the protective screen of artillery fire landing just beyond them, Canadian troops raced across "No Man's Land" with little resistance. They swarmed up the Vimy Ridge slopes to the brink of the enemy trenches and the speechless Germans were blasted from their dugouts by hand grenades dropped directly on top of them. Many Germans stumbled down behind the Canadians and were taken prisoner. While the enemy offered some resistance, the troops were so well versed in their duties, that when an officer fell, a sergeant immediately took over. If the sergeant fell, the corporals and privates simply carried on. By afternoon, two front lines were taken. By April 12th, the Canadian Corp controlled the ridge. The Germans fell back to the plain beyond, except for one bump in the ridge at the northern end called the "Pimple." That stronghold was taken care of by an Alberta rancher, Brigadier-General Edward Hilliam, who led his 10th brigade against them and evicted the Prussian Guard Grenadiers in an hour.

The victory was still costly with casualties reaching 10,602 including 3,598 men killed. German casualties amounted to over 20,000.

This battle, incorporating methods and tactics never before seen, was considered the turning point of WWI. Vimy was a glittering triumph amid the ongoing tragedy and failure of the Allied offensive. The Canadian Corps was commended for its bravery and recognized as an elite fighting force—a defining moment for Canada as a nation.

Jones was there, though he left no record of his own activities. We do know that on May 1, 1920, he received the official warrant from the Military Forces of Canada appointing him Warrant Officer Class Two in the Overseas Military Forces of Canada and back-dated to April 19, 1917. Now he was a non-commissioned officer, undoubtedly an award for exemplary performance in that great battle.

CHAPTER 7 - HILL 70

S till flying high from victory at Vimy Ridge, the Canadian Corps continued operating around Arras, France with a diversionary job redirecting attention from the French front, thus hiding Allied maneuvers, for their upcoming offensive in Flanders.

And while the Canadian Corps was building its reputation, Jonesy, quite unconsciously created his own legend and standing among his buddies as a non-drinker, a man who didn't swear, who walked away when the language became too crude. He prayed regularly, read his Bible, and if that sounds sissified, they considered him one of the toughest, bravest guys to ever mount a fire step. He was a warrior and the hero of the 13th Battalion.

For the first time, the Canadian Corps was under Canadian command, that of Lieutenant General Arthur Currie. He proved a superb tactician and one of the best military minds of all time. He used his troops carefully, likely sparing thousands of lives. On the other hand, he was incredibly insensitive to the rank and file who disliked him intensely but did their jobs.

His first orders were to capture the town of Lens in northern France. The Germans considered it impregnable and needed it for the rail access. The British needed its coal to support their war manufacturing. Currie was to carry out a ruse by keeping German troops occupied while the British and French launched attacks in the Somme area. This was not an enviable assignment as the Germans had recently introduced flame throwers and blistering Mustard gas into their arsenal.

Currie was expected to make the usual frontal attack on Lens and his men could undoubtedly take the town at the cost of many lives. A better plan, though more difficult, was taking Hill 70, the higher ground north of town. There would be fewer casualties than having the Germans sitting up there raining bombs on their heads.

Currie's countermanding orders riled the British Army's

hierarchy, but Field Marshall Sir Douglas Haig, commander of Britain's forces, reluctantly approved, predicting failure. Hah!

As at Vimy Ridge, Currie carefully laid out an area behind the lines representing Hill 70. Every unit drilled until they knew exactly what they were to do, meanwhile keeping up a steady bombardment, and, yes, gas attacks, on the hill.

Evening of August 14, 1917, Canadian artillery began heavy bombardment of the hill. They severely damaged trenches and blew openings in the barbed wire. Hours later at 4:25 a.m. the troops went over the top with Company Sergeant-Major Jones in the 1st Division on the left, the 2nd Division in the middle and the 4th Division to the right. The 3rd Division was kept in reserve.

Ten battalions advanced up Hill 70 protected by that rolling barrage of artillery fire and took their objectives in twenty minutes.

Now for another Canadian innovation. Drums of burning oil were dropping into the trenches. Flames and smoke spread over the hill. Airplanes, buzzing low over the battle site spotted pockets of resistance and radioed the positions to the artillery who re-calibrated their big guns and accurately shelled the locations.

It took until 9:00 a.m. before the Germans managed to organize a counter-attack and set off explosives and Mustard gas shells. Canadian troops had gas masks, but because their vision was restricted and it was an oppressively hot day, many removed them and suffered severe blistering to their skin and lungs.

On August 16th, two days into the battle, "D" Company of the 13th Black Watch was having a difficult time. Short of officers, Company Sergeant-Major Jones became the tower of strength through that endless day. In the gathering darkness, Major Macfarlane found him effectively carrying on his duties and they discussed several matters.

Sometime later, with the Highlanders taking another terrific barrage, Macfarlane came across Jones again and thought this paragon's crown had slipped. Sergeant-Major Jones was leaning against the dirt wall of the trench, his head on his arm. When questioned, his responses made no sense. Too many swigs of rum? How unlike the Sergeant-Major. He ordered him below to sleep it off and only later, when he found the sergeant lying face down on his bunk, did he wonder if something was wrong. He turned him over and discovered blood streaming down Jones' face. He'd been struck by a flying piece of shell–his left eye gone.

"Why didn't you say something?" Macfarlane asked.

"Because you'd surely send me off the line. I want to carry on no matter what."

"You must go for help Jones," Macfarlane insisted.

"No, I just need a little break. I can carry on," Jones protested struggling unsteadily to his feet.

"Please go for help, I insist." Macfarlane had too much respect for him to issue an outright order.

"Alright," Jones slowly agreed. "I guess you're right sir."

And Company Sergeant-Major Jones was passed back through the lines and shipped to England for healing.

The Germans, determined to retake their hilltop, counter-attacked 21 times. The Canadians beat them off every time, though 1,505 were killed, 3,810 wounded plus 487 injured in the gas attacks. Forty-one were taken prisoner by the Germans. On the other hand, the Germans sustained 20,000 casualties with 970 taken prisoner.

Haig's prediction was gloriously wrong and the Canadian Corps's reputation was etched in stone. The attack was brilliant, though given little space in historical accounts.

Major Macfarlane's recommendation that Jones receive a Bar to his Distinguished Conduct Medal for carrying on his duties despite being injured at Hill 70 was granted.

Back in England, Jones quickly recuperated and returned to the battle scene 28 days later, a newly-minted lieutenant.

Hill 70 was a small part of the much larger Third Battle of Ypres which blundered on disastrously for months before bogging down. Endless heavy rains and heavy German bombardment, mustard gas and machine-gun fire turned the battleground into a quagmire. Something had to be done.

CHAPTER 8 - BLOODY PASSCHENDAELE

Loss of an eye was not stopping Lieutenant Bill Jones. He only needed one eye to aim a rifle and there were battles to be fought. This muddy, heart-breaking struggle and savage loss of lives had to end.

New plans were laid.

Two years earlier in 1915, German chlorine gas had driven the British back to Ypres, Belgium. From that point, a ridge ran from the east to the south of the town of Passchendaele. It was then occupied by the Germans and was the only high ground looking over a pancake landscape.

This small town with the difficult spelling was the key. If the British could just get beyond Ypres, take the ridge, free the town, they could head north and drive the Germans from the Belgian coast. The enemy was uncomfortably close to England.

The Germans knew their lofty eerie looked over potential battlefields, though these were low-lying reclaimed marshy lands. They would flood quickly once shelling began compounded by the usual heavy rains in the area. Expecting an attack, they retired from their front line to the Passchendaele Ridge freeing up the flat marshy zone for the Allied troops to bog down in.

They did. By late October, 1917, the 3rd Battle of Ypres, begun some three months earlier, had gone through a series of muddy engagements. Exhausted Australians actually captured the Ridge leaving Passchendaele the only obstacle on the way north. Losses by British, Australian and New Zealand troops were appalling. It was time for the Canadian infantry to pull off another impossible task.

General Currie, at his tactical best, drew his plans on a map and denoted various advances by red, blue and green lines. The 3rd Division, with two brigades was stationed over the largest area, known as "Army left." "Army right" was the 4th Division with one brigade. Separating these Divisions were the impassable Ravebeek swamps. Three hundred and twenty-six canons carried on a

36

thundering assault for four days prior to the actual attack.

That battle began early morning of October 25th with heavy mist turning to rain. Troops advanced 50 meters every four minutes protected by artillery barrage keeping pace just ahead of them. The speed of their advance was deliberately slowed from that at Vimy because of the mud problem and, unlike Vimy, where they advanced in a single line, this advance contained seven lines due to the uneven terrain. Because of the slower advance, the foot soldiers in "No Man's Land" were at greater risk from German artillery. In the first wave of fighting, 2,481 Canadians were lost.

Four days later, the 3rd and 4th Divisions reached the Red Line lying east and north of Passchendaele. The 4th Division had also reached the Blue Line, but owing to a fierce German counter-attack, their next objective, the capture of Decline Wood, was abandoned. The enemy then reoccupied some Canadian positions that had not been fully secured. This was fixed during the night on October 27-28th with the 44th and 85th Battalions pelting the enemy with grenades followed by man-to-man bayonet fighting.

Meanwhile the 3rd Division, under intense artillery fire, backed off until reinforcements arrived, then continued advancing.

Exhausted troops perform poorly and Currie had this eventuality built into his plan. During the first few days of November, he had the 1st (Jones') and 2nd Divisions relieve the 3rd and 4th Divisions. By 4:00 a.m. on November 6th, they were in position. Five hours later, with little resistance, Passchendaele was firmly occupied by jubilant Canadians. Jones' 1st Division had a little more work as one company of the 3rd Battalion was isolated in the bog and they quickly took care of this.

Then came a setback to the final assault objective of securing the high ground north of Passchendaele. Attempts were made on November 10th by the 1st and 2nd Divisions but they managed only to position British troops for the winter on Passchendaele Ridge.

The Allies had advanced nine kilometres but did not break through enemy lines. The Germans still occupied Belgian ports. Five months later in the spring, the Germans greedily took back what they had lost.

Canadian casualties were 15,654. All, in all, both sides

suffered 250,000 casualties. Was it worth it?

Lieutenant General Sir Launcelot Kiggell, Haig's Chief of Staff, exclaimed after visiting the fighting zone: "Good God, did we really send men to fight in that?"

And Lieutenant Bill Jones? He headed back to England intact for officer training.

CHAPTER 9 – FINISHING THE JOB

To remedy the shortage of trained officers, Canada established an officer training school in 1917 on the south coast of England at Bexhill-on-Sea, Sussex. Non-commissioned officers serving on the front lines were selected for further training, unlike the British method of selecting officer material from the country's universities and best schools. The Canadian way provided the best army in history--fighting leaders who had worked their way through the ranks and understood the intricacies of war from the ground up.

Bill Jones had become a legend within his 13th Battalion and, unsurprisingly, was selected for specialized training at Bexhill under commanding officer, J.A. Critchley. Wearing the white band around his hat denoting an officer-in-training, he received instruction in proper parade ground drill maneuvers, physical training, correct saluting protocol when meeting a more senior officer, bayonet practice that involved stabbing suspended stuffed canvas bags or bags lying flat on the ground. There were endless lectures and strategy discussions. The process was very thorough but the whole time he was in training, he was champing at the bit to return to the scene of action.

Training completed and the white hat band removed, he was ordered in March, 1918 to Surrey, England to take command of Frensham Pond Camp, an Isolation Camp for Canadian troops destined for the 20th Reserve Battalion. This was not the front lines.

On July 20, 1918, he wrote to the headquarters of the Canadian Overseas Military Forces, Argyll House, Regent Street, in London, expressing his wishes to return to the front.

On July 30, 1918, he received this response:

"TO: Lieut. W.M. Jones,
       20th Canadian Res. Battn.,
       Bramshott

I am directed by the Chief of the Canadian General Staff to acknowledge receipt of your letter to him of the 20th instant.

Although your desire to return to your service unit in the Field is highly laudable, I am to state that it is regretted that no exception can be made to the policy which has been laid down and that, therefore, you cannot be made available for service in France in any front line unit.

(signed) "J.H. McLorg" Captain, D.A.A.G.,
for Brigadier-General, Adjutant-General, O.M.F. of C.
McL/GM"

Undoubtedly the loss of his eye lay behind this. Though Jones did not feel hindered by it, the military was determined that he was. They had other plans for him, and Jones was left gnashing his teeth in frustration.

The Great War dragged on endlessly, battle lines see-sawed back and forth, the human toll was unconscionable but the Canadian Corps would fix it again.

By February, 1918, with new tactics learned from the Canadians, the Germans had 178 divisions ready to attack. On March 21st, 2,500 guns opened up on the 50-mile British line and pushed them back beyond the Somme River with the French suffering the same fate.

The Canadians, encamped between the British to the left and the French to the right, waited for the same treatment. Twiddling their thumbs, they sat … and sat … and it never came. War historians contend that the German High Command utterly feared attacking the Canadian line. The Canadians had never been defeated, and why this time? What new tactics had they dreamed up in the dark corners of winter?

Haig wanted the Corps to work defensively with the British but Currie convinced him the Canadians should go on the offensive. Through Canadian tactical trickery, the Germans were convinced

40

that a major assault would occur in Flanders but the Canadians actually moved in complete secrecy south to Amiens, France. The code word for the operation was *"Llandovery Castle."*

Contrary to international law, a German U-boat torpedoed a Canadian hospital ship, the *Llandovery Castle*, carrying Canadian nurses and wounded on June, 1918 at a cost of 235 lives. Instead of helping, the U-boat ran down and destroyed lifeboats and bits of wreckage with survivors clinging to them. Only one life-boat carrying 24 survivors was saved and outrage over this callous event gave wings to the feet of the Canadian Corps. The incident was later deemed outright murder at war crimes trials.

Instead of softening the enemy with artillery, the Canadians, on August 8, 1918, 4:20 a.m., used another new tactic. They simply moved forward with tanks. The astonished Germans found ten divisions of Canadians and Australians advancing from their rear! By 1:15 p.m. German lines were breached and the Corps sped 13 kilometers into German-held territory. The price of these impressive results was 4000 Canadians killed or wounded. German casualties amounted to 27,000 with 5,000 taken prisoner.

During the next two days, the German lines were pushed back another 24 kilometers, 10,000 prisoners were taken, 25 French towns were liberated and the Germans quit trying to split the British and French armies.

The Canadian Corps had turned the tide of war! Now began what would be called "Canada's One Hundred Days."

Meanwhile there were 15,000 German prisoners who had to be dealt with. Lieutenant William Jones, now 23 years old, got that job. He returned to France and took command of Company 213, the prisoner-of-war camp, at Orival, Foret Duay. He was not happy, but at least he was on the same continent as the war. The logistics of caring for all those non-productive humans were huge. Getting supplies was difficult at best.

A week later, the Canadians were ordered back to Vimy and given three days to come up with a plan to attack the Drocourt-Queant line. They developed a zigzag track. As they progressed forward, and the Germans brought in reinforcements, they altered their direction leaving the enemy wondering what those blasted Canadians would do next. By September 2, 1918, the Canadians had destroyed the line and the Germans saw the handwriting on the wall. Quartermaster General Erich Friedrick Wilhelm Ludendorff, "manager" of the German war effort, admitted to Kaiser Wilhelm: "We have lost the war: poor Fatherland."

The Germans retreated behind Canal du Nord and shortened their line to compensate for losses. As their next objective, the Canadian Corps plowed on toward the 30-meter wide canal where a dry section remained to the south. Anyone advancing through there was a sitting duck but this was the logical crossing place. Not entirely approved by the British, the Canadians advanced on September 27th. The Germans knew the enormity of losing this position and rushed in six divisions. The Corps bulldozed across, then split their forces in two, one heading north, the other south creating more confusion. By October 11th, they had advanced 37 kilometers into enemy territory and liberated 54 towns. Joyful people danced in the wake of the Canadians.

By the middle of October, 1918, most of occupied France and parts of Belgium had been removed from German grasp.

At the same time Lieutenant Jones received new orders to Denain, France, just below the Belgian border. His job, as Assistant Town Commandant, was billeting 40,000 troops. This was still not the battle front.

There was one more job for the Canadian Corps. By November 5th, the troops had crossed the Belgian-French frontier, pushing the Germans further and further back. That day, the Canadians liberated Valenciennes. By some quirk of maneuvering, the Canadians were not invited to the town's celebrations. The less successful British forces needed a morale boost and attended the liberation ceremony as the victors.

The Canadians entered Mons by November 9th. Rumors of armistice were circulating but no one knew the terms, and Currie, not being sure, ordered Mons taken. The city was liberated, cheering crowds lined the streets waving at the troops and this was the only recognition Currie ever received for his actions. Despite his splendid, innovative tactics he was viciously criticized for this final attack, felt unnecessary by some because it cost more lives.

On this same day, November 9th, a dejected Kaiser Wilhelm II abdicated from the throne.

On November 11, 1918, at 11:00 a.m., the Great War was over. The killing was ended.

And Jones? On that same day, he took command of Mons under Quebecer, Captain Cinq-Mars. He was responsible for billeting another 40,000 troops and the administration of refugee affairs. The powers-to-be recognized his organizational abilities, but Jones was not happy. He wanted to rejoin his 13th Regiment and be part of the Army of Occupation.

A week later, Jones left Mons without permission. He headed to Rath Heimar on the Rhine, where his beloved 13th Black Watch Regiment was busy and rejoined them. He should have been court marshaled (!) but everybody was too busy to bother with small details of insubordination.

He did make a proper request afterwards though to join the Army of Occupation with his battalion, and with a sigh, someone in the higher echelons said: "Well let him have what he wants. He's bound to be effective wherever he is."

On November 18, 1918, at 11:00 a.m., the formal Armistice was signed in Redonthes, France. It took another year to hammer out the formal "Peace Treaty".

On February 19, 1919, Lieutenant William Morris Jones was demobilized to Halifax, the war over except for the parts forever seared into his memory. He was 24 years old but had gained a hundred years in staggering experiences.

The statistics of the Great War are mindboggling. In their book, *Pictorial History of the Great War*, (1919) by S.J. Duncan-Clark and W.R. Plewman, reveal that Allied war expenditures amounted to $200,000,000,000. Words cannot adequately describe the amount translated into today's dollar.

From the British Empire, United States, France, Italy, Russia, Belgium, Serbia and Rumania, 41,364,700 men enlisted for the Allies. For the enemy, Germany, Austria-Hungary, Turkey and Bulgaria, 22,350,000 enlisted. They were outnumbered almost two to one.

Allied losses amounted to 6,422,738 with 18,437,684 casualties. The enemy lost 5,000,000 with 15,050,000 casualties. In a country of just over 8,000,000, Canadian military deaths amounted to 64,944, plus 1,204 from Newfoundland which had not yet joined Canada. Casualties, including Bill Jones, added up to 149,732.

The loss of life was mind numbing.

And while there were many other events in the Great War, this account simply follows the known trail of William Jones and what he reluctantly divulged about his activities.

CHAPTER 10 – RECONSTITUTING

In the dead of winter, 1919, Bill Jones landed in Halifax with his memories, scars and medals and began picking up the life he'd left five years earlier. A teenager then, now he was an adult who had survived some of the worst experiences imaginable.

But what was ordinary life? No uniforms, no bully beef. He was on his own. No more taking and giving orders to be obeyed unquestioningly. Now he could question.

There was no help for veterans, neither support nor pensions for those who had slugged through that agonizing war. Bill called it "reconstituting myself." Now he was a peacetime civilian making his way somewhere, but where?

He returned to earlier goals.

Bill immediately contacted the Presbyterian Church and they sent him to their Home Mission Field. He was based at St. Peter's Presbyterian Church in extravagantly beautiful Neil's Harbour, Cape Breton Island. He had three preaching posts in this area of long beaches, sea-side cliffs and rounded, forested hills–a place where a man could remake himself.

In a letter dated January 6, 1971, one of his parishioners, Mrs. C.M. Pearl, of Neil's Harbour wrote: "... I think it was in 1919 that he was with us . . . . He had just come from overseas and they sent him here to take charge of our church and one at Ingonish. I remember him saying that one night at Ingonish, after service he could not stay at Ingonish for the night so walked all the way back to Neils Harbour, a distance of about twelve miles. . . .

"He was well liked here and my mother liked him very much. I think everyone did. He was always willing to help. . . ."

Bill probably enjoyed that long walk, perhaps worked out his next sermon and thanked God for His protection through the war. He was alive! So many were not.

Bill worked on the Home Mission Field from February until

August, 1919, then headed to Pinehill Theological Seminary at Dalhousie University in Halifax still determined to be a medical missionary in Africa.

He enthusiastically embraced student life and led so many social and religious groups he barely had time to study. Life and people were so interesting.

"Shucks!" was his favorite expression in those days and Jonesy found more uses for it and could give it more expression than most people could give half the dictionary.

"For Parsons Only", an undated tribute to Jones of their university time by classmate and parson Dr. Frank Archibald of Moncton noted: "Yet we didn't even need to hear that word (shucks) to know that it was Bill Jones coming down the hall. Without ever turning to see him go by, we would know him by his very step. It was somehow different from other fellows' step. There was a downright firmness in it–but not conceit, if you know what I mean. It was the step of a man who knew at all times just where he was going, and what is more, exactly what he planned to do when he got there. And, my word! What things he did when he got there!

"... he made his presence felt in every class. You would turn aside to look at him, and when he spoke, you just had to listen. And what an organizer; I wonder if they have ever had the like of him before or since.

"On summer holidays he would put to sea, and, on his return, to our eager questioning, he would regale us with his stories. At one famous Pine Hill "At Home" he was accused, as an old sailor, of having a wife in every port. The mock trial that followed was one of the highlights of all the years of college life."

Apparently Bill, the defendant in a mock trial, was marched onto the stage and made to stand in the prisoner's dock which was a wooden barrel. Charges were read that, as a merchant marine sailor, he had a wife in every port. He was questioned to gales of laughter, and Bill would open a huge book he was holding to find his answers. What they were, we don't know, but the room was rolling on the floor. Collecting himself, the 'judge' intoned, "Prisoner in the barrel, you are found guilty." Bill's 'lawyers' had failed to intimidate the judge who continued, "And your sentence: either that

46

you be hanged by the neck until dead, or that you take Hebrew I."

"I'll be hanged," Bill responded off the cuff.

Bill took an active interest in the betterment of student life. In 1921 the university declared that a student missing *any* classes would be dismissed. He and his friends took exception to this.

"We will not tolerate this infringement upon our rights," Jones cried. "And we hereby give our notice accordingly."

Lieutenant Billy organized a revolt and gave a memorable speech saying exactly what he thought. At one point, wearing a bowtie as a moustache, he led a group of protesters to emphasize his point.

News of the uproar hit the Halifax newspaper which published the glaring headline, "Students Threaten Strike." The Faculty reinstated the students' rights of 10% absence and his revolution was fondly recalled for decades.

On the side, Bill became involved in starting boys' clubs.

Fit from the battlefield, he loved and excelled in sports and made a formidable opponent in boxing and participated in long-distance running, sailing, canoeing and swimming.

Father and son were opposites. Frank, materialistic and acquisitive, dealt with the realities of the world in his law practice. High-spirited Bill lived on a plain of enthusiasm and hope that sat poorly with his father. An optimist to the core, he only wanted things to be better and a lot of petty things just did not matter to him. They had serious words and sadly their differences were never really resolved. Frank found his son, Billy, incomprehensible.

Education was a joy, but he had to work to pay his way. During the summers of 1920 and 1921, Jonesy served with the Canadian Government Merchant Marine. He moved through the ranks of AB (able seaman) standing watch to Quartermaster in charge of the helm, compass and signaling, Bo's'n (boatswain) in charge of rigging and anchoring and Acting 3rd Mate.

In 1920, he crewed on the *S.S. Princess* and his pencil-written notes indicate their destination was South America.

When school year ended in 1921 he signed aboard a larger vessel, *S.S. Volunteer*, Voyage No. 10. His notes show they traveled to the "Eastern Parts of South America, Clarke's City: Queensboro, Newcastle-on-Tyne; Chriantini (sp?) on Gaspé, Philadelphia, Halifax." In case of trouble, his particular assignment was the starboard lifeboat.

The following summer, 1922, wishing for a change of pace, Bill worked for the Canadian Geodetic Survey under Capt. W.C. Murdie of Ottawa. They were developing a uniform system of surveys, maps and geographically referenced information about Canada. Little did he know the surveying skills acquired here would stand him in good stead at another time and place.

CHAPTER 11 – A WORK INTERLUDE

For financial reasons, Bill finally had to drop out of university, but no ordinary job would do. Still a young man seeking adventure, he landed the dangerous job of rolling logs for Price Brothers Pulp & Paper Co., in Kenogami, Quebec. This company town, some 214 miles north of Quebec City, was a world leader in the industry.

Bill made an immediate impact. Chris Martin, a new friend there, described him as: "A great character and a great man, and a very great friend of mine over a long number of years. A man to lean on in emergency and who had great strength mentally and physically. I can remember so many incidents I could almost write of them to fill a book. He arrived in Kenogami, P.Q. in 1924 unheralded but in a very short time had made an impact on many, many lives which they will remember for life.

"I can remember him entering the dining room of the King George Hotel, a powerful figure, not tall but thick shoulders and going like a C.P.R. train of those days, full of steam and all eyes were turned on him, he was a magnetic personality." (From letter dated July 28, 1971)

During his two years there (1924-1925), the welfare of the community's youth became his hobby. Within weeks, he formed a "Cub" pack, soon followed by Boy Scouts and Girl Guides, the first ones north of Quebec City. Bill wanted young people to be taught proper values, justice and fair-play and what better framework in which to promote this.

By 1925 the first Scout and Cub camps was held at nearby Lac St. Jean. Campers were given the following list of articles to bring—and each had to bear the boy's name or mark:

"Blankets	2 or more
Uniform	complete
Heavy coat	

49

Fatigue suit	Suit of old clothes.
Boots	1 good pair, 1 pair old
Shirts	2
Handkerchiefs	3 coloured or white
Bathing suit	1
Stockings	3 pairs
Belt or braces	
Cheese cloth	3 yards (fly protection)
Soap and towels	2
Tooth-brush and paste	
Brush and comb	
Darning needle and yarn	
Needle and thread	
Buttons	6
Boot laces	2 pair
Jack knife	1
Table knife	1
Spoons	2
Forks	1
Plates	1
Cups	1

Writing pad, pencil, envelopes and stamps.

Knapsack: Make a cloth (duck) sack the length of the boy, about 26 inches wide. Roll the sack up till you have just enough space left to hold the boy's kit. Tie two ropes to each corner by which the sack is carried. Such a sack can be used as a mattress when unrolled, and stuffed with hay etc."

They neglected to mention clean underwear!

Chris Martin further writes: "Memories of this camp include Bill eating blueberry pie and pork and beans all off the same plate saying it gets mixed up anyway. Again throwing a handful of coffee into a can and making the finest coffee I have ever tasted. That was his way, he excelled in whatever he did. His was a dominant personality, you felt his presence and when he said something, you remembered it."

Bill started a night school and community club, activities surely welcomed in this isolated town with its long, dark, bitterly cold winters.

An ardent canoer, it was here that Bill acquired his much loved birch bark canoe, a craft he used for over thirty years.

Chris recalls: "We circled Lac St. Jean, Quebec, by canoe in 1926 and what an experience that was. He taught me more in the week of camping than I ever knew was possible. I can think of him sitting over the front of the canoe getting shaved or 'dolled up' as he called it to have a civilized meal at Island House on the Lake, a house owned by Price Brothers for their employees, the next night we were almost eaten alive by the largest mosquitoes and black flies I have ever seen. I was nearly crazy but Bill, imperturbable as usual swatting one and saying that's a big one Chris. He really was a wonderful companion. We visited the 'Peribonca' and the 'Mistassini' Rivers and 'Pointe Blue' the Indian reservation and were made very welcome and Chief Carter of the Indian reserve and Bill had so much in common, the chief being an ex-army man.

"Some of the greatness of this man Bill Jones must surely have been his physical condition. I can see him now picking up a log from the lakeshore and carrying it up the beach which 2 or 3 normal men would have found difficult and how apparently tireless he was in a canoe, seemingly able to paddle on and on."

Jonesy actually canoed from Kenogami to Montreal. As the crow flies, the distance is at least 250 miles, but on the winding rivers, the trip was considerably longer, but he saved the cost of a railway ticket.

While building up his financial kitty at Price Brothers, he never lost sight of his long-term goal of returning to university and then Africa.

CHAPTER 12 – JONES THE BUSINESSMAN

Jones enrolled in premedical science, languages and military studies, an eclectic mix at best, at the University of Toronto. Were his goals wavering? He never thought for one minute that the terms of settlement of the Great War had ended the matter. He wanted to be ready if it happened again.

His brother Doug, his business ventures flourishing, wrote from Edmonton, Alberta on April 27, 1926:

"Dear Brother Bill:

Just a few lines to you to let you know that I am still in the land of the living and am getting along fairly well.

Conditions throughout our part of the West are very materially improved over what they have been during the past three or four years, with the result that we expect the season of 1926 will prove to be a very successful and profitable one for us. Business has already opened up very considerably, and while there is somewhat of a lull now due to seeding operations being general we expect that in the course of another two or three weeks the season's business will be in full swing. . . .

I suppose you are buckling down to your studies now in anticipation of your exams. I certainly wish you every success in them, and hope that your results this year will be such as to give you a very great amount of encouragement.

. . . .Have you altered your plans for the summer months? If so I would like to know just what you intend doing. From what you told me you were certainly very fortunate in many respects in your surroundings in Quebec, and I suppose that in view of your stay being of a temporary nature wherever you go for the summer it would be hard to find a better place.

Please remember me to Mr. and Miss Hart. Also try to drop

me a few lines letting me know how you are getting along, sometime in the near future.

With love and best wishes, I remain,

Your loving brother,
"Doug"

Address: c/o Hayward Lumber Co. Ltd., Edmonton"

Jones again faced financial shortages and discontinued his studies for good having completed an arts degree. He would go into business.

From 1926-1927 he was the senior partner and proprietor of Jones & Clouston, a grocery or provision store called "J.C's". This venture flopped.

The following year he joined R.B. Rice & Sons, Real Estate, in Toronto where he worked for four years as a salesman learning the ropes, his infectious enthusiasm likely benefitting sales.

The Great Depression struck on October 29, 1929. Despite the nosedive in business, he optimistically headed out on his own in 1933, established Jones Realty Service at 21 King Street East, Toronto and struggled through the depression doldrums specializing in industrial and business real estate.

Jones Realty Service letterhead. He was in business! Provided by Bill Jones Jr.

Times were tough and as a one-man operation, he managed the office, showed properties, answered the phone, did the paperwork and legwork. He never could afford a clerk.

FOR SALE OR LEASE

ADAPTABLE FOR MOST REQUIREMENTS

For Price, Terms and Other Information inquire of

JONES REALTY SERVICE

21 King Street East, Toronto ELgin 0986

A typical "Realty Ad" describing one of his listings attractively printed in dark blue ink on pale blue paper. Inside, the brochure indicates the floor plan and property's attributes. Bill Jones Jr. collection.

Nevertheless, Jones purchased an older home beside Lake Ontario at 45 Lakeshore Drive, New Toronto, Ontario. The fireplace was a joy that supplemented the balky furnace. He owned not so much as a hotplate and perhaps the open fire allowed him campfire-like cooking. He re-shingled the leaky roof, dredged up huge stones from the lake, floated them on a raft and rebuilt the deteriorating breakwall.

Ever interested in young people, he taught a boys' Bible class in New Toronto's Century United Church for years.

CHAPTER 13 – SWEETHEART APPEARS

He met her at university. She was a medical student. Even more exciting were her similar long-term goals. Her name was Helen Scott and she lived at 977 Main Street East, Hamilton.

A busy man with multiple interests, Bill did not seem to have had any previous close female relationships, but he quickly learned the art as they became better acquainted.

Their biggest difficulty was the distance between Toronto and Hamilton so letters became their favorite, cheapest means of communication. They missed each other something awful every minute they were apart.

"Thursday evening, Oct. 17/35

Hello Sweetheart,

It is good to sit down and have a quiet talk with you, only I would much rather be there with you in front of the open fireplace. You know I'm as jealous as the dickens of you having our fireplace and our moonlight all to yourself. It just isn't fair and I object strenuously. Some of these days I'se just going to come right down there and park right beside that fireplace and lord help the person who tries to make me get away from it. I've got several weeks to catch up on you young man and by gosh I'm going to do it too! I'se a vicious woman when I gets going. Don't get awful scared Honey. I'll have a little mercy on you, maybe. I am really longing to be there with you though and I'll be glad when our allotted time is up and all is ready.

I have been quite busy and the results are pretty good. I wasn't going to tell you yet but I think it might cheer you up. Dad and Mother are getting us a lovely electric stove and our kitchen suite. Isn't that grand? I have warned Mother that she is not to get us anything extravagant. The stove is a Moffat range like Mother's only not as large. Of course it is much more modern and I think it is a little beauty. I know you will be pleased with it too. Our kitchen set has not been chosen yet.

So you see my Darling, we are not doing too badly. We have the necessities for our home now I think and we will have a swell time fixing the house up.

I completed my house dresses today. They are ironed and folded and put away. I haven't bought my stockings yet but I have the money for 6 pairs and also money for gloves, hat and shoes. One of these days I'm going to have a grand time spending it all. This Saturday I am going to get material for my dress. I was going to get it last Sat. but I was too sick to go out of the house.

So the place is damp eh? I guess I better buy you and me some red flannels. I think red ones would look cute on you! They would be sort of appropriate eh what!! Do horses get all excited when they see red? Maybe I better get you blue ones! I always did love you in blue anyway. And now that problem is argued and settled. Blue ones it is.

Your letter did not arrive until quite late this morning and I just about had a fit. I don't think I could have done a thing all day if it had not come. About 11 o'clock the postman brought it and I was considerably relieved. It won't be long until we won't have any letters at all will it. Gosh, what a stack of them I have. Not one has been destroyed from the very first. Someday we will have a lot of fun reading them over. What a love story you could write Honey! I bet every page of it would be censored!

You haven't written me a poem for a long time Sweetheart. In fact you didn't even finish the last one. What a man. I'll have to start writing poems myself if you quit! What a threat that is!

....Well my Darling I hope today has been more prosperous than yesterday. Keep up hope. The change in government and the war is bound to put a crimp in all business. Someday things will be much better and the future more hopeful.

Heaps of love Sweetheart. I can't tell you how much I love you too and long to be with you. I feel sure that happiness lies in the path we are taking and both of us will be happier with a new outlook

56

on life.

Hugs and kisses,
Your Helen"

"Monday evening,Oct. 21/35

Hello Sweetheart,

How's my wounded lover tonight? You certainly looked terribly abused last night when I observed that cut in your face. You want to take better care next time. Honey, I really am convinced now that you do need a new eye. The other has seen too much and just cannot see anymore. It has earned a long, long rest. Don't you dare worry about my glasses. They are alright. I am not even thinking of them and the family has not even noticed the break. (Excuse me. I just sneezed and now I'll have to run for a hanky. I don't keep 'em in my hip pocket for emergencies like you do!) Here I am back again I haven't got a cold. Just a good healthy sneeze that cleared my head a lot.

I enjoyed picking up this sheet of paper tonight and reading "Here I am" on it. [Note: in Jones' handwriting, in pencil, he had written diagonally across this sheet of notepaper: "Here I am". Below it Helen wrote: "I wish you were."] Please walk in the front door and convince me that you are. We will stay up tonight Honey to sit beside the fire. It is raining quite hard and is most uninviting where the fire is just begging us not to leave it. When I drop off to sleep you can carry me upstairs and tuck me in. Now be good and I'll let you crawl in beside me. You see I have one eye open a little just to see what is going on! I do hate to miss anything.

What a day! I really think I have been sleep walking most of it. I stretched out on the chesterfield this afternoon but I was disturbed every few minutes with the phone and door-bell ringing. Say, do I look awful dirty to you? People persist in trying to sell me soap. I use Lux and I like it better than any other. I got so mad at a dame today I just about slammed the door in her face. I guess it doesn't hurt to sample new things if you have the money but if you

57

haven't, it sort of makes you mad.

. . . I picture you out at the house just now. I hope you make yourself a hot cup of tea to go along with your lunch. Please don't neglect yourself anymore Sweetheart. You worry me a lot. I would give anything to see you well and happy and contented. You certainly did look all in Saturday night.

I hated to see you go this morning but it wasn't so hard as usual when I knew I would be seeing you on Wednesday which is not so far away now is it? I thought I would go up town today but changed my mind and decided it would be better for me to go on Tuesday. I am uncertain as to what I shall start on next in the line of sewing. I had thought of pajamas but I find I can buy them cheaper than I can make them. I need a dressing gown so I think I'll make one if I can do so cheaper than buying one.

Well Sweetheart I wish you were here to talk to me or not to talk as the case may be, just as long as you are here.

Now you hop into bed early and get some sleep. You are going to need it. I'll tuck you in and call you in the morning with a hug and kiss. Heaps of love for you alone Dear and lots of kisses and hugs.

Yours Helen"

"Tuesday evening, Oct. 22/35

Hello Sweetheart:

Well Honey it won't be long until I'll be seeing you. I'll be leaving here on C.P.R. at 4:45 p.m. and will arrive at Union Station at 5:40 p.m. If you are not at the Station, I'll wander up to the office.

Your letter was quite cheery and bright this morning. That's the spirit. I was more than glad that the glasses did not worry you. I never even think of them and no one has noticed the break yet.

This has been a very sultry day. Last night too was just as bad. It seemed impossible to sleep....

I went uptown this morning and needless to say, spent all my

58

money. I got the slip for your Mother and I am sure you will like it, if it doesn't scare you to death to look at it. Then I bought six pairs of stockings that I was supposed to get a couple of weeks ago. . . .

. . . . I saw all sorts of things I wanted uptown but couldn't get unless I robbed a bank or helped myself as I went along. After I spent all, I walked on up to Aunties and had lunch with them. Aunt Margaret gave me another pair of pillow cases and two white linen towels and also a hand painted box that she had given to her years ago along with about six handkerchiefs. Aunty Em gave me a crepe de chine slip. I feel guilty accepting all the things they give me but I can do nothing. They say they are sorry they cannot give me more. Can you imagine that?

I came on home and have most of the washing on in the washer. I suppose it will continue raining for a couple of days so I can't get it out on the line.

Well Sweetheart, I'll run along and do a little work so I'll be able to be with you tomorrow. Thanks for tucking me in but don't go away please.

Heaps of love and kisses.
Ever your Helen"

Still at odds with his father, Bill was going to Digby to personally announce their imminent marriage. Helen would wave goodbye to him at the station.

"Frank Jones, K.C.
Barrister-At-Law
Notary Public, etc.
Digby, N.S.
Nov. 8th/35

Miss Helen Scott
Hamilton, Ont.

Dear Helen:

59

You can justly reproach me for not writing to you sooner, but as Bill informed me that you and he had screwed up your courage to make the perilous plunge into matrimony on or about the 16th of this month, I decided to wait a little longer and make one letter do for the occasion–I find it necessary to economize my energies as much as possible at my age. So you will please make allowance for that, and excuse any apparent negligence on my part. On the eve of your marriage, I wish to assure you that I have the greatest confidence in you and the highest respect for your family; and I am quite sincere in saying that I heartily approve of the choice my son has made. I am quite sure that he will find in you a true and capable helpmate, and I wish you both long life, happiness and prosperity.

I am enclosing herewith as a wedding present, to you a cheque for Fifty Dollars. I am sorry I can't make it more at present, but will try and supplement it later on. In fact, if things go well with me, as I hope they will, I trust that I shall be useful to you and Bill in time of need if ever that should arise. Bill has been having a pretty hard pull to get established in Toronto but I have great hopes that he will make a complete success of his business. He certainly deserves it. But for a time he will have to practice the strictest economy and care. It should not cost him very much for living expenses after you and he get settled down. I hope to be able to make another trip to Toronto and perhaps further west before very long and I shall certainly look forward with eagerness for an opportunity to visit you.

Mrs. Jones and Helen (my wife and daughter) have departed for New York for the winter, so at present I am baching it. I don't know just what arrangements I shall make later on.

I trust that your parents, Margaret and the other members of your family are all well. Please give them my best regards. With love and best wishes.

I remain yours sincerely,
'F. Jones'"

A warm friendly, congratulatory letter on first reading, but Bill considered the paltry $50.00 wedding gift from his wealthy father an insult.

"It was a cheap shot," Helen said of it.

Their wedding day was nearing. The dress was made, the trousseau was complete. The air vibrated with excitement.

The wedding took place on November 15, 1935 at Sherbourne United Church in Toronto. Bill Jones was 40 years old. Though late in the year, they went canoeing for their honeymoon. He claimed getting married was the most exciting thing that had ever happened to him.

Their time together in the house by the lake was brief. Immediately following the honeymoon, Helen's father took ill and she returned to Hamilton to help care for him. This was a dreadfully lonely time for both. Apart so soon, they managed with letter writing and visits. Thankfully, her father soon recovered and she was back with Bill and life was good, snuggling in front of the fireplace on a chilly night, camping holidays, their garden, a cat and dog for pets.

CHAPTER 14 – ELBOW FLEXING

Before Bill and Helen married, they agreed that if war erupted again, he would enlist should the need arise. They knew the issues of the Great War had not been settled to everyone's satisfaction.

Germany, the unhappy loser, kept its belligerent tendencies toward nationalism intact. France, Britain and the United States had all reached their wartime objectives. They had reorganized European boundaries as they saw fit and Germany was reduced to a nonentity. What was there to worry about?

The 1920s were a peaceful time of growing affluence. The League of Nations settled international disputes in a civilized manner though its powers were limited to persuasion and moral and economic sanctions. They preached disarmament and isolating an aggressor was within its powers.

Europe, however, revolved around the German problem. If it could be settled, everything would be settled; if it remained unsolved, Europe could only expect an uneasy peace.

What was "The Problem?"

By 1921, German frontiers were settled by treaty but disarmament inched along slower than the Versailles Treaty terms dictated. The army ceased to exist as a major fighting force. Their growing resentment was fueled by reparations payments to France who wanted their full damages reimbursed and their demands increased as Germany recovered economically.

Americans conservatively proposed a fixed sum, but even Lloyd George, Britain's Prime Minister, knew this was beyond Germany's capacity to pay. He hoped the Allies would make a reasonable demand and Germany a reasonable offer and that these two efforts would coincide but it was impossible because of Britain's and France's divergent views. Germany was unwilling to cooperate and deliberately kept their economic affairs in confusion. Meanwhile their private armies and nationalistic right-wing organizations flourished.

Italy, as well, was unhappy with its small gains and parliamentary disorder left the country ripe for Benito Mussolini.

The 1920s prosperity was flawed by over-extended credit. When the 1929 depression sank the economy, Italy, Germany and Japan declared themselves victims of economic warfare with its protective tariffs and ruthless competition.

Economic unrest and memories of the huge cost of war caused the victors to focus inwardly. Britain tried appeasing dictatorial regimes. The United States adopted neutrality. France secured itself behind alliances and the defensive Maginot Line.

Germany paid reparations to France until they could pay no longer. Having lost everything, national paranoia settled in.

Expansionism, nationalism, internal and external conflicts conspired to stir the pot.

At a 1932 Lausanne conference, the German slate was unwillingly wiped clean after 13 years of growing suspicion and grievances on both sides. The French felt they'd been swindled; the Germans felt they'd been robbed.

On January 30, 1933, Adolph Hitler became chancellor of Germany, tore up the Versailles Treaty and removed Germany from the League of Nations. A massive rebuilding of the army, navy and air force began with no reaction from the democracies. The following year, Hitler sent his armies into the demilitarized Rhineland. Testing. Testing. How far could he go before anyone complained?

Italy had a decades-old hang-up regarding Ethiopia. They had failed to conquer it in 1896 and it still rankled them. Mussolini decided to erase the embarrassment. From Italian Eritrea, he sent forces into Ethiopia on October 3, 1935, then more troops from Italian Somaliland resulting in an easy victory against the poorly-equipped Ethiopians. The League of Nations imposed an embargo against Italy for their behavior, but forgot the most vital item–oil.

The Spanish Civil War erupted in July, 1936 from conflicts between Spain's liberal-leftist republican coalition government and General Francisco Franco's rightists. Hitler and Mussolini sent

63

planes, men and supplies to Franco; Soviet dictator Stalin gave military equipment to the leftists. The United States stayed neutral and Britain and France banned the shipment of war materials to Spain. Thousands of anti-Fascist volunteers from Britain and the United States served with Franco.

Franco won (1939) and inadvertently strengthened Hitler's and Mussolini's positions in the Mediterranean.

Remember, Hitler was Austrian, but chancellor of Germany. From 1934 on, he sought *anschluss* or union between these countries. In February, 1938 he threatened invasion if Austrian chancellor Kurt von Schuschnigg did not admit Nazis into his cabinet. A month later, Hitler invaded Austria and integrated it into his Third Reich.

Claiming Germans in Sudentenland, part of western Czechoslovakia, were being persecuted, Hitler began agitating on their behalf. The Czech government tried dealing with the threats peacefully by offering concessions to the Germans. In September, 1938, Hitler demanded that Czechoslovakia cede the Sudetenland to Germany.

The situation was discussed at the Munich Conference later that month and Britain and France concluded their smaller ally should capitulate to Hitler's demands after he promised no more expansion plans. Poor little Czechoslovakia had no input.

Neville Chamberlain, Britain's prime minister grandly hailed this agreement as bringing "peace in our time." They would "never to go to war again."

Six months later, (March, 1939) Hitler occupied Bohemia-Moravia and made Slovakia a German protectorate, effectively destroying the remainder of Czechoslovakia. Then he needed Memel on the Baltic Sea giving him a new door on the coast. Next he wanted the narrow strip of land, known as the Polish Corridor, which separated East Prussia from Germany.

Western powers could no longer keep their heads in the sand. Hitler's promises were meaningless; his territorial ambitions limitless. Britain and France frantically prepared military resistance against the Nazis. They guaranteed to help Poland against German aggression and began coalition negotiations with Russia.

Convinced that Britain and France were plotting to throw Germany's strength against the USSR, Russia signed a ten-year Nazi-Soviet Pact of nonaggression on August 23, 1939 and secretly agreed to divide Poland and the Baltic states between them.

Hitler was thrilled.

Blitzkrieg! On September 1, 1939, German tanks charged across Poland's borders blowing holes into their defense lines. Luftwaffe bombers destroyed their air force and communications system. German foot soldiers finished the work on the ground.

On September 3, 1939, Prime Minister Neville Chamberlain pronounced on the BBC that Britain had declared war on Germany. Oversized newspaper headlines screaming "BRITAIN DECLARES WAR" were anxiously read, hashed and rehashed.

Bill commented dryly to Helen: "Here we go again."

They talked. Was it time to sign up? He wanted to be a fighter pilot. What about his real estate business? How would Helen manage financially? How long would this go on? Would it be like the Great War? Worse? Would he survive? He always knew there would be more conflict and for this reason he and Helen put off having children. He didn't want to leave a widow and child with no support.

On September 17, 1939, Germany's Soviet allies marched into Poland stopping at a line running from East Prussia to the Bug River. Hitler and Stalin split the country in two: the USSR got the eastern half; the Germans the western half including Gdansk and the coveted Polish Corridor.

Stalin, with the expansionism virus, forced the Baltic states of Estonia, Latvia and Lithuania to accept Soviet garrisons, and simply incorporated these states into the USSR.

Next came Finland. On November 30, 1939, Stalin's Red Army invaded and was surprised by the effective Finnish resistance in the deep winter snows. In December, the League of Nations condemned their actions and expelled the USSR. At the end of February, 1940, Stalin sent in his best troops and by their sheer

65

numbers, the Finns finally gave way. Finland was forced to cede strategic ports, a naval base and airports.

The British Royal Navy took control of the high seas forcing German merchant ships into neutral ports. The Germans responded with a deadly submarine campaign. On the day war was declared, contrary to orders, Oberleutnant Fritz Julius Lemp, commander of German U-30 which was lurking off the Scottish coast, sank the *Athenia*, a Canadian liner bound for Montreal. Fearing reprimands, the submarine slunk off without reporting the sinking. One hundred and eighteen people died. Outraged newspapers screamed: "Athenia Torpedoed." Hitler was furious with Lemp, but later swept the event under the carpet.

German troops overwhelmed Denmark in April and Norway in June forcing the Allied withdrawal from those countries.

Neville Chamberlain's doomed leadership was replaced on May 10th by Winston Churchill who fired Britain up with his memorable promise of nothing but "blood, toil, tears and sweat" and a relentless fight against the Nazis. His inspirational speeches rallied the country in its darkest, longest days.

Hitler continued his action plan. On May 10, 1940 he occupied defenseless Luxembourg. The Belgians and Dutch fought back blowing up bridges, blocking roads and flooding vast areas, but when help came from Britain and France it was insufficient and too late. The Netherlands was taken in five days; the government and Queen Wilhelmina escaped to England. The Belgians surrendered after two weeks of struggle against tanks and parachuters.

Allied troops, isolated by the German advance, appeared doomed when one of the strangest armadas of wartime occurred. Over 850 navy vessels, private yachts, steamers, fishing boats, anything that floated appeared. Protected by the Royal Air Force, the ungainly convoy crossed the Strait of Dover to the beaches of Dunkerque and evacuated 338,000 British, French and Belgian troops between May 26 and June 14th. The legendary retreat, a near military disaster, was turned into a victory of wartime propaganda.

The whole world wondered agog at what Hitler would do next. By June 14th the Germans swept into Paris forcing the French to sign an armistice on June 22, 1940. The unbeatable French army evaporated when confronted by German tanks and mechanized equipment.

With France so easily defeated, Mussolini, who had remained neutral, joined the Nazis, declared war on June 10, 1940 and invaded southern France to prove his intent.

With France's easy fall, Hitler assumed Britain would simply accept his control of the Continent and ask for peace. To his chagrin, this did not happen. He turned his Luftwaffe over to Hermann Goering to begin the first real air battle in history. Goering called it "Operation Sea Lion." Approximately 160 heavy bombers unloaded their deadly cargoes over London for 57 nights. The RAF was greatly outnumbered, but their agile Spitfire fighters, aided by new radar, shot down 1,733 German aircraft, though lost 915 of their own planes. This fiery resistance was unexpected. The Germans, unable to withstand the heavy losses, postponed the operation in October.

Meanwhile, the Russians coveted Romania for its oil and seized Bessarabia and northern Bucovina, and by November, 1940, Hitler forced Hungary and Romania into alliance with Germany. Bulgaria was next, then strategic Yugoslavia lying in the midst of his path south.

For Bill Jones the time had come for action.

CHAPTER 15 – WITH NINE DOLLARS IN HIS POCKET

With Hitler's army blasting all over Europe, Bill felt the call, but realized his age and glass eye were formidable obstacles. He managed perfectly well with one eye, but the authorities flatly turned down his offers to serve. Two visits to Ottawa proved fruitless.

After the Russian invasion of Finland in November, 1939 Bill was impressed with their heroic resistance. He wrote to New York to the 'Finnish War Veterans in America' on December 26, 1939 offering his services. He gave his military credentials, candidly admitted to losing an eye but that it was no handicap whatsoever. Apparently his services were not needed.

Bill and Helen prior to World War II. Photo courtesy of Bill Jones Jr.

Finally, with his typical do-or-die determination, Jones made arrangements for his business and then it was time to go. He was participating in this war one way or another.

He left with mixed feelings as he kissed Helen goodbye and was already missing her the moment he stepped out the door. He had already petted Jingo their spaniel and Ruffles the cat. Nearly 45 years of age, he had a young man's excitement at the prospect of joining the air force and fighting Jerry in the air. Bill strode off leaving 45 Lakeshore Drive in his wake. It was July 6, 1940. He had $9.00 in his pocket and was confident it would get him to where he was going.

Hitch-hiking and walking were his means of transportation. He left the old car for Helen and was heading for Ottawa again.

He wrote Helen on the morning of July 7th from Port Hope where he slept outdoors, and remarked how he'd washed "by a babbling brook." "Just as I finished, along came a flock of geese to see this strange creature splashing in the water. They seemed to hold a pow-wow and evidently decided it would be better to keep their distance." Of his last lift, he said: "The last Samaritan was a hearse from Oshawa. He turned into the Catholic cemetery just before he reached Port Hope. I made a clean get-away!"

By July 15th, he had reached Smiths Falls and with two more lifts and a bit of walking, he reached his destination.

In Ottawa, he found a room for .50¢ per day or $3.00 per week at Mrs. L. Prefontain's house at 132 Slater Street where he dreamed of screaming over New Toronto in a Spitfire. He'd swoop low over their house and rattle up Helen's dishes.

"By the way," he wrote Helen, "I landed here with $7.50 cash and food enough for a day and a half, having paid .75¢ for bread, butter, tomatoes, cheese, cucumbers, cookies last night, also .05¢ for envelopes, .15¢ stamps, .25¢ Toronto car fare (I have 3 tickets still) all the rest went for drinks along the way."

Money was tight for the Joneses and the $9.00 presented a hardship. He thanked Helen for the sacrifice.

Bill was prepared. He sailed through the recruiting office processing. Next came the dreaded eye test but he had memorized the eye chart letters and that test went well, though the doctor became suspicious. He placed a candle in front of Bill's good eye and got the expected reaction but none whatsoever when he placed it in front of his left eye. He actually singed Bill's eyebrow.

The doctor was apoplectic. The glass eye was that good. Bill was equally furious for having been found out. He would later see the funny side of the examination, but his next letter to Helen, omitted the whole scene.

As a compliment to the eye maker, on January 30, 1946, the *Toronto Daily Star* wrote a piece on Dr. Clifford Taylor, the only man in Canada making glass eyes. He had made at least 75,000 for veterans and regarded one of his more flattering successes as the case of an unnamed man trying to enlist. He nearly passed the eye exam because he had memorized the chart. The eye was that good!

On July 16th Jones wrote:

"Hello Sweetheart:

Here we are miles apart but still I can imagine you here right beside me.

Well Honey I have nothing yet in a definite way but by tomorrow afternoon I may have a final decision. In any case I'm afraid the Air Force is definitely out of the picture for the time being, at least as there is no possible way of overcoming the ruling that rejects me.

Yesterday (Monday) I had two meetings with Gen. Turner (General Sir Richard Turner, an old friend) – he seemed very glad to see me and went out of his way to make contact for me with different officials. He found out that Ralston would be at the Parliament House in session during the afternoon and if I were lucky I might see him for a minute or two between sessions. I proceeded to the House about 4 p.m. The guard stopped me and was not going to let me pass as I had no written instructions. I took the bull by the horns and <u>bluffed</u> (I hear you accusing me of such practice) it out by asking him to inform Col. Ralston that 'Jones of Digby' wished to see him for a minute or so. Immediately he contacted Ralston's secretary. I was invited to his suite of offices but I surmised the trap as I could only see the secretary in evidence. These secretaries are the mischief to get by. However what I wanted was an introduction to Major Power, Minister of Air, from Col. Ralston. She at once made arrangements to see Major Power. Just as I was leaving the suite to visit Power, I met Ralston face to face. He nodded and asked me into his private office. A battle royal ensued. He took me wrong and we battled for fifteen minutes until I saw we could get nowhere as he thought I was just another job seeker. However he modified his attitude toward the end and became quite civil. He dictated a letter of introduction to Col. Gorseline and asked him to consider my case as special. Which meant a job in the army as C2 category. Not satisfied with that alone, I headed for Major Power this morning and had much better satisfaction–it seems that at present a C2 man cannot be taken into the Air Force on the Administrative staff but I am assured that my case is going to be given special consideration and I am to hear from Col. Stewart in a few days. But that is too slow for me as I cannot wait. So this afternoon I followed along Ralston's leads and I was sent over to the Forestry Corps where Major Ferguson seemed very glad to meet me and requested me to wait over until tomorrow p.m. in order to have time to look into my case. I have decided to wait and see what develops. Between you and me it may just be so much hooey. I never saw so much slip shoddy methods in my life as one sees here. All seem scared of the job they hold and try to carry out instructions to the minutest detail fearing they will be criticized....

Well Sweetheart, I must run to the letter box now. Heaps of love and a big hug and kiss. Ever Bill"

He was not thrilled with the bureaucracy. Helen would learn later what really happened with The Honorable Colonel J.L. Ralston, Minister of Militia, an old friend of Bill's father.

After an hour-long harangue, Ralston had had enough.

"You are here wanting to become a fighter pilot. I damn well wouldn't fly with you," he shouted, banging his fist on the desk.

"I darn well wouldn't invite you, sir," Bill replied.

The Minister phoned the Chief of Medical Services and

asked for the official ruling concerning one-eyed men.

"Listen," the Colonel said, "the Chief of the Medical Services says the Medical Association has recommended closing the door to all one-eyed men as it would be an unfair risk to the public Treasury."

Jones had further discussions with General Turner and they concluded he should go to England where the rules were different. Unhappy with Jones' treatment, Turner gave him a letter of recommendation.

As a final shot, Jones asked Ralston's secretary to thank the colonel for his efforts and to: "Please tell him that I'm leaving for England!"

On July 18th, Jones wrote: "Well, Sweetheart, I set out for Montreal today and if lucky there, I shall soon be on a boat for England." He was unsinkable, tenacious. "I have no doubt in my mind that I am doing the right and only thing open to me. . . . My one great concern and worry is yourself and what I am doing."

Helen did have his war pension cheques to help eke out an existence.

By Thursday, July 19th, he wrote Helen from Montreal. With the remains of the $9.00, he had splurged on a .05¢ bus ride to speed him out of Ottawa. "I had not been walking ten minutes before I heard a horn honk and a car and trailer pulled up alongside the curb and asked if I wished a ride. Two Frenchmen on their way home to Montreal they were, and very jolly fellows. Gee, did I appreciate the break!! They stopped at several places en route to whet their whistle and even wished to treat me to anything I wished, even soft drinks. But I considered myself so fortunate to get the ride that I readily declined further hospitality."

He wrote that General Turner gave him a fine letter of introduction to Brigadier, the Honourable P.J. Montague, C.M.C., D.S.O., A.A. 7 I.M.G., who was at the Canadian Headquarters in London, England. Turner hated seeing him resort to this and his parting words were: "Damn it all Jones, it's a shame to see a man like you treated in this way. Good luck to you my man."

In Montreal, Bill took the first room he came to. Cost him .50¢. He had a good sleep, a bath and a change of underwear.

His next stop was the Canadian Government marine offices to try booking working passage to England.

He wrote again that day saying he had connected with a steamer bound for Bristol, England. His "private yacht" was the *S.S. Darcoila* skippered by Captain Anderson. It was owned by a Glasgow firm and chartered by the British Government. He began work as a seaman the next morning replacing a sailor who had fallen overboard and drowned in the St. Lawrence the previous day. He reassured Helen that they would be part of an escorted convoy crossing the Atlantic.

To Helen he requested: "Your prayers and support are all the world to me. I am doing what I am doing for you and I trust your life and happiness will be secure and enduring." He reassured her that money should be coming shortly and Mr. Fenwick, their banker, would likely be content with less than $25 that month on their almost paid off mortgage.

On July 20, 1940, Bill reported on board at 7:00 a.m.. He wrote Helen: "The Bo's'n (boatswain), the fellow below the mate, from whom the crew take orders, kept us busy all morning taking aboard provisions including ice (2 tons), about 6 whole muttons, 2 whole creatures of beef, a frozen pig or so, 2 crates of eggs, a 200 lb. barrel of salt beef, a whole cheese and a half, ten bags of potatoes, turnips, 3 bags onion, a quantity of rhubarb, green lettuce, carrots, green onions, two larger hampers of oxtails, hearts, liver, etc. frozen biscuits, condensed milk, canned butter, jam, cereals, rice, tapioca, etc. for dessert, crates of bread and a mixture of other groceries for the cook. You see we are well stocked.

"We worked until 8:30 a.m., had breakfast of liver and bacon, oatmeal porridge, bread, butter, coffee. We then carried on loading the stores until the rain came on. We then covered over the hatches with huge tarpaulins and be that time we were prepared for lunch. Roast beef, potatoes, cabbage, rice pudding, bread, butter, jam and tea.

"I would die laughing if you could have seen me. It is really

73

a lark for me. I think I have had about as much sea experience as anyone in the crew. The sailors are eight in number–3 Newfoundlanders, 4 Englishmen and yours truly. The firemen, with whom we have nothing to do are Hindoos. (8 of them). . . . Then there is the captain, 1st & 2nd mates, steward, assistant steward, cook, carpenter, 1st, 2nd & 3rd engineer. Donkeyman, 2 oilers, 2 deckhands, a cat and a chicken. . . The boat is all steel of course and about 3000 tons gross weight. A boat about the size of the larger lake boats but of slightly different lines."

Bill thought the English sailors better educated, but particularly enjoyed the Newfoundlanders with their strong, interesting characters.

This is wartime, he reminded Helen and wrote: "I shall tell you a secret now but don't spread it about as we must be careful. Our cargo consists of all kinds of building materials, lumber, beaverboard sheeting, nails and such like going to Greenland & Iceland for Canadian and British troops. We are headed there first and then we believe we go to Bristol. Be very careful to whom you give this information as it would be extremely valuable to the enemy. From what I have told you the enemy could easily piece together the entire British plans of what is doing in Greenland and Iceland. It is best to say nothing to anyone. I want you to know all I can possibly find out because it will give you an inside picture of things and you can enjoy deducting your own conclusions. It is the next best to you being with me. Of course once I leave Canada, I shall have to be very careful what I put in my letters because all mailing coming into Canada is subject to censor."

He arranged a little code with Helen. "When I suddenly talk about the weather, you will know we are about to sail to some port, and I shall always manage to work in the name of the port immediately after."

And "By the way," he gleefully wrote, "we are paid 10£. 12 s. per month and a bonus of some sort besides, when the trip is over. I don't know how much it will be. If we are torpedoed we get another bonus. Gosh I'd like to be torpedoed fifty times if it would hurt nobody or not destroy the ship or cargo. What a bonus you would have!"

After posting this letter, Bill went shopping with his remaining $2.00 and purchased: a "fountain pen .25¢, toothbrush .10¢, Snap (handcleaner) .15¢, soap .11¢, towel .05¢, paper & envelops .15¢, ink .05¢, spoon & fork .10¢." Now .72¢ remained of the $9.00 and he never explained what became of that.

"Wed., July 24/40
On our way down St. Lawrence River

Hello Sweetheart:

How is my girl today? We got away about noon yesterday. It was very pleasant running down the St. Lawrence River. For awhile this morning we were held up by fog, we dropped anchor and kept our bell ringing periodically answering those of the lighthouses on a point of land nearby.

I was so glad to get a letter from you before leaving. It cheered me up mightily. I am very sorry that I could not run to Toronto to see you before leaving but such is our misfortune. Never mind Dearie, we shall look forward to a very happy reunion as soon as it is possible.

The shore of Orleans and Londre look very familiar. I can picture myself in our canoe on our way from Chicoutimi to Quebec. A fellow by name of Labaree made this trip with me. I hope someday to take a trip with you up the Saguenay. (I am sort of lying in my berth writing this note, so please excuse the scrawl.) Some of the boys are on deck, others sleeping. It will be my turn at the wheel from 8-10 p.m. Then I shall be ready for anything that I may be called upon to do until our watch is relieved at 12 p.m. We have roughly four hours on duty and eight hours off right around the clock...."

Three days later. they steamed through the Strait of Belle Isle in another pea-soup fog. A fog horn to the south boomed through the thickness. Bill took his regular watches and trick at the helm. In his spare time he wrote to Helen.

"I have a great deal to account to you Sweetheart already. Some of it is very funny and you would die laughing. I make a few notes in a small notebook that I have from day to day just to aid my memory.

"One of the boys, Fred, is a real 'card.' He has had a varied experience and to hear him recount them is first class entertainment. Last night he kept the whole forecastle awake until quite late telling how he got into difficulty once by signing on as a ship's cook without having had the slightest experience. Honestly it would put any audience in fits of laughter. He was to have dinner ready for twenty-five men on board at 12 o'clock. By twelve o'clock the potatoes were as hard as rocks, the great big cabbage that he thought should make three meals, shrunk to such a small quantity he had to keep adding more and more of it until he had the whole cabbage in the pot and even then it wasn't half enough. He was going to give them sago pudding for dessert, but you can imagine his troubles when he put a pint mug full of dry sago per man into an ordinary pot. He said it was all over the stove, galley floor, and what he couldn't throw over the side of the ship as it would run over. The pot was so badly burned that it was useless. Then as twelve-thirty came along and no dinner ready, the men became restless with impatience and one after another would visit the galley and help themselves to a half-cooked potato until by the time he thought he had things ready to serve up, he found that he hadn't even a potato per man left. He said he took what was there of the dinner to the mess room, set it down on the table and vanished. He said the entire crew was much annoyed and was raging with anger. He didn't show his face until supper time. His attempt to make bread that night ended up in dough being scattered from end to end of the ship so with that he decided to chuck the job."

As Bill had no means of mailing this letter, he kept adding on.

"Friday, Aug. 2nd – Sighted land, this a.m. Now lying at anchor. Have been playing bridge all evening and am finishing this note in case we get an opportunity to get ashore and mail it."

Then using their pre-arranged code, he informed Helen of where he was.

76

"The general appearance of this place reminds me of the shoreline of Iceland when we visited Reykjavik years ago, but of course the weather is not quite as wild and bitter as that of Iceland. Treeless hills, rugged, peaked and volcanic in appearance meet the view on all sides."

He concluded with, "Goodnight, Dearie, and hearty dreams. I miss you terribly but don't you worry about me. A heart full of love and hugs and kisses to comfort you. Love to all the family. Ever Bill"

Until Italy entered the fracas, the Mediterranean was a minor theater. It became tremendously important when Mussolini declared he was building a Mediterranean empire at Britain's expense. While seaman Jones was sailing to Britain, Mussolini took his first step and overran poorly defended British Somaliland.

"Sunday, Aug. 10th/40

Hello Sweetheart,

A day of rest again. Some of the boys are still indulging in a few hours longer in their bunks. I have had breakfast, porridge, egg & sliced ham, fried potatoes and coffee; washed out my towel, shirt and hung them on the line today and here I am talking to you. We could find plenty of interesting things to do if you were only here, i.e. if you wouldn't freeze to an icicle getting here.

Yesterday afternoon half of the crew were permitted to go ashore for the first time since our arrival here. I drew 10 Kronin (the equivalent of eight shillings, or $1.60 our money).

The first thing I did was to look for a telegraph office but on learning it would cost $2.00 to $3.00 to send a short message I could not indulge. . . .

I then looked around for something that might be interesting and typical of life here but had no luck. All shops were closed, it being Saturday afternoon. I looked over the central part of the city (43,000 people) and saw a very impressive looking parliament building, somewhat resembling an old French farmhouse only a bit

77

larger. A monument or two, statues of early settlers and statesmen are to be seen nearby, and about the only piece of grass in the place is to be seen in front. The streets are very narrow and only one or two are paved. Shopping district is quite concentrated but of course the shops are not at all comparable to modern standards. However one sees the usual classes of business, jewelers, barbers, grocers, bakeries, dry goods etc. and as always, restaurants. By the time I had surveyed the major part of the city I came across three of our boys so we pooled what money we had and looked for a place to eat. We indulged in a cup of coffee and something that resembled a slice of buttered brown bread with a very thinly sliced portion of cured fish on it; and half a dozen so-called cakes, which resembled small coils of rope. Plain, unflavored food seems to be the characteristic. Well, after the 'meal' we looked up one of the two picture houses here. We had to wait until 7:30 before we could get in as 'theatres' only open here in the evening. For the equivalent of .50¢ we got a seat and saw a six month's old picture, so I understand, entitled "In the News" or something like that. It was well acted, and the plot, somewhat similar to a detective story, was interesting to say the least. Oh, yes, just before the show we started to look for fish hooks so as to fish over the ship's side after working hours is the chief past time for many of the boys. Since all shops were closed we had to do some tall scouting. Finally we came across a sail maker in a little old shack who very kindly took us to a nearby telephone and get in touch with a hardware merchant who very kindly came down to his store and opened up for us. We purchased fish hooks, Lux soap, (2 bars for .40¢ - what do you think of that?), knives, tobacco & cigarettes. I wanted another towel as one of mine had blown overboard, but on pricing towels I could get nothing under three Kronin, so I thought it would be better to see a picture, determined to make the one towel last until we see England. Well, after the picture we roamed about until we came to another restaurant where we had a cup of tea each and two small cakes each for which we paid the equivalent of .45¢. You can see how small the purchasing power of money is here, no doubt times are not normal in the business field.

There is a hot spring just outside of this city and an attempt is being made to lead it in concrete ducts so that all houses can be heated by it. I shall explain this phenomenal undertaking later. You can have a bath, which two of our boys had, at the public baths, a most unattractive looking building, for 2 Kronin. . . .

. . . I have been greatly worried about you Sweetheart. I don't know how you are making out financially and I have no way of getting aid to you until I reach England. My pay is accumulating and so far I have about fifty dollars coming to me. In addition to our regular wages of 10£, 12 s. we get a bonus of 5£ per month.

If you can manage until I can send you some, which I shall do by cablegram, I shall send it to Royal Bank of Canada, College & Spadina branch just as soon as I arrive. I'm very sorry indeed to have you worry as you must be doing.

I miss you terribly Sweetheart and am ever thinking of you. As yet no letter has arrived from you and before we leave I shall get another chance to enquire at the post office. The other half of the crew are going ashore today and I shall get one of them to post this letter. Heaps of love Sweetheart and a great big hug & kiss.

Ever Bill"

The *S.S. Darcoila* set sail again and on August 21st they sighted St. Kilda's Island off the Scottish coast.

"Hello Sweetheart,

While our good ship is rolling from side to side causing things to slide about the cabin and generally adding confusion to an otherwise quiet company, I shall do my best to have a quiet chat with you.

So far our voyage has been uneventful and apart from rain, fog, some wind (especially during the past forty-eight hours) there has been little to add interest to life from day to day. The routine of ship life goes merrily on and somehow or other the skipper manages to find enough work or activity to fill in the hours that one is not actually sleeping. Between the various navigational duties, such as steering, look-out, standby, we have managed to paint almost the entire ship from topmast to waterline. You would have your odd joke if you could see me dangling about in a bo's'n's chair trying to get a paintbrush to contact a mast that somehow or other has the habit of moving about with the ship. I'm certain you would see something funny in the spectacle. It's good fun though and to repay us for our effort, we have a ship each day looking more like a cared-for, respected merchantman as all freighters should be....

So far I have just one month's pay coming to me. Approximately $75.00 with the discount–it will likely work out to $65.00. I have to buy a suit of clothes and a pair of shoes ... I shall cable you $25.00 just the minute I am paid and shall send it to the Royal Bank of Canada ... Be brave Sweetheart– s you have always been and things will turn out as we had hoped they would."

On Saturday, August 24, 1940, the *S.S. Darcoila* tied up at Barry Docks in Wales. There had been no sightings of the dreaded German U-boats, possibly because their route had taken them far north of the Arctic Circle.

The $9.00 had carried him all this distance. Now there was a pay cheque from the shipping company.

CHAPTER 16 – THERE'S ALWAYS A HITCH

With time on his hands, Jonesy wrote his sweetheart about Barry, a Welsh town looking out across the Bristol Channel.

On Sunday, August 25, 1940 he wrote: "The Bo's'n and I went up to the village last night and saw about everything of interest in this South Wales coaling station. The Bo's'n related a description of this seaport as he remembered it years ago. It must have been a wild place. But at present it is just the usual seaport–stores out to get the pay envelopes of the sailors, the odd theatre, reasonably sanitary streets and quaint English architecture characterizing the public buildings. Of course, as England is a free country you find beer & liquor for sale at the world famous English 'pub.' The usual bar counter, tables and saw-dusted floors. The bar maid, tough and beer soaked… Needless to say, I indulged in a glass of ginger beer and a glass of limeade and to please the Bo's'n, a small glass of sherry."

He discovered a curiosity: "One novelty is a stamp vending machine. You drop in a penny or ha' penny and out comes a corresponding stamp–somewhat convenient. I understand these vending machines are all over England. You find one or two in such a village as Barry."

That evening, the ship's carpenter, Owen Williams a sailor, and Bill attended a national church. The preacher spoke in Welsh. Williams, a Welshman, understood it all but Jonesy understood nothing except when he occasionally broke into English. Curiously, the sermon discussed unemployment and forced idleness going hand-in-hand with the deterioration of the races. Odd content for a sermon, he thought.

As to danger: "I wish I could give you an account of air raid precautions but we must reserve that until you come (optimistic hey what). I want you here too. Selfish do I hear you say. Well you should be here and I mean it. There must be some way to make it

81

possible …. As far as danger is concerned, either I'm blind, dumb or dippy–there is mighty little. Of course when a raid is on anything <u>might</u> happen which might be said of the possibilities of accident even when one shakes apples from a tree to his chums below."

Bill priced new clothing in Barry for the next stage in his life. A decent suit cost $15.00 to $17.00, English shoes $3.00 to $4.00. He needed little else for the moment, and would Helen please send his great nephew, Bill Anthony's address.

Writing from the privacy of *Darcoila*'s fo'cas'le, on August 27th, he told Helen about a hitch in his plans, a little glitch.

He had signed on for six months and was frozen in that job because of new wartime rules. He had to serve the remaining three months. "It seems that all merchant seamen are given Naval status for the duration of the war so virtually we are in H.M. Navy. Gosh, I would get hung up on something like that! However I am not discouraged and even if I have to stay with the ship for another three months (the articles have already been running for three months) I shall finally get my discharge in England. . . . Have you been canoeing since I left home? How does the house look now? I expect the taps and everything else cause you constant worry. . . .

Heaps of love and keep your spirits up Sweetheart. Love & kisses. Ever Bill"

In his next letter, he explained how he circumvented the 'regulation.'

Captain Anderson advised Bill that he could not break the articles he'd signed and Bill, undoubtedly, reiterated his plans to join the RAF. Liking the efficient, affable grey-haired seaman and recognizing his eagerness to sign up, Anderson approached Barry's shipping master, explained the situation and Jones' potential. The shipping master grinned, then visited Barry's mayor. They concocted a technicality to bypass the rules and formally declared William Jones a Barry citizen. Gave him a ration card to prove it!

Bill stayed on the *Darcoila* a little longer and lovingly admonished Helen with: "Gee why aren't you here to let me hug you. I would take you right away to some quiet Welsh village and what a time we would have!"

"Hello Sweetheart: Just think, Sept. 1st so soon.

I am still aboard ship at Barry and expect to leave here for London tomorrow noon. (Sept. 2nd)

The Captain has been very good indeed. He has consented to release me if the immigration authorities are agreeable… He told me (and I hesitate to tell you as you will think I'm conceited and I'm not – in fact I was always modest) what do I hear you say– anyway I shall tell you just what he said: "Jones," said he, "I am d-m sorry to let you go. I wish I had a crew like you. You are the best man aboard. The others are all bluff. But," he continued, "while I have no authority to release you, I shall do everything possible to assist you and if you have influence in London you may go for a weekend and see what you can do, and I shall do all I can at this end to get you off the articles, although I don't want you to go."

The plot worked and Bill was discharged fair and square.

Bill later described his frugality: "I have been busy trying to get clean since yesterday noon. You should have seen me. The entire crew was amused at my appearance. I kept one of my shirts for a work shirt and all that is left of it is the collar band and buttons. I had to cut the sleeves off weeks ago and since then rips and tears have had their run (a pun). The pants that I got from Ira are a scream. You know how well I can use the needle, well enough said, there were gatherings here and there until the blessed things became so small and tight they resembled nothing I have seen in style catalogues. My shoes, well, the heels came off some time ago. The holes in the soles became so large that I could just put them on upside down as easily as right side up. However, Sweetheart all has worked out splendidly. I have twenty pounds sterling and can soon equip myself."

He purchased trunks, vest, socks and boots in Barry and would stop in Cardiff for a suit the following morning.

Helen was having problems with the cranky furnace and Bill promised to address that issue when his plans were finalized.

He predicted enthusiastically: "By another three or four months we shall be well on the road to air supremacy and unless we

83

are silly enough to lose our heads in the meantime, there will be little chance of "Jerry" gaining a foothold here."

On Monday, September 2, 1940, Bill travelled to nearby Cardiff, was stalled there briefly while the Germans visited overhead—his first real taste of war. Sirens sounded nearby and everybody dashed for the air raid shelters. But he sat outside the Immigration office and calmly wrote Helen: "I had rather an interesting day yesterday. I left the ship to go to Cardiff about 2:30 p.m., right after dinner. I took the bus to Cardiff (fare 1 s. 3d.) and visited the central park. The municipal buildings in Cardiff are really magnificent as you will see from the picture post cards I am sending under separate cover . . . ."

The all-clear siren finally blew and he concluded: "Well I said good-bye to the ship's crew and I rather hated to do so. . . . Capt. Anderson told the Shipping Master that he hated to sign me off but here I am. They helped me get a passenger's registration card and now I am as good as a subject of these islands. I can go anywhere without fear of being detained. Also, since I carry a seaman's certificate, I have the privilege of half fare on the railway to London."

He was nearing his goal.

The *S.S. Darcoila,* departed Barry for Philadelphia as part of Convoy OB-217. On September 26, 1940, mid-Atlantic between Newfoundland and Britain, German submarine U-32, skippered by Hans Jenisch, torpedoed the steamer. Master William Anderson, and the crew of 30 were all lost and but for the kindness of Captain William Anderson, Bill Jones' story would have ended here.

CHAPTER 17 – CONVOLUTIONS OF BUREAUCRACY

The Battle of the Atlantic began June 1st, 1940 with the Germans hoping to subdue Britain by starving them out—hence the loss of the *Darcoila* and so many like her.

Invading Britain came next, but Hitler concluded it was impossible to cross the English Channel until the RAF was blown from the skies. The Battle of Britain began with daylight air raids in August, 1940. "Der Führer" hoped to draw out British fighter planes, destroy them and eliminate the air force, but he did not reckon with the new-fangled radar. Somehow the British always knew when he was coming and after several months of startling losses, he resorted to night raids only.

Bill Jones was marching straight into these raids but made a small detour to Chippenham, some 25 miles east of Bristol. Miss Gladie Slade, a Great War acquaintance lived there. He wrote:

"Bristol & Chippenham
Tues. Sept. 3rd/40

Hello Sweetheart,

Just leaving Bristol Stn.

Again I find myself on trains en route for Chippenham to see Miss Slade. I just got her on the telephone to let her know I shall arrive at 11 a.m.

How are you this beautiful morning? Gosh Hon, I am lonesome for you. It is cruel to have to move around like this without you being here to enjoy it with me.

I arrived at Cardiff too late to continue on to Chippenham as train connections were too bad. I made many purchases of clothing. Here they are: 1 suit–blue gray with light blue or red pin stripes–3£

18 s., 2 shirts--1£ 3 s., 1 pr. Socks–2 s. 11 d., 1 suit pajamas–11 s., 1 pr. Braces–3 s., 1 tie–2 s., 3 hdkfs–1 s 8 d., 1 valise–3 s., 1 hat–11 s., 2 collars–1 s. 8 d.

I had a sponge bath at a hand basin (in a) gentleman's lavatory, which was presided by the attendant reserving the entire establishment to me by closing the door. Here I changed from sailor to dear knows what–you can name it. I then got a bit to eat and looked for a room which I found at a nearby rooming house for 3 s. 6 d. This morning I reached the station at 8 a.m. and have been traveling since 8:40. . . .

Well Sweetheart, there are raids over some part or other of these Islands almost every day. But our defense forces are strong and are doing wonderful work.

Heaps of love Dearie and will write when I reach Chippenham. A big warm kiss and hug and then more.

Ever Bill

Gee Hon. I have no picture of you. Please supply me with one I like. You know, the original. Just crawl in an envelope."

He found Gladie Slade, her sister, Mrs. Glidden, a bed-ridden invalid and Mim, another sister, who looked after her. Mrs. Glidden was married to Rev. Glidden and they had an adult son Arnold, who suffered from a chronic throat infection.

They welcomed Bill into their home and to Helen he wrote: "After a bite to eat yesterday we sat around the invalid sister and talked our heads off. Then we went over to the main part of Chippenham, visited an antique shop, saw some wonderful antiques, examined the very ancient buildings, then visited the very old church, read some of the funny memorials on the walls which date back to 1670, then admired the handmade slate roofs and later thatched roofs of the quaint shops which line the narrow winding street."

Bill and Rev. Glidden talked until midnight, then he made himself reasonably comfortable on a four foot chesterfield. During the night, air raid sirens woke everyone except Bill who slept right through the event.

Bill left Chippenham on September 5th, heading for London and next day he wrote home on letterhead from Cranston's Waverley Hotel, Southampton Row, London, W.C.I.

"Here I am at last," and told her he had already phoned and made an appointment with the person he wanted to see. Then he explained about the air war above his head: "We had the longest air raid from Jerry last night ever experienced. He caused the warning to extend to seven and a half hours duration. A record so far. The extent of damage was I believe very small. It was almost unbelievable to see the entire capacity of Lyons' big restaurant, the dining rooms of many of the largest hotels and the entire premises of most restaurants entirely opened up to the public, free of charge of course, as air raid shelters. Most of these buildings are concrete and reinforced steel. No serving is allowed and all tables are cleared of their linen and utensils. The people lie down on the floor to sleep or sit in chairs leaning over the tables half asleep. Honestly, to sit and look over the scene causes in one the queerest reaction. To think of such places in peace time bristling with business and admission based on the extent of one's pocketbook, now to be so changed as to become a charitable shelter, without charge."

He discovered that: "Everything is being regulated extremely well here. Rationing, while on a reduced scale, still provides ample food value and people have no thought or notion of complaining. For instance, one gets 1 cube of sugar for a cup of tea. Three ½" diameter balls of butter for a meal. Eggs are .08¢ each and very hard to get. Everything is evenly distributed and no favoritism, this is a fact I believe."

Bill next presented himself at General Montague's office.

Initially, the general wanted to pass him off as just another wannabe, a one-eyed one at that, but soon became entranced by Bill's determination. Montague mapped out a plan. In minutes Bill was introduced to more generals than he had ever seen. He was sent to Major Cameron who decided he needed to meet his close friend, Air Commodore Critchley who was away for the weekend. (Critchley was Bill's commander during officer training at Bexhill.)

87

Bill hoped and prayed he would remember him and splurged on a new pen for 5s.

His inquiries at Canadian Headquarters produced the whereabouts of his great-nephew Bill Anthony stationed just 14 miles away at Walton-on-the-Hill. To pass the weekend, Jonesy telegraphed that he was coming that afternoon, boarded a train and was off.

Seeing a familiar face from home was wonderful and he found that his great nephew was a dispatch-rider chasing all over the countryside on a motorcycle and loving it.

On Sunday he attended church, then he and Bill caught a bus to nearby Richmond to visit Miss Slade's married niece, Mrs. E.M. Glidden (Betty for short). Betty was a teacher and they liked her immediately. She shared a house with another teacher, Miss Day, and the school principal, Miss Sendamore.

The following morning, the teachers drove Bill Anthony to his base and Bill Jones caught an 8:30 a.m. train to London. He met Major Cameron and was told to go straight to Torquay, in Devon County in southwest England and report to Critchley.

He boarded the 2:30 p.m. train and arrived 12 hours later at 2:30 a.m. in pitch darkness. After sleeping briefly at the Palm Court Hotel, he telephoned Critchley only to discover he had returned to London the night before. Bill was interviewed at length by the wing commander who suggested he take an instruction post. He filled out another application, hurried back to London hoping to catch Critchley and spent the night exploring the bombed out areas.

Bill wrote to Helen: "And Heaven help old Jerry if he lands foot on these islands. Each raid adds fury to the peoples' determination to give him a good trimming. . . Jerry has about as much chance of winning his objective as the proverbial snowball."

On Wednesday, September 11th, Bill finally met Critchley. As to the interview he wrote Helen: "Critchley asked me to be content with an instructor's part for awhile. He could see no possibility of becoming a pilot right away as there are so many on the waiting list who have had aviation experience and therefore have prior opportunity to serve in that capacity. He assured me that should I have an opportunity to serve in a more active capacity that

88

he would release me and not prejudice my plans. On those terms I accepted his offer and was advised by him that I should hear from him Friday, September 13th."

The war was becoming more of a reality and Bill wrote to Helen: "So much is happening over here, experiences happen so quickly and there are so many of them one finds it difficult to keep things in order. This is what has happened to Betty since Bill and I visited her Sunday. Monday afternoon at 5:30 Betty & Miss Sendamore were returning to their house after school on bicycles (as most people move about here these days). They had just entered their house when they heard the noise of aeroplanes. They looked out the window and saw nine planes flying quite low. Naturally they thought they were British. No sooner had they withdrawn from the window when they heard a terrific explosion, then another and several more. The house shook badly and as soon as they recovered their senses then ran to the back door. The lady living next door shouted to them that her house was hit by a bomb. Betty and Miss Sendamore ran to her and there they saw the entire front of the house blown in, all windows, pictures and fixtures completely broken and every wall of the building cracked and moved considerably out of place so that it was not safe to remain inside. The bomb had made a big crater (hole) in the lawn just in front of the house and the windows in all the adjoining houses on both sides of the street (except Betty's house which was undamaged except for one or two tile shingles, which were broken) were missing altogether or badly broken, as the result of the force of the explosion. It was not long before the firemen and police arrived and ordered everybody out of the area for several blocks around. (No casualties resulted in this particular area, although several houses were tumbled to the ground.) Betty and Miss Sendamore took their handbags with just their personal toilet kit and went back to the schoolhouse. There they have been ever since. The school authorities have built underground shelters of concrete to protect the children by day, in the event of raids. The staff use these shelters every night. They try to sleep on wooden benches and cover themselves with a blanket. Of course few sleep at all during the hours of a raid, and Jerry has been over here, I understand, every night this week."

89

Home-owners or renters dug shelters in their yards. Cold, damp and chilly, they held the barest necessities. The day after this bombing, Bill borrowed tools, scrounged lumber and began building bunks in the dugout shared by Betty and her housemates. That night they invited him to use the school's shelters where he promptly fell asleep and slept through Jerry's 11:00 p.m. and 3 a.m. visits. Everyone was weary in the morning and just as they sat down for breakfast, enemy planes roared over again. Finally at 9:30 a.m. they finished their meal. Despite disruptions, everyone carried on and Bill became accustomed to this new norm. While writing to Helen he would casually mention: "I hear the guns (a-a + anti-aircraft) so I presume the enemy are overhead. Yes, I hear the drone of engines. They are very high up."

And "By the way Sweetheart, I shall be a Lieutenant in the air force or a corresponding commissioned rank and from that point promotion is possible to air commandant (equivalent to Lt. Colonel in the army)."

Bill missed his beloved canoe but discovered he could rent a Peterborough canoe (This thoroughly Canadian product had somehow found its way across the Atlantic.) and he and Betty went paddling on the Thames. They found a tiny spot to land, built a fire and brewed their tea but he longed for it to be Helen poking the embers and saying things in her "funny Irish way."

By September 17th the ladies' dugout bunks were finished and they returned to 23 Marchmount Road. Not caring to sit idly waiting for word from the RAF, Bill made himself useful to the three women and the school where they taught. At one point they were sticking cheesecloth to the windows and Bill was varnishing it thus creating shatterproof glass.

Finally he heard from Critchley who had signed his application and forwarded it to Major General Montague. For some reason they wanted his Great War decorations. Did they doubt him?

A few days later he wrote: "Our day is greatly shortened because of the raids. Every evening it is now a routine to go to the dugout immediately supper is over and prepare the blankets etc. before it becomes dark. At nine or nine thirty the warning (siren) is

90

sounded and everybody, except those on duty or like myself, who prefer to stay in the house, go to their shelter (dugouts) for the night. It is about six a.m. that the 'all clear' goes (sirens again) and people return to their houses for an hour's sleep before going to work. Queer life hey what? ... This district is his favorite course to London and the Midlands, so we hear his countless machines in steady streams milling their way above us. The odd plane on its homeward journey, when flying over us will drop the odd bomb."

Another brief message from Critchley advised the wheels were turning and on September 28, 1940, Bill wrote:

"Hello Sweetheart:

My it was good to receive your letter yesterday dated Sunday, Sept. 8th. My girl was in bed with a cold. I do hope you are all better now Dearie. You must not overtax your strength in any way. I trust that Marjorie will not be too much for you to care for. (Note: Marjorie was a youngster that Helen was taking care of.) If you think she is at any time, please make other arrangements and spare yourself for my sake.

I received a letter from mother also. She is greatly worried as she has not heard a word from me. I have written her from each place I have been stationed long enough to write and I can't understand whatever has happened to my letters. Please keep her informed as you get news from me, Dearie, and that will help her a lot....

I was surprised to hear that both Doug and Cecil are in the army. (Bill's brothers.) How in the world did Doug ever manage it? Yet I with twice the physique could not get to first base. Unfair I calls it .... A great big hug and kiss and shake that old cold off right away. Sorry I'm not there to keep you tucked in. Ever Bill"

A formal acknowledgment from the Secretary of State arrived stating his application was being given immediate attention, and he complained to Helen: "Gee, am I tired waiting! Surely I shall not have to endure such inactivity much longer." A month had passed! His new friends encouraged him and meanwhile, he studied the Air Force manual and installed electricity in the ladies' dugout at each of their bunks.

He was summoned to appear before an Air Force selection committee on October 15th at 3:30 p.m. and decided that if he did not make it through, he would join the merchant marine. He was not quitting.

The 40-minute interview Bill left confident that he had passed muster since they sent him across the street for a medical examination. That went well. They noted his left eye, but gave no indication on what affect it would have. He returned to Richmond to await further instructions.

He missed Helen terribly; wished she could join him. The waiting was distressing; he felt he was taking advantage of the kindness of friends, his ship income was dwindling and it was time to take action.

"Hello Sweetheart," he wrote. "The 23rd of Oct. How the time flies. It does seem a strange thing but how many twists and turns I seem to make on the 23rd of something. Sometimes it almost haunts me. This morning I moved from 23 Marchmont Road, Richmond, to 9 Bonamy Street, Bermondsey, way out in the east end of London. Yesterday was the seventh day that I was asked to wait for instructions. Well I just couldn't think of waiting idly any longer, so I set out yesterday to look for something to do. I just followed my nose more or less from the heart of London and tramped in the direction of the most destruction. It wasn't long before I came to a great amount of damaged and demolished buildings. (Please note they were chiefly old shacks and of little or no military value.) When I considered it about favorable I decided to look up a local labor exchange. I soon found one and when they were able to grasp the full details of my case they got busy and found me a job. Within an hour and a half I was employed. The foreman instructed me to report at 8 o'clock this morning. I have to work …. My work is very light, removing debris from a factory which a bomb has caused."

Two days later he sent more information to Helen: "You were no doubt surprised to learn that I am working for a living. I started last Wednesday and have worked three and a half days. It is most menial work but necessary in the face of such destruction. Everybody is doing something to help in this struggle and my patience just became exhausted. I had to do something useful so I scouted around until I got this job. We are removing debris from a factory building (Cooper, Dennison & Walkden) which came jolly near being put out of business altogether. Fortunately production is being maintained and we are helping to clear away the mess caused by a bomb which landed plumb on the stock room .... I was determined not to be idle and it gives me great satisfaction indeed to be self-supporting at least. I work from 8 a.m. to 4:30 (with half-hour for lunch). We get 1s 5d. per hour. Yesterday I drew 1£ 12 s. which is the pay for 3 days (24 hours).

"My room is quite comfortable. An elderly lady, 65 years, has managed to remain in her home, as very few people have in that area, and is glad indeed to have me with her. I pay her 8 s. a week for the room. The windows are broken out and a large hole is in the roof of the house, but at least there is water. I have a sink just next to my room which is very convenient. I still have to burn candles for light upstairs. There is electric light downstairs and a small coal stove in the living room. I am privileged to use the living room whenever I desire. (There goes the air raid warning, the weird noise of the sirens gives one the creeps. We have had three warnings already this morning.)

"I have so far only managed to get tea and buns to eat. As the entire district has been badly wrecked, there is not a restaurant for blocks. One night I did manage to get a slice of fish and chips. I am not suffering for something to eat, Dearie. I can always make a meal. I am just describing the conditions as they are. I have thought of getting the lady to cook my meals for me. It will cost more but I may do so, at least one meal a day.

"When I tell you I inquired of twenty or thirty houses in the district before I could find one room even fit to live in you will have some idea of what it is like. People leave the area at six o'clock in the evening to sleep in the tubes and to visit relatives for the night as far away as Richmond. The few people who remain, like the old lady, take shelter in their dugouts. I prefer my bed on the second floor. People are spending from twelve to sixteen hours per day in

93

their dugouts these days–yet the work goes on and the spirit of the people is wonderful. . . . It is an experience of a lifetime to pass through the tubes (subways) and see the thousands (millions) of people lying down side by side, to spend the night. They do it so willingly and merrily, children, young people, middle aged and old are all there, night after night, sleeping in their blankets, coats or whatever they have."

Bill was relieved to find Walter & Wilsons had installed a new furnace in their house but had no idea when their bill could be paid. At his job he got into steam fitting, carpentry and digging and described himself as "happy as a clam in mud."

Mrs. Doran, his landlady stuffed him daily at noon--maybe a nice lamb chop, mashed potatoes, baked beans, Brussels sprouts, apple sauce and rice. This hardly seemed rationing. For other meals, he bought bread, cheese, butter, tea, sugar and whatever else he fancied.

Despite war's grimness, it had its moments as he described on October 27, 1940: "Bill (Anthony) is looking splendid. He is a Lance Corporal (one stripe) and is now acting full corporal. He is very keen about his work and is mighty anxious to get on. He had a narrow escape this morning. A bomb fell a hundred yards or so away and shook the house that he was sleeping in. He said as he heard the whiz of the bomb getting louder and louder, he felt himself getting smaller and smaller until he felt the plaster from the ceiling fall on him. He jumped and said he never dressed quicker in his life. He ran out to see what was hit. Fortunately nobody near was injured. Then five more bombs fell in quick succession. The funniest thing that he witnessed was in one case a bomb divided a house in such a way that an elderly gentleman who was in the bath tub suddenly found himself fully exposed on one side. Bill said one wall was completely blown away and here the old boy was looking over the side of the tub down on the spectators. His clothes had been hanging on the wall that was blown away. The spectators had to put a ladder up for him to come down and also to supply him with clothes."

On weekends, Bill visited people like Betty's married sister,

Olive Garvin, a 20 minute walk away at Blackheath. "Her husband is a doctor," he wrote Helen, "in the army, but living at home in Blackheath. When I arrived at the door I was drenched to the hide. My legs and feet were quite wet. As soon as I entered the house, Olive took me into the sitting room where two of her girlfriends were seated before an open fire. One of the girls is a sister of Dr. Garvin, the other is a graduate of the same nursing school that Olive graduated from before she married. Immediately Olive made me take off my shoes and socks–much to my embarrassment, but not the least bit to the surprise of the others. Olive is like that. She is candid like yourself and never stands on ceremony. She served tea and later supper. Dr. Garvin was on duty and would not be home until sometime today. It was raining so hard at eleven o'clock when I was about to say goodnight that Olive made me bunk down on the chesterfield for the night. She and Miss Garvin (who by the way, works in the Foreign Office) slept in the basement where the other tenants of the house sleep."

It galled Bill that he was doing nothing as the war progressed. Mussolini had just sent 200,000 troops into Greece via his puppet state Albania expecting an overwhelming victory but his attack was badly planned. Though the Greeks had an obsolete air force and lacked mechanized equipment, they expelled the invaders a month later in mid-November. 'El Duce' (Mussolini) was greatly embarrassed.

In the dark of November, Jones commented to Helen on the re-election of Theodore Roosevelt to the presidency for the third time and gave her detailed instructions on changing tap washers.

He became a regular at the home of Douglas and Olive Garvin and Olive became grist for his letters. On November 11, 1940, letter #11, he noted to Sweetheart.

"Olive Garvin is a scream. She does everything in her own original way and I'm sure you would die with laughter at some of the things she does. Her housework is a hit and miss proposition. She cooks as she feels. Sometimes she achieves a successful effort and to her surprise something good will come out of the oven. It doesn't fizz her a bit if it turns out any other way. She serves it up just the same. The other day (Sunday) she took an apple pie out of

95

the oven and let it drop on the kitchen floor. We heard a grunt and before we could inspect what had happened she was busily scraping it up on four different plates and without any apology was carrying it in to us with a mere casual remark "excuse the broken appearance. I had to scrape it off the kitchen floor." A mouse had eaten the top crust when it was on a plate on the kitchen shelf, and had left little black deposits all over it. Olive brushed them off and assured us that the mouse had not eaten much because it found the crust to be "too tough"."

He added: "Why I am obliged to wait so long for word from the Air Force is a mystery to me . . . I am determined to join the Air Force. . . but there will be a limit even to my patience. One thing is certain I can join the army now at any time or the merchant marine."

The damp, poorly-heated English homes were his Achilles heel. "The open fire feels good as I have not been warm since yesterday. I got such a drenching last night, and it was so cold, I have not been comfortable since."

November 15, 1940 their fifth anniversary was a lonely one, and he reminded Helen of their kiss at the altar of Sherbourne United Church. She had looked so sweet. As an afterthought he added: "Our guns are barking away but still the drone of his (Jerry's) engines is very audible. The temperature here in my room must be very low. My nose is cold and I can clearly see my breath. Mrs. Doran is in the shelter at the rear of the house. I am the only person in the house."

He was now covering the roof of the damaged factory with rubberized roofing. He and the foreman knew little of the process but were figuring it out. He enclosed a 1£ note in his letter for which she could collect about $4.30 Canadian at the bank.

November was dark with "Rain, rain and still more rain! Every day it rains at least three or four hours." Nightly there were air raid sirens accompanied by the distant thump of bombs. Heavy drapes were hung over windows so not the slightest speck of light leaked out for the enemy to spot. The homes were chilly and damp with most of their window glass blasted out and replaced by bits of cardboard. Tiny coal fires barely warmed a sitting room. Bill conveyed the atmosphere to Helen. On November 21st, he wrote:

"By the way, I have never described a journey from my 'digs' to Blackheath. I rush home from work as black as I usually look when working, give myself a complete sponge bath, change into my dress-up togs and run for the bus. Thousands and thousands of people do the same thing evidently just about the same time of day, because all streets along Old Kent Road (refer to London map) seem to be swarming with running people, carrying anything from a roll of bedding to coat, umbrella. Those carrying bedding are running to nearest shelter, others are scurrying from work trying to get a bus, train or other vehicle to carry them to their homes or places of abode for the night. You have seen University Avenue at rush hour in the evening. Picture such a highway with trucks, buses, trains and cars all hurrying to get along, with pedestrians in groups waiting at the 'stops' and many others running or nearly so, trying to make their way along as best they can. Public conveyances have proved to be so inadequate to carry such a mob in such a short time, that the Government has decreed that owners of private vehicles and trucks are obliged to stop and pick up anyone that is at the usual bus stops.   For this the owners of these vehicles are permitted to purchase an additional quantity of gasoline. Pedestrians so picked up are not obliged to pay but they may contribute whatever they wish to the driver of the car. The government has assumed full liability insofar as personal injury is concerned (a touch of real socialism hey what?) What I do is to try to gain foot room on a bus if my patience is good enough–if not, I walk, rain or no rain. I arrive here (distance about 3 miles) at about 6:30 p.m. We have supper at 7:30 or 8 and then we read, write or study until 10:30 or so, have a cup of chocolate and then I walk home. . . ."

In December, he reported to Helen: "You will be amused when I tell you how cold it was when I visited the little cubicle at the rear of the house. Most English houses in this area have no conveniences inside. A tap and sink is about the limit of plumbing installed. Gee, as I sat there, I was thinking of you and could not picture you having to experience such crude and cruel exposure on a frosty morning."

Still no word from Critchley and Bill discovered that the Germans had devised something new during a visit to 23 Marchmont Road:

"Miss Sendamore and I talked before the gas grate until almost nine o'clock. She related the terrible experience they had had Friday night when sixty or seventy high explosives were dropped in that neighborhood. Fires were started in all directions. Fortunately Betty had stayed with her Friday night. They were alone in the dugout and were evidently quite brave. They went up to the surface in the midst of it and as they said, the many fires and flares round about made it as light as day. Planes were humming overhead in great numbers. Many buildings were burned in the business section and two incendiaries pierced the roof of the school. There were extinguished immediately by Wheatly, the man in charge. Miss Sendamore and Betty went out to offer assistance in putting out an incendiary bomb and took the pail of sand and a shovel with them. Just before they arrived at the bomb, a gentleman was throwing sand on it when it exploded and injured him so that he had to go to hospital. Lucky indeed for Miss Sendamore and Betty. This is the new kind of incendiary bomb that Jerry is using. It burns away and when it is bothered or touched the d-m thing explodes and scatters missiles about. Jerry is a fiendish sort of fighter and will stoop to the lowest and meanest tricks."

Meanwhile, Bill struggled to forward money to Helen from Lloyds Bank, Richmond, to the Bank of Nova Scotia in Toronto. England did not want its currency leaving the island.

On December 19, 1940, Jonesy noted that his RAF application was still alive and being favorably considered. A recent communication expressed concern over several missing teeth in his lower jaw and that he needed to get replacements. They were keeping him waiting just for that! He made an appointment with a dentist and the work was to cost four guineas.

Christmas parcels arrived from Canada and Bill was invited

to so many gatherings it became a dilemma where to go.

By Christmas Eve he had received his "eight new teeth, Dearie. Four molars on each side of my lower jaw. They feel like mountains. When I eat I don't know what I'm chewing. But what a mouthful. The dentist filled my front tooth so that as far as teeth are concerned, I am well equipped. One advantage of a plate is that one is free to lend it to others. So far I haven't had any requests."

Christmas day was a whirlwind. At 3:15 a.m. he, Douglas, Olive and Betty drove off in pitch blackness. Wartime regulations reduced the light emitted by headlights to the size of a .50¢ piece. They arrived in Blackheath by 8:00 a.m., attended church with Rev. Glidden and returned home to Christmas dinner. There was an excellent roast beef served with two kinds of potatoes, mashed turnip and Yorkshire pudding, followed by fruit pudding with custard sauce. Plain fare, but sumptuous enough. An afternoon walk wore off dinner and while there, Bill opened three parcels from home containing practical gifts of blue socks, short bread, shaving cream, toothpaste, sweets, a delicious cake, tea and cheese.

Helen's parcel arrived on December 29th and he found gloves, more socks, pajamas, undies and a flashlight. He also received a certificate that day from the dentist confirming his dental work for the Air Force. Hopefully this was the final holdup.

The year turned to 1941. The weather was below freezing and his landlady complained that her laundry froze on the line.

His job would last another couple weeks. Now in charge of roofing, he had four men under him and work was keeping him physically fit.

On January 2, 1941, he wrote: "Hello Sweetheart, Please excuse this writing as I'm sitting by the stove fire, lights out as the meter requires a coin, trying to see. I can follow the lines but can scarcely see the spelling. Mrs. Doran is next door and I don't know the combination of the meter. People in this country don't get what they can't pay for as they use it. It's somewhat of a nuisance having to put coins in the electric meter, gas meter etc."

Days later, the plant superintendent informed Bill that he was increasing his pay by a third.

His landlady kept life interesting and he wrote: "Mrs. Doran was funny the other day. The previous night had been very cold. I noticed that my tap upstairs was frozen. I asked Mrs. Doran if it ever got any colder in England. She was astonished by my question and said, "Why, how could it get any colder, didn't it freeze water?"

January 7, 1941 – "Wednesday evening I called on Rev. Mr. Moore whom I heard preach last Sunday. He and his daughter live in a house without a roof and sleep in a public shelter every night. He gave me a rather vivid picture of religious conditions in England, and seemed to be a bit sad that the church has fallen into a state of unpopularity on the whole. His wife and two youngest children are evacuated to a safer spot in England. The daughter who is staying with him is about nineteen and is employed at a gas company's office nearby." Soon after, fire gutted the upstairs leaving him with only one useable room for a study and sitting room.

To assist the war effort, Bill became a Warden and spent several evenings a week on fire duty or rescue work in the event of bombings. His elderly landlady was hospitalized following a stroke and he remained in her home tending to things there.

And finally, the orders with "O.H.M.S." printed on the envelope arrived on February 14th, sort of a Valentine.

CHAPTER 18 – FINALLY!

At last! The six month wait was over.

Bill was measured for his new blue uniform and he gave Helen his new address as: 54 Group, R.A.F., Alta Vista, Higher Warberry, Torquay, Devon, the most popular winter watering hole in southern England with picturesque hillsides overlooking the English Channel.

He excitedly wrote: "I only wish you could be here Honey, we would have a rare old time in the Old Town tonight. Gee am I glad! Your prayers have all been answered and I owe it all to you. Whatever lies ahead, this much by way of accomplishment goes down to your credit. Keep up your prayers and perhaps some day I shall be seated in control of a great big Spitfire helping to give Jerry his dues. Please don't fail me now Dearie. No half-hearted prayers or opening one eye. That won't do. So far and for some time my duties will be to carry on as a beginner. I take the usual elementary training then am kept on administration and special duty work. I must not be left in a rut. I want to fly and fight."

Bill said goodbyes to his landlady, Mrs. Doran, and his new friends. He bought medal ribbons, rosettes and oak leaves for the tailor to add to his uniform and by February 23rd was outfitted in his dashing uniform at a cost of 46£ with 40£ to be reimbursed by the government.

He arrived in Torquay and wrote: "Torquay is a very hilly spot. The hills are steep pinnacles and I believe there are seven such formations. Houses and buildings cling to the slopes on steep curves like so many scabs. Streets are narrow and winding. The shopping centre–Union Street–is quite well representative of most chain store companies. All in all it is a most pretty spot. The waterfront, of course, is the great attraction. Sandy beaches and a wide concrete promenade along the entire front provide room for the thousands of tourists who flock here every summer. At present, of course, there are few tourists here."

Bill was billeted at Belmont House, a boarding house owned by a Mrs. Downing and mainly occupied by London evacuees and elderly people. His room was large, airy and cold as the garage back home. There was a wide old-fashioned wooden bed, a single iron bed, a tall dresser with a mirror, and an old fashioned bureau with endless drawers. There was a fireplace with a coal grate, a wicker-topped table, a commode with hand basin and water pitcher and a chamber pot on the floor. The bathroom was three doors away. Meals were poor. "Hot water is available on Friday in case anyone should require a bath. I don't think it is used very much as people on this side have not yet become educated to the idea of daily or bi-weekly bathing. A toilet next to the bathroom appears to be more popular than the bathroom."

Bill Jones was in uniform, posted, and content for the time, to be under Critchley's command.

Life was instantly regimented starting with morning parade before breakfast. He was assigned all sorts of odd duties. Instead of being there just for instruction, Bill would also be an instructor. He took his turn as Duties Officer which often fell in the evenings until midnight. There was guard mounting and regular night-time duty. His careful letters home were now censored and he did much of that writing during night duty. Some Sundays he took the church parade and heard the chaplain, Squadron Leader Buchan.

He made the acquaintance of a fellow officer and his wife by the name of Phillips. From them he learned he would earn about 1£ per day, prompting another attempt at Lloyd's Bank to send money to Helen. If this failed, he felt Helen should find some way to come to England.

There were off-duty activities like the Spa Baths for swimming and weekly dances at the City Hall where he once actually asked a young lady to dance and admitted: "I then saw Miss Pipe (rather a peculiar name) home. It was a long walk in the pitch blackness of blackout. The journey was uneventful except for the misfortune of Miss Pipe running full force into a stone wall which jutted out on her side of the sidewalk (pavement as it's called

102

here). She struck her forehead an awful wallop and it was only a minute or so before a bump the size of an egg appeared just above the eye. No doubt her eye will be black today."

In mid-March, Bill received a perfect hand-knit sweater from Helen, along with butter, a rare luxury, and cigarettes which Bill handed to the smokers. He longed for chocolates!

He immediately began taking courses, beginning with machine guns. It was half through but he resurrected past memories of the Lewis gun, learned the parts of newer guns and scored 84 on the test.

Bill Anthony took a week's leave in Torquay where he slept until noon every day. They took in picture shows like *Pride and Prejudice* starring Laurence Olivier and Greer Garson, attended a vaudeville show and took long walks through the countryside.

Jones was mastering Morse code and could soon rattle off six or seven words a minute. Once he got the sound of the dot and dash fixed in his mind, letters gradually became nothing more than combinations of dots and dashes. He plugged away at algebra and logarithms until his head was dizzy.

During this time, Hitler was on the move, unhappy that British troops and aircraft were aiding the Greeks, and that Bulgaria and Yugoslavia had reverted to neutral positions. He needed them under his control. On April 6, 1941, Hitler sent a blitzkrieg into Yugoslavia where the pro-Nazi regime of Prince Paul had just been overthrown. (Prince Paul ruled the country as Regent until the future King Peter reached the age of 18 in 1941.) They struck Belgrade and forced the country's surrender ten days later. Simultaneously, Hitler moved troops into Greece smashing through their defenses and Britain hastily withdrew from the Greek mainland. Germany overran the country.

Torquay was comfortable and war was a distant disturbance aside from the occasional drone of very high airplanes. The sun shone warmly on the peaceful hills

On April 9, 1941, Bill reported to Helen: "It is my turn for duty again tonight. Everything is quiet, most of the troops are asleep

103

and I'm sitting here in a comfortable wicker chair before a very cheerful open fire. I see you running about doing the chores, washing, cleaning, cooking and then wishing that you were here. My how those hours must be long for you. They are mighty long for me. I know they must be longer for you. You are a mighty brave and wonderful girl Honey." He added: "I have armaments off; signals test will be Friday; law, navigation and several other subjects are at various stages along the way. Perhaps by another two months I shall have completed my work here. I then hope to be posted to a flying school, if I'm lucky." Bill wrote about his friendship with the Phillips, the Allans (he was the adjutant) and the Glovers (he was the squadron leader). They enjoyed walks along the cliffs, had tea at the Glen Hotel and enjoyed long conversations. And: "Tomorrow evening we have a swimming gala on at the Spa Baths. I'm in the officers' relay race. We had a try out this afternoon. I wasn't quite the slowest but very nearly. I'm never a speed artist it seems–wish I were. But I didn't fall out."

Days later, he wrote: "I take time out this beautiful sunny, warm afternoon to chat with you. It would not require very much imagination to know what we would be up to if you were here. I'm sure the beautiful cliffs would find two very affable and extremely amorous people among its visitors. Then we would have a game of tennis, tea at the Queen Hotel, a show at the Palace Pier and then a dance at one of the many halls or hotels, then to bed. What a weekend we would have. Church tomorrow morning, more tennis, a glorious walk along the sea line. This is the spirit of spring and the beauty of this part of England is just unequalled. From my window I hear the song sparrows as we would listen to them at 45 Lakeshore Drive. The entire countryside is a picture of freshness and wondrous beauty. . . . Our Squadron kept the cup for water sports when we competed the other night with Nos. 1, 3 & 4 Squadrons. I swam in the officers' relay race and as usual, came in last. It was good fun though. I wish I could swim well. Some of the chaps are excellent. . . ." And finally: "Heaps of love this Easter day. And do justice to that chicken, send mine to me all made up with love. I love you more than ever if that is possible. A great big hug and kiss. Ever your Nurts"

Helen's finances were an ongoing nagging concern and he reported that the Royal Bank would forward 10£ per month to her-- and he got 97% on his signals test.

Jones' duties and work intensified.   In April, he was appointed training officer for his first "Flight" of 50 recruits and Bill feared he would become so swamped that he'd never have the opportunity to fly. This well-educated group included three BSc's, four MA's and nine school teachers. The cadets worked like Trojans, had high moral standards and refrained from wine, women and song. He often sat late into the night marking 50 test papers. Not a year earlier he had been shingling and painting their house.

Graduation photo of Jones' with his "Flight" of 50 men. He is in the second row from the bottom, second from the left. Photo courtesy of Bill Jones Jr.

Teaching cut into his course-taking yet he received 94% on the gas test, but was disappointed with a 76% in hygiene. He should have taken more time, he told Helen, noting that his supervisor was Lord Ratendan, the Duke of Wellington's son. A week later, he reported the lord had incorrectly added his score and he had actually received 86%. Bill was the one officer actually completing the exams and failed to understand why the others were content to just train the others.

Missing Helen terribly, he dreamed up ways to get her to England to ease their financial situation. He met with Assistant Section Officer Elaine Waterman from the Womans Auxiliary Air Force and she unsuccessfully suggested the F.A.N.Y.S. ('Fannies' for short) who did dispatch riding, chauffeuring, clerical and supervisory work.

Germany and her allies now dominated most of the non-Soviet European continent. They exploited Europe for its resources, industrial plants were geared to German war needs and millions of Europeans were forced to work in Germany's war plants. Political dissidents, Jews, Slavs and gypsies were interned in concentration camps and 6,000,000 were exterminated though this horror was only later discovered and vague rumors were held in disbelief.

On May 20, 1941, Hitler dropped 3,500 German paratroopers on the British held island of Crete. Most were killed, but a second wave captured important defenses and overwhelmed British troops. Hitler had another stepping stone to North Africa.

At this time, Jones wrote to Helen: "Last week I simply got so knotty, mentally, that I couldn't think 'nohow'. It was a piece of good luck when Adjutant Allan and his wife, Mr. & Mrs. Inkeldon and the officer W.A.A.F. and I went over to Totnes Sunday a.m. and were able to spend the day on the river Dart in a great big clumsy row boat. The Dart is a tidal river and there is nothing but mud on all sides when the water recedes a bit. We soon became plastered with mud but that didn't matter, we were able to have our lunch on the river bank about noon, and later on and much farther down the river, we had supper over an open fire which we made. By that time the tide was about half out and what a struggle it was to row back up the river almost three miles with tide and wind against us. We arrived back at the pub at Totnes, had a bit of a clean-up, coffee and waited in the lounge until a bus came along. We waited for three buses but they were so crowded that we couldn't enter them. Then

106

we hailed a truck on its way to Torquay and what a trip we had. Everyone enjoyed it thoroughly. The weather was bright and sunny and everyone acquired their first suntan. I longed for you to be with us Dearie and at times I really felt miserably lonesome."

Two days later Bill reported that his squadron won almost every event in a "swimming gala" the previous night, including hilarious skits, an officers' relay and kept the cup despite Jones being a slow swimmer. Two weeks remained in their training and the brief river respite with friends left him able to grapple with the final courses on aircraft recognition and navigation.

Next day, Bill had more small-boating adventures. "Miss Waterman (the W.A.A.F. officer) and I went canoeing on the river Dart. It was a bit cloudy and dark when we reached Totnes (the point from which we set out in the canoe), and we paddled downstream to Dittisham, or very nearly there and found a sandy piece of shore, amidst mud flats on all sides, on which we decided to have our dinner. The rain had begun by this time and it poured torrents until we left for home at 6 p.m. We turned the canoe upside down and supported it with props and then sat under it while a cheerful fire did its duty by boiling the kettle. In due course the rain became constant dripping from the side of the canoe, drenched the cushions, the floor covering, the only thing we had to sit on and by four o'clock we were wet through, notwithstanding the fact that we had our mackintoshes. We had a second fire about 5 o'clock, reheated the left over tea from dinner and ate part of the food we had left and then decided to paddle home. It poured all the way up river and were we wet! However it was real jolly fun. Miss Waterman never had an experience like it in her life and she enjoyed it thoroughly. One of her sergeants was to go with her but at the last minute found that she couldn't manage it. Honey you should have been there. You would have died laughing."

By June 5th, Bill had written his last two exams but was not hopeful of great marks in the difficult navigation course.

On June 11th he had an interview with Critchley. To Helen he wrote afterwards: "Honey it was just another Ralston affair. Critchley lost his head entirely and went off on a tangent. I simply couldn't get anywhere. The Squadron Leader who accompanied me was most sympathetic with me after the interview and couldn't understand why I should have been treated so beastly. However, I held my head and took an awful lashing. He was simply unreasonable and blind with prejudice and overbearing manner. . . . These fellows have a warped conception of their own importance and they are misleading the entire country. A day of reckoning is coming I feel and I hate to think of what might eventuate. . . . Needless to say I am somewhat unhappy mentally after being hopeful that I would be given at least a hearing. I have finished the courses here and am the only officer to have done so since they started. It makes me jolly well mad to think that this fact is not recognized."

June 16, 1941 he wrote: "Well Sweetheart it's an ill wind that blows no good. After that experience with the A.O.C. (Critchley) last week I was not feeling too happy as you may judge from my letter. All day Thursday and Friday I tried to think my way through this perplexed position I had found myself to be in. I had come to the conclusion that I had better seek a way out of the Air Force as it would be hopeless to achieve anything after that battle with the chief. Lo, and behold, Saturday morning the Wing Commander sent for me and apologized for the way the A.O.C. had treated me on Wednesday and informed me that the A.O.C. had relented from his stand and that I am going to be sent on to the Bomber Command. Boy, oh boy! . . . I'm afraid I was sort of dazed. Gee Honey to think of actually getting there after such an uphill climb.

"Am I lucky for once in my life. The unpleasant thing is I shall not be able to tell you what we are doing from day to day as such must be kept most secret. However you will no doubt be able to put two and two together. That son-of-a-Critch certainly played a great one on me. . . .

"I expect to get my moving orders very soon–probably in a very few days."

On June 21, 1941 he reported: "Friday night, when passing by the Wing Headquarters, Critchley called me over to where he was standing and informed me that I am going to the bomber command

108

in the Middle East (Mediterranean). Gee I was so happy I could hardly refrain from being excited. He was awfully funny and called me all sorts of horrible names, whimsically. He was really funny. Jolly good of him hey what. After the terrific abuse he gave me that memorable Wednesday. It all seems to be like a dream Sweetheart. I certainly didn't think I should have such an opportunity as this. Almost everyone here is envious and some are very jealous and upset about me getting such an outstanding appointment. I attribute it all to my stand with Critch the other Wednesday. Most of the officers here are very pleased that I have it and keep asking if I can ride a camel. Well, Dearie, at last after almost a year of effort we have achieved our aim."

Hitler dreamed of conquering the Slavic people of Eastern Europe and the USSR giving him the additional *lebensraum* (living space) where he would establish German colonies served by the 'inferior' Slavs. He began preparations in December, 1940.

"Operation Barbarossa," began June 22, 1942 when he launched a blitzkrieg with 121 divisions on a 3,200 km. (2,000 mi.) front stretching from the Baltic Sea to the Black Sea. They moved into Leningrad. Moscow was approached by forces moving east. To the south, they marched toward the Ukraine and Kiev then planned to turn south to the Crimea, cross the Don to the Caucasus and finally to Stalingrad on the Volga River.

Hitler surprised the Soviets. In 18 days, the attackers advanced 640 km. (400 mi.), captured 300,000 prisoners, 1,000 tanks and 600 big guns.

CHAPTER 19 – INTO THE WILD BLUE

After purchasing his tropical kit including cork helmet and shorts, Jones took a week's leave and the train to St. Andrews, Scotland to gain some personal flying experience.

He visited headquarters there and his friends the Phillips, who had recently transferred there. He saw Lord Haddington, who kindly requested the wing commander to take him flying.

To Helen he wrote: "Here I am writing on one of the most exclusive letterheads in the world. I don't suppose the Fathers of this 'Royal and Ancient Golf Club of St. Andrews' would rest long in their graves if they were aware of my presence here. Such a breach of the sanctity of this place. And yesterday was a red-letter day here, by the way. The first game of <u>Sunday</u> golf was played on the St. Andrew's links. There is almost civil war in this community and I'm certain there'll be someone burned at the stakes. Such contempt and disgust, if not horror, one hears from the locals regarding this sacrilege of yesterday is expressed in today's newspapers, in the phrase, 'the introduction of the Continental Sunday!'"

Another day he wrote: "All officers here are honorary members of the Honorable and Ancient Golf Club of St. Andrews. It is the oldest club in the world, the place where golf had its origin. Phil took me over to the premises this a.m. I was most impressed by the appearance of the clubhouse and the place is steeped in traditions, convention and such conservative atmosphere. Earls, dukes, etc. comprise the membership. The monarch of course is a member. I'm an honorary member."

Jones actually stayed at Inchcape Private Hotel and never did tee off in front of the massive club house.

As to the first flight: "Tame I calls it. Hardly as much thrill as rowing a heavy rowboat about the harbor of Toronto. Still it's better than walking and I know you'd enjoy it as much as I do.

What shall we have Honey a seaplane? Well today I go on a much longer jaunt. I do wish I could tell you full details."

Next he reported: "What a thrill I had this a.m. We were pretending chasing an enemy. Gosh of all the twists and turns we made. It was great. I only wish I could manage the controls. It looks easy enough and I think I could easily do it. In fact it looks to be as easy as driving a car."

Added to this: "A funny thing happened last night. My batman suggested that I fill the sink with cold water for morning else I'd find the water too hot to wash in and usually, in the morning, the cold water would not be running. I turned the tap full open just before getting into bed and as no water came, I left it open and put the plug in the drain. I went to sleep and left the sink stopped and water tap open. I awoke about five o'clock, heard a terrific downpour of rain, turned over and went off to sleep. The next thing I heard was two (they were censored from the letter) who had entered my room and shut off the water. The blessed water had come on during the night, filled the sink and flowed all over the floor. There had been no rain except on those poor chaps on the floor below me. Gee I felt sorry."

On July 6, 1941 he sent Helen's letter with an airman returning to Canada. No censorship this time and he wrote more details of his upcoming plans and how much he had enjoyed flying.

Jones returned to Torquay for final orders. He visited friends, said goodbyes and tracked down his trunks which had gone missing when shipped from St. Andrews to Birmingham.

Bill was still unable to send money to Helen and was declared ineligible for additional separation pay because he came from outside the "sterling" area. "Stupid regulations," he called them. Helen took in two girls as paying borders.

Meanwhile, despite an aversion to communism, Churchill promised Stalin economic and technical assistance against the Axis invaders. On July 13, 1941, Russia signed a mutual-aid pact with London followed by additional offers of help from Washington.

CHAPTER 20 – ORDERS TO THE MIDDLE EAST

He wrote: "Aboard train July 30th/41. Hello Sweetheart. Here I am at last on my way. I wonder where! At any rate I have got my kit for the Middle East. We must make our own deductions. What a job I had last evening getting away from Torquay. I was orderly officer right up until 6:45 p.m. when I received instructions to pack and catch the 8:54 p.m. train. But even then my uniforms were at the tailors being repaired and adjusted. Several other items were also scattered 'all over the shop.' It kept me right on the hop to get everything packed and ready by 8:30 when the transport called for me. Sorry I'm not able to give you an address but at this moment I haven't the foggiest idea where mail should be directed."

The following day at sea: "It is a very nice canoe Dearie. A first class one in fact with all the frills that go with it. To see the quantity and quality of food served one wonders if there is a war on." He was aboard some luxury liner, and part of a large convoy. Bill found it interesting that: "There are many of the opposite sex aboard–girls of various organizations. They seem to be getting a tremendous thrill out of it. It is wonderful to see the intermingling of the sexes in this war. It adds a real sense of cooperation to the picture, which impresses one with the seriousness of the job we have on hand. I fully believe it will go far to break down the superficiality of the male attitude toward women as women are proving themselves fully capable of performing a man's work."

At the time of sailing, both Britain and Russia had occupied Iran forcing its pro-German ruler, Reza Shah Pahlavi, to abdicate on September 16, 1941 in favor of his son.

The sea trip was many weeks long and life soon fell into a routine. There were drills in case of enemy attack, tame to an old seaman like Bill, but to the greenhorns, it was a matter of getting to the right place and understanding port and starboard. He spent hours reading, chatting with passengers and talking shop with crew members. A regular task was censoring mail. With very little opportunity for exercise, he ate sparingly, often asking only for soup, a portion of fish and dessert.

Days were much the same as the ship pressed southward in gentle swells. By August 6th, beyond sight of land, they headed east. He wrote: "Another day and still I am not within sight of you. Headed in that direction though but only for a day or so likely."

A week later, he informed Helen that his mailing address would be: "R.A.F., Middle East Command, Cairo, Egypt." So now she knew his ultimate destination–sort of.

Afternoons passed with shipboard games: deck tennis, quoits, swimming, running. It was warm and sunny, the sky filled with big white clouds and the sea deepest blue. The occasional porpoise accompanied them to everyone's delight.

While Jones rode the southern seas, US President Roosevelt and Prime Minister Churchill met on a navy vessel somewhere off the Newfoundland coast and signed the Atlantic Charter on August 14, 1941, a counterthrust to possible German peace offensives and a statement of postwar aims. Within a month, the USSR and 14 other allies endorsed the Charter.

By August 26, 1941 Jones wrote: "The familiar constellations we used to watch revolving about the North Star are fast becoming lost to view whilst the newer and less familiar formations of the southern sky appear each night. The Southern Cross has not yet come into view but Mars is already appearing as a ball of fire. . . .

"At a port of call recently (likely continental Africa) we were entertained by native (black) salesmen in their (here he drew a tiny sketch of a native canoe) small, perilously frail canoes. (It is my ambition to take one of those native dug-out canoes back home with me.) The natives are scantily clad in a part of a shirt or just a cloth (loin). They are all men who come out to us and many dive for silver coin, others try to sell oranges, bananas, mangoes, coconuts,

113

monkeys, knives (sheath), sandals, small basket containers, cow horn racks (a group of polished cow horns mounted on a piece of wood to be used as a hat rack.) Rain poured almost incessantly and one felt clammy and depressed pretty much all this time. The shoreline appeared to be green and trees resembling the hardwoods of Canada intermingled with palms gave the landscape a decidedly attractive appearance."

By September 1st the balmy, tropical weather became cooler, "similar to Canadian temperature at this time of year. In fact I could easily imagine that we are just off the Nova Scotia coast." With the cooler temperatures, Jones gave a talk to the passengers on the "Canadian Outlook."

By September 3rd he wrote: "I might say we are well out of sight of the North Star and the Southern Cross is clearly in view each night. We have passed under the sun and would likely see icebergs in the Antarctic if we continued in our present direction."

The Southern Cross does not become visible until 25°N. Lat. and they were now well south of the equator heading for the Cape of Good Hope. Sea water temperature dropped from 78° - 82°F. to a chilly 58°F.

The seas gave the ship a pleasant roll for a veteran sailor. "Several things slip and slide all over the place. One has to be careful in walking or he will likely find himself running down hill. There was quite a commotion last evening as the glasses slid off the tables. Apart from the roll of the ship there is no departure from the daily experience of sea, sea, sea. (Gosh I just caught my ink bottle. It was in the act of taking a grand slide off the table.) I am seated in my cabin before the dresser alone with you. Two bunks are on my right (mine is the top one), two other bunks are on my left, a dresser facing me and an "L" on my right running to the side of the ship to the porthole and, at the end of which is a wash sink with running hot and cold water. We have electric lights over each bunk, electric heater and air vents for warming and cooling, large wall mirrors, and heavy battleship linoleum covering the floor with thick mats to step out on. Fawn colored and wool blankets and white sheets and very comfortable mattresses. The woodwork is all white enamel, furniture polished birch, clothes press large and ventilated. All in

114

all, it is first class accommodation."

Continuing south, they watched seals cavorting and rumors circulated of upcoming shore leave and there was a bricf lcg-stretching opportunity at some port in South Africa where Jones and two other officers were hosted by a Mr. and Mrs. Lubke, a South African married to a woman from Ingersoll, Ontario.

The ship began steaming north in the Indian Ocean.

On September 14, 1941, he wrote: "Hello Sweetheart, What a beautiful day it is. Notwithstanding the fact the sun is directly overhead, the temperature is not oppressive. I spent quite a long time this morning, stripped to the waist and below the knees trying to acquire a suntan. I am many shades darker than I was when I left England still I'm not as dark as you have seen me at 45 Lakeshore.

"Just think, Dearie, it is almost six years ago since we established our little home at 45 Lakeshore. We certainly didn't anticipate anything like this did we Sweetheart? I keep living over and over again all our associations and it's wonderful how green and fresh the memory of them is. I find myself running away on one of our weekend excursions to the north, or reveling in the memory of doing the chores at home. What good fun we had and what fun we are still going to have. I can truthfully say that on this sixth anniversary I am more intensely in love with you than ever before in my life and were it not for the war I would delight to my heart's content to assure you of the fact in full reality. I realize only too well what you are enduring and it grieves me deeply to think of being separated from you. Hope for happier days never ceases to give me courage and compels me to pursue this road no matter how difficult it may be."

And his last shipboard letter:

"At Sea
16-9-41

Hello Sweetheart.

Sitting on a sunny deck wearing only shorts. What a life and they calls it war in the Middle East. . . .

115

We have every reason to believe our days are few aboard this palatial liner. In fact I redistributed my kit this morning in preparation for disembarkation. Whatever next comes into this adventure, life I know not but whatever comes, I'm ready for it. . . .

I have been puzzling my wits to know how to remit money to you. Just what new regulations have come into being since I left England I don't know. In any case there must be some way for me. I can't believe it will long stand that a married man, just because his wife is living outside the Sterling area, is not entitled to separation allowance. It just doesn't make sense and more especially when a man has money of his own that he should not be able to send it on to you. My bank account at Lloyds, Ox & King Branch, London is slowly building up. So far I can't see why one should require much money out here though I'm told that the cost of living is quite high. I shall even find out all there is to know about it.

The heat is quite intense at present. Last night, many of us carried our blankets up to the top deck and slept under the stars. I hadn't anything but my khaki trunks on–not even a shirt. There was a strong wind for most of the night but it was very warm. You would have reveled in such. It was the nearest thing to those rocks on our point at Echo that I've experienced.

Well Sweetheart, I must run off now. Heaps of love and a big big hug & kiss and happy dreams.

Ever your Nurts."

The ship traveled through the Suez Canal to its final destination and life became even more secretive and classified and a whole segment of Bill's activities become largely lost to time.

CHAPTER 21 – THE MIDDLE EAST

First stop Cairo, Egypt. It was September, 1941.

Second stop– the Island of Cyprus--Bill's first assignment.

Of this posting, he said: "As Crete had just then fallen, and it looked as if Cyprus was in for a to-do, I jumped at the chance."

Long a British colony, Cypriots were staunch Allied supporters, particularly after the invasion of Greece. Over 6,000 volunteers fought under British command during the Greek campaign and 35,000 Cypriots served in the British forces.

The island escaped actual war except for limited air raids but was an important Allied supply and training base, a naval station and significant air base.

Jones' job was Ground Defense Officer for Royal Air Force members based there. He discovered that not one of the 4,000 RAF personnel was armed and promptly requisitioned rifles, taught them to shoot and organized the defense of Cyprus with effective rifle defense tactics. He effectively developed his own system and successfully fulfilled the assignment.

Six months later he was transferred to the Western Desert to provide similar training for 205 Group, a heavy bomber group that formed part of the Mediterranean Allied Strategic Air Forces (MASAF). Jones served under Air Commodore Gayford.

This African war would play a key part in the Allies' eventual success.

A British army contingency had long been posted in Egypt protecting the vital Suez Canal. As long as Britain controlled the Suez, Nazi Germany could not use it. With Allied bases in North Africa, they held the potential to attack what Winston Churchill called the "soft underbelly of Europe," meaning Italy and Yugoslavia. Hitler greatly feared that possibility.

Two players came to the fore in this match.

Major-General Bernard Montgomery, (1887-1976), was compared to a ferret and nicknamed 'Monty,' and unlike many senior British officers, he went out of his way to meet his soldiers. He lived an ordinary lifestyle and though his command base was a luxurious North African house, he lived in the garden in a trailer (caravan). He was a teetotaler, anti-smoking, but ensured his men had access to cigarettes and felt that if a soldier needed a woman, why then he should have one.

Field Marshall Erwin Rommel, (1891-1944) was in the 1940 German push to the English Channel heading the victorious 7th Tank Division. The following year he was placed in command of the Afrika Korps in North Africa. A brilliant tactician in desert warfare, he drove the British from Libya to El Alamein by June, 1942. His success got him the nickname 'Desert Fox.'

Following Italian reverses at Tripoli, Hitler sent more troops to Africa to clear out the Allies.

In March of 1941, while Jones was in Cyprus, Rommel attacked the Allies in Libya and pushed them back into Egypt. Only coastal Tobruk, in northeastern Libya, held out. British General Wavell designed "Operation Battleaxe" to maintain their tenuous hold on Tobruk but failed. Churchill fired Wavell and replaced him with General Claude Auchinleck whose attack on Rommel in November, 1941 forced a retreat.

The Desert Fox re-organized, then bulldozed his way to Gazala in January, 1942. The Allies lost Tobruk by June. Thirty-five thousand Allied troops were taken prisoner and Churchill deemed it a "disgrace."

By July, 1942 Rommel was within 70 miles (113 km.) of Alexandria, a situation so dire that Churchill traveled to Egypt. He fired Auchinleck and placed General Harold Alexander in charge of British land forces in the Middle East and Field Marshall Montgomery commander of the Eighth Army.

Montgomery designed 'Operation Bertram' to convince Rommel that most of the Eighth Army was heading south. Dummy tanks were set up and a dummy pipeline was built. The ruse was successful. The real plan was 'Operation Lightfoot'with Mont-

118

gomery knowing Rommel's attack would come from the south. He dug in his tanks and waited.

Monty was reinforced with more men and U.S. equipment, while most German transport ships heading for Benghazi, Libya, were sunk by ships and planes. The attack came on August 30, 1942, at Alam el Halfa, south of El Alamein. The Germans were beaten back by the Eighth Army, a prime example of army and air force co-operation.

Actually, Rommel was on sick leave in Austria. His replacement, General George Stumme, died of a heart attack the following day and Hitler ordered Rommel back to Egypt.

On the night of October 23, 1942, Montgomery began a five hour, thousand-gun artillery barrage. Two British columns moved forward and cut a deep salient into German lines. Rommel counter-attacked. Monty's troops withstood for two weeks, but after being bombed day and night, they abandoned the battlefield and returned to Libya.

Churchill angrily accused Montgomery of fighting half-heartedly. Monty ignored him and developed a new offensive, 'Operation Supercharge.'

On November 1, 1942, Montgomery's Eighth attacked the Afrika Korps at Kidney Ridge. Rommel resisted but soon ran low on resources. Three days later he ordered his troops to withdraw, but was overruled by Hitler. The Eighth Army broke through Nazi lines and Rommel was forced to retreat.

A sudden rainstorm on November 6th turned the desert into an impossible quagmire and prevented the British from entirely cutting off Rommel's army. Down to 20 tanks, the Germans did reach Sollum on the Egypt-Libya border.

Two days later, the Allies invaded Morocco and Algeria under General Dwight D. Eisenhower leaving Rommel's depleted army facing war on two fronts. On November 12, 1942, the British Army recaptured Tobruk.

During this whole El Alamein campaign half of Rommel's 100,000 men were killed, wounded or taken prisoner. He lost over 450 tanks and 1,000 guns. The Allies suffered 13,500 casualties, 500 tanks were damaged but 350 were repaired.

Churchill said of El Alamein: "Before Alamein we never had a victory, after Alamein we never had a defeat."

Until just before El Alamein, Jones was busy in the Western Desert serving as RAF aerodrome defense officer. His ground defense scheme magnificently coordinated army and air force personnel into a defense unit for the area in the vicinity of Kilometer 40, on the Treaty Road, West of Alexandria.

It wasn't all work though. Jones had leaves and went sight-seeing despite the blazing war. On January 1, 1943, on letterhead from the Luxor Hotel, Luxor, Egypt, Bill wrote:

"Hello Sweetheart,

Having bummed another piece of paper I shall try and give you some idea of what I have seen today….

We (my guide and I) set out to see the valley of the Tombs of the Kings this morning leaving the hotel at 9 a.m. We had to sail across the Nile (about half a mile wide at Luxor) then row up another small stream finally taking an old Ford, which was waiting for us on the other side of the Nile, and drive about five or six miles to the Libyan Mountains–a range of treeless hills running about 500 feet high. Just plain rock and dirt similar to what one sees in Egypt when away from the valley of the Nile. Well up in the hills, like a long ravine, one sees several holes resembling openings of mine shafts. These are the openings to the tombs, some 70 or 80 already formed of former kings and in other parts of the hills another ravine –the valley of the tombs of the Queens and still another part of the hills called the valley of the tombs of the Nobles. All together some hundreds of tombs already discovered and the promise of many more yet to be unearthed….

To think that one must indulge in erecting one's own monument long before one dies seems to be mighty queer to me.

Now for my bath. Please wash my back Honey. A big heartfull of love and kisses galore for my girl on her Birthday. Happy dreams and now turn over and sleep. I know you are weary.

As ever Your Nurts"

CHAPTER 22 – SOME VERY UNUSUAL TRAINING

Jones' highly effective training methods captured the ears at Army Council headquarters in Cairo, Egypt.

"Are you Jones?" Colonel-in-Charge Kinmount confronted him one day in early 1943.

"Yes sir."

"Well, I've got a proposal," he continued and invited Bill to transfer to the army for an even more challenging task. Then he surprisingly asked, "Will you jump?"

Jump? It only took a second to work out the meaning and another to consider it before Bill replied, "I'll jump. Anywhere!"

The Colonel offered no further clues, but explained that it was quite unusual to transfer from the Air Force to the Army, almost a step down. He would have to be discharged from the Air Force and re-enlist in the Army as a 2nd Lieutenant.

"You will then be promoted to the rank of major," the Colonel continued, "to be confirmed immediately."

"Sir, I'd like to request that I be allowed to wear the uniform of my old Great War regiment, the Royal Black Watch."

"Well," said Colonel Kinmount thoughtfully, "I believe Major General Rennie of the Black Watch is in Cairo and I would suggest we have lunch together."

The major general understood past loyalties and consented to Bill's request stipulating only that he wear the red hackle in his beret (the feather plume) of the British Imperial Regiment.

"You will be a member of the Imperial Black Watch this time and not the Canadian."

Bill was tickled. He was so proud of the Black Watch name, British or Canadian.

And parachute jumping from an airplane! That might be the closest he ever got to solo flying.

As soon as the paperwork was completed in February, 1943, he was shipped to Haifa and Ramath-David near Jerusalem for two months of para-commando training. He learned about guerilla warfare, espionage, spying. He had no idea where this was going, but the prospects were certainly heady.

Bill's letter to Helen indicates it wasn't all work:

"King David Hotel, Jerusalem, Palestine, 10-2-43

Hello Sweetheart,

Just a line to wish my 'Valentina' all the happiness in the world. Here among the relics of a very old civilization one sees little to suggest St. Valentine. Jew and Arab bedecked in beard and kalabash, milling about in the narrow alleys of the old city, set the visitor back to days when pastoral life in all its simplicity and extremes of inequality characterized life here. . . . Tradesmen are seen here making their wares in the same crude simplicity as their ancestors did two thousand centuries ago. But here in this hotel, outside the walls of the old city, one lives in an atmosphere of the ultra modern. The "King David" was built at great cost only a few years ago and reflects all the glitter and superficiality one sees in the western world. Such contrast as the two extremes of civilization causes one to wonder and consider whether or not life has missed its point on purpose. The King David certainly could never be used or entered by the vast multitudes of poor who live in the hovels of the old city. . . .

A big hug and kiss and happy dreams–may the same come true. May St. Valentine never fail to supply arrows for cupid's bow and perfect his aim for all time. A great big heart of love to my Valentine.

Ever, Your Nurts"

This letter curiously reached her by some convoluted route. The 3¢ stamp is Canadian and the handwriting pure Jones. Notes scribbled on the envelope say: "Washed up on Gibralter--found,"

"Found in Egypt," "Forwarded to Canada S.S. Slowboat," "Forward: Mrs. Wm. M. Jones, 45 Lakeshore Drive, New Toronto, Ont. Canada," "25-2-43," "Via England," "Lost at Sea." Somebody carried it to Canada and mailed it from Digby, Nova Scotia. The letter took two months to reach Helen.

In an undated letter, he wrote:

"F/OW.M.Jones   #215
MO4 Middle East Forces

Hello Sweetheart:

Just returned from five days' trip about this beautiful country. [Palestine] I am more than pleased that I was able to get about and see so much of interest and to see collective farming at first hand. I am deeply impressed with the possibilities and fully believe that collectivization is the answer to many economic and social problems. I wish I knew more about it that I could give you a first rate picture of it as it works here. One sees units of from ten to fifty families living together on from two or three hundred acres to twelve hundred or more acres depending on the funds available and the suitability of the land for agricultural purposes. . . .

I put a pack on my back and hitch-hiked altogether about four hundred kilometers–walking about thirty kilometers each day to keep fit and strong for my next job.

I feel so selfish at having seen so much during the past few days that I could weep for you to be here. You were ever in my thoughts and wherever I went you are as well known as myself because I tell them all about you. I still haven't a picture of you and it will likely be quite a while before your mail reaches me.

My heart is full of love and happy dreams and a big hug & kiss.

Heaps of love, Bill"

As noted in the return address, Bill was now part of MO4 (Military Operation No. 4). Churchill had created this very classified army secret intelligence department to work with M15 (British secret intelligence service) and the Special Branch to monitor and combat subversion and disorder.

With an inkling of the task ahead, he gently warned Helen that communications might become very sparse, if any.

Bill Jones completed the intensive, grueling and unusual training including six practice parachute drops of which he dryly remarked, "The first one was the hardest."

While Jones' mysterious guerilla training progressed, on March 20, 1943, Montgomery attacked Rommel at the French Mareth Line in southern Tunisia. Joined by Eisenhower's First Army, the Allied forces overran the Axis troops from the west and the south and pushed the Germans into the northeast corner of Tunisia. By May 7, 1943, Tunis and Bizerte had fallen and five days later 250,000 German Afrika Korps and Italians surrendered.

Now back in Cairo, Bill wondered what this training was all about.

"How about Yugoslavia?" Colonel Kinmount asked.

"Why not. As well there as anywhere."

The colonel explained, "We believe we may have been backing the wrong horse in Yugoslavia. You will be parachuted into Croatia on a dark night to find out the facts."

"Is it a people's movement?" Jones wondered.

"We believe so, but we know very little about it, only what we have learned from escaped prisoners who have returned to us via Yugoslavia and reported that they were guided and protected by members of a partisan resistance movement. Here are some reports you can read to see for yourself."

Bill Jones knew next to nothing about Yugoslavia but he learned fast. Alright! Now he was a spy!

That Jones was selected by intelligence officials for a mission was unusual: middle aged, white-haired, spoke no Slavic languages, one-eyed, but determined to try almost anything.

CHAPTER 23 – THE COUNTRY AND THE PLAYERS

Though its history began in the dark ages, Yugoslavia was actually established on December 1, 1918, a kingdom comprised of Serbs, Croats, Slovenians and several minority groups.

The country embraced 96,000 square miles including 1,000 miles of spectacular Adriatic seacoast. Only 28% was arable and much is ruggedly mountainous. In the 1940s, the population was 16 million comprised of 8.25 million Serbs, 1.5 million Croats, 1.5 million Slovenes, half a million Germans and smaller numbers of Rumanians, Albanians, Magyars and other Slavic people, an uncomfortable mélange of nationalities, traditions, languages and religions–Orthodox, Roman Catholic and Islam.

There were seven provinces:

Slovenia, to the northwest, is mountainous with a mainly Roman Catholic population of 1.5 million. Despite outside pressure, they maintained their language and culture, were well educated and deeply religious. Ljubljana, a university town, is the capital.

Croatia, south of Slovenia, is a vast plain, a patchwork of fields. Croats considered themselves Central European rather than Balkan. Their language is similar to Serbian. Cultured, refined, well-mannered and mostly Roman Catholic, Zagreb, another university town, is their capital.

Dalmatia, bordering the Adriatic Sea, is barely 35 miles wide, best known in Yugoslavia as a vacation destination. It is isolated from the rest of Yugoslavia by rugged mountains, and inhabited mainly by Croats and some Italians.

Bosnia and Herzegovina is west of Serbia below Croatia.

Wild, high mountains alternate with thickly forested valleys. Sarajevo, Bosnia's capital, was where Austrian Archduke Franz Ferdinand's assassination precipitated World War I.

Montenegro meaning 'Black Mountain' is a tiny province on the Adriatic inhabited by remnants of tough, fearless warrior tribes who waged continuous struggles for liberty for centuries.

Serbia, the largest province, lies east of Bosnia and Herzegovina and has the longest history of independence among the provinces. The people are hospitable, friendly, courageous and mainly Orthodox. The countryside is covered with maize fields and rows of sunflowers. Belgrade is the capital.

Am anonymous joke considers their ethnic diversity: "A Serb (short-tempered, high spirited) sits on a tack. He curses and throws it away. A Slovene (industrious, thrifty) sits on a tack. He pockets it for future use. A Bosnian (hardworking, dutiful) sits on a tack and says: "The Party may have directed that this tack be placed here. I will put it back."

Yugoslavia, 1943

The Royal House

Beginning December 1, 1918, King Alexander I ruled amid fierce Balkan politics. Assassination was an occupational hazard. In 1934, while traveling with the French Foreign Minister in Marseilles, France, the trigger was pulled by Vlado Chernozemski, a member of the Internal Macedonian Revolutionary Organization which was agitating for separation from Yugoslavia. Chernozemski was beaten to death by onlookers before police arrived and this was the first assassination ever caught on film because it occurred right in front of a photographer.

Queen Marie, his 34-year-old widow, remained in Belgrade with three sons, the oldest being 11-year-old Crown Prince Peter Karageorgevich. The great-great grandson of Queen Victoria, he was crowned King Peter II on October 11, 1934, two days after his father's death. Partly because of this British connection, Britain supported him and his army in Yugoslavia far too long.

The late king's cousin, Prince Paul, was appointed regent until Peter's 18th birthday, a daunting task for the inexperienced Prince who soon showed the same lack of force as the late king.

Prince Paul wanted to remain neutral but Hitler wanted the Balkans at any price. The worst mistake of his life was allowing himself to be pressured into signing a pact with Hitler.

King Peter II came of age in 1941, was in power three weeks, then swept from the throne by occupying Germans. In Britain, he headed the Yugoslav Government-in-Exile. He urged his country to fight the Germans though the Royal Army had been eliminated. He then unwisely backed the underground resistance forces of General Draga Mihailovich and associated his name with the Chetniks, a resistance group working in the pockets of the Germans. He was formally deposed in 1945.

Though the Germans overran the country in 1941, it was the only time they had complete control. The unexpected resistance from the common people soon liberated half the country. The Nazis were forced into a defensive position to hold what they occupied and maintain their goal of controlling transportation routes heading

127

south.

Colonel Dragoljub-Draza Mahailovic

He was born on April 27, 1893 in South-West Serbia. In October, 1910, Draza Mihailovic entered the Serbian military academy and participated in Balkan wars against Turkey in 1912-13. He served in the Serbian army during World War I in Albania, then returned to the academy for higher education.

Between 1927 and 1935, he was deputy chief, then chief of staff and commander of the king's guard. A stint as military attaché in Sofia followed and a promotion to colonel. The following year in Prague, he gained experience in the field of intelligence work and became interested in guerilla warfare.

In 1939, he presented his superiors with a reorganization plan by nationality for Yugoslavia's armed forces reasoning that nationally pure units increased cohesion and fighting capabilities. His superiors despised the plan, punished him with 30 days in prison and publicized his disgrace to the army. A year later, he served another 30 days for participating in a quasi-political/cultural gathering organized by the British military attaché in Belgrade.

Following the German invasion, Mihailovic was appointed deputy chief of staff of the 6th Army district in Mostar, an utterly insignificant position. There he played his own subversive role working both sides of the fence, assuming authority he did not have and controlling a resistance movement.

The Chetniks

Following the Yugoslav Royal Army surrender in April, 1941, Serbian soldiers set up *chete* (bands) named after armed irregulars who once harassed invading Turks in the 19th century. The most significant group, controlled by Mihailovic, operated from the highland region of Ravna Gora in western Serbia.

Mihailovic ordered these units to avoid large-scale fighting with the Germans known for their terrible reprisals. They occasionally joined German, Italian and Croatian units against the
128

Partisans who they considered to be communists.

Menacing skull and crossbones flag of the Chetniks.
Their motto was: *Za Kralja Otadzbinu. Sloboda ili Smrt.*
(For King and Fatherland. Freedom or Death)

The Ustasi

In 1884 Josip Frank, a Jewish convert to Catholicism, started a movement called *Pravasi* or the *Frankovci*. Ultra-nationalistic, they fostered hatred towards the Serbs. Composed of wealthy Zagreb residents, clergy, towns-people and Croatian undesirables, they organized local terrorist gangs. In the 1930s, the movement, led by Ante Pavelic, was secretly revived as a terrorist organization calling themselves the *Ustasi*.

As the war progressed, Roman Catholic Croatia was gripped with religious fanaticism. An archdiocese newspaper of Sarajevo claimed: "Until now, God spoke through papal encyclicals. . . . They closed their ears. . . . Now God has decided to use other methods. He will prepare missions. European missions. World missions. They will be upheld not by priests, but by army commanders. The sermons will be heard with the help of cannons, machine guns, tanks and bombers." The Ustasi swore oaths to eradicate the Serbs and their Orthodoxy. The Croatian primate, Archbishop Alojzije Stepinac, provided his blessing.

After invading, the Germans created the Independent State of Croatia and Pavelic instructed Croatian soldiers to: "Use your weapons against the Serbian soldiers and officers. We are fighting

129

shoulder to shoulder with our German and Italian allies."

The Ustasi began systematic massacres of Orthodox Serbs in their country. They buried 250 people alive in a Serbian village in Bjelovar. In Otecac, the priest was tortured to death and 331 Serbs were murdered. They planned to exterminate one portion of the Serbian population and force conversion to Roman Catholicism on the other part.

Clergy were tortured and mutilated. The Ustasi arrived at villages, assembled the inhabitants and ordered conversion to Catholicism. Those refusing were locked inside the local Orthodox church which was then set on fire. Thousands were killed by the most heinous methods until even the German leaders thought the group had gone completely mad.

Approximately 700,000 Orthodox Serbs were killed for their faith. Ante Pavelic was called the 'Butcher of the Balkans.'

The White Guard

This was the Royal family's and government's army, there to protect them rather than the populace. Its loyalties became questionable.

Marshall Josip Broz Tito

He was born in 1892 in Kumrovec, near Zagreb, Croatia. While working at the Daimler automobile factory in Vienna, Austria during the Great War, he was conscripted into the Austro-Hungarian army. On the Eastern Front in 1915, he was captured by the Russians. Oddly, Tito participated in the Russian Revolution with the Red Guards, learned a new ideology and later became an activist in the outlawed, underground Yugoslav Communist Party.

In 1935, Tito worked in Moscow with Comintern (Communist International) whose aim was "by all available means, including armed force" to bring about the "complete abolition of the State." In 1938, he became General Secretary of the Yugoslav Communist Party.

After the German invasion, Tito organized resistance in

130

Belgrade, Serbia. He rallied and unified diverse political, religious and national elements and was named Supreme Commander of the People's Liberation Army and Partisan Detachments.

His headquarters were in Drvar, Bosnia and as an unidentified newspaper described: "Now he (Tito) lives in a large room in a small wooden hut with maps pinned on the wall and a big desk covered with papers. He invariably wears a khaki-grey uniform without badges of rank and big black jackboots, a forage cap (the Partisans called it a *Titovka*) with red star and a revolver tucked in his belt."

Tito was an honest, frank outstanding, magnetic leader and military genius.

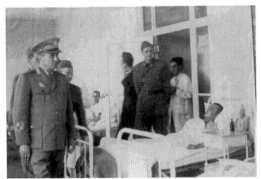

Josip Broz Tito visiting a hospital in Yugoslavia.
Photo courtesy of Joe Maloney.

The Partisans (National Liberation Army, NLA)

Resistance to the German occupation was spontaneous and in June, 1941, the first Partisan detachments were formed in Serbia.

Throughout Yugoslavia, new groups sprang up in hamlets, villages and towns. Each had its leader and fighters. Contacts were made with nearby communities and groups connected to form patrols, companies and brigades. People joined regardless of nationality or religious denomination. Their goal was to establish democratic freedom. They were the Peoples Liberation Army or simply the Partisans.

Masterful guerrilla warfare techniques evolved. They armed

131

themselves by whatever means. A group of villagers would hide in ambush with only a stick or their bare fists. They would creep up behind a lone Italian or German soldier plodding by, point the stick and shout "*Stoi!*" (stop). The enemy usually surrendered. He was dispatched, his weapons, uniform, the much-needed boots, grenades and ammunition were removed and the body buried. Now they could tackle a bigger enemy patrol. More arms were taken and the scale of ambushes grew.

The Partisans attempted collaboration with the Chetniks, but found them unwilling to do anything and eventually learned that their leader, Mihailovic, opposed any action against the Huns.

In Struganik, September, 1941, an angry Tito met with Mihailovic who insisted it was too early for action but claimed he was loyal to the Partisans and would leave them in peace.

In December, Major Bosko Todorovic, commander of Chetnik headquarters for East Bosnia, contacted the Italians proposing a cessation of hostilities and joining together against the Partisans leaving them alone against the Germans and their own traitorous countrymen.

Information about Partisan resistance was leaking to the Allies and Jones was to discover who they supported as well as the loyalties of the Chetniks and Ustasi.

German Propaganda

With the invasion of Yugoslavia, the Germans carefully nurtured age-old vendettas between Serbs and Croats and denounced the Partisans. It was psychological warfare using 'divide and rule' ploy to exploit religious and racial hatreds.

German propaganda claimed the Partisans were the enemy to both. To the Catholic Croat, the Partisan was a Serbian bomb-throwing, bewhiskered communist. To the Orthodox Chetnik (Serb), the Partisan was as a bomb-throwing Croat Communist.

CHAPTER 24 – *ZDRAVO!*

Winston Churchill was anti-communist and anti-Bolshevist, though during his 1943 Cairo visit, he saw the need to extend Allied support to the Soviet Union in order to defeat the Nazis.

While there, Captain William Deakin arrived at SOE (Special Operations) headquarters to reveal intercepted enemy communications and suggested a British mission be sent to Yugoslavia, despite Tito's communist leanings. This partisan army was becoming quite convincing.

Churchill agreed, noting: "The less you and I worry about the form of government they set up, the better. That is for them to decide. What interests us is which of them (the Chetniks or Partisans) is doing the most harm to the Germans."

The wheels were set in motion and Major William Jones was conscripted for the mission.

Graduates of "Camp X" who were in Egypt were asked to volunteer for a task in early April, 1943. Narrowed to six Canadians of Yugoslav background, the first two parachute drops would be somewhere in the mountains of Yugoslavia.

During World War II, Camp X, located on Thickson's Point, Lake Ontario, between Whitby and Oshawa, was the only secret-agent training school in North America. It was so classified, not even the Canadian War Cabinet knew of it. Canada, Britain and the United States sent agents to the barb-wire enclosed enclave to be trained in the shadowy methods of another form of warfare.

Graduates carried on some of the most dangerous acts of guerilla warfare and espionage of World War II. Their work became the stuff of movies and books with some of the most renowned being Sir William Stephenson (*A Man Called Intrepid* by William Stevenson), J. Edgar Hoover (late director of the FBI) and Ian Fleming (creator of Agent 007 James Bond).

On a dark night, April 20, 1943, the chosen six, were divided into two groups and briefed by Captain Deakin. They boarded Halifax bombers at the British airfield at Derna, Libya and, 1,500 miles later, parachuted into their homeland.

The first group was led by Stevan Serdar, a Camp X graduate. Code-named HOATLEY 1, Serdar, accompanied by two Quebec miners, landed in eastern Bosnia where there had been vicious fighting between Germans and Partisans. The Partisans took them to their headquarters where Serdar established their credentials. To celebrate, the Partisans wrecked havoc on a nearby German stronghold the following day.

Suspicion did underlie initial Partisan enthusiasm, but 10 days later a Partisan recognized Serdar, having fought with him in Spain. Trust grew and they were allowed to use their radio. Confirmation from Tito's headquarters established complete trust.

The second group, code named FUNGUS (Jones would work with this group), was led by Sergeant Petar Erdaljach, a stonemason. The other members were Vancouver shipyard worker, Sergeant Paul Pavlich (another Camp X graduate), and Sergeant Alexander Simich, a Serb. On a full moon in April, 1943, they jumped unseen, hoping not to be found by the wrong people. Within 24 hours, they were taken to Croatian headquarters. Like the HOATLEY 1 group they too were viewed with suspicion. With no written orders or identification, the Partisans wanted to shoot them assuming they were disguised German agents.

Tito was contacted and his response was: "Radio set must not be taken away from mission. You can ask them if they do not need two sets, to lend us one. But I underline—only if they give it to you freely and without pressure. Give them necessary information about Chetnik (Ravna Gora) treachery and/or enemy forces but no information about our forces until we give you the details." Tito was being careful.

Days later, a Cairo radio operator received the first messages from behind Partisan lines and for weeks FUNGUS was the only link between the British and Tito.

To establish rapport, Simich suggested they bomb Italian forces at Krivi and outlined details. He felt the Partisans appreciated

134

their arrival and realized the British had been misinformed about the situation. They desperately needed Allied aid and he soon found proof that the Chetniks, Ustasi, and Germans had buried young and old alive, a hideous thing to report.

Telegrams in cipher flew to headquarters. A sampling from Paul: "5/5/43.nr. 3: 19 march 30,000 germans ustasi ten day offensive on partiz in slavonia stop wrecked burnt villages brusnik lipovac cicote evicvare zvacev omelj and drenovac stop partiz counter attack retook all. m.e. paul.

"5/5/43 nr. 5." April 16 partiz. routed 1,600 quote slavonski zdrug taking colonel bosnic 10 officers 600 men 3 guns 100 mm 13 mg. 25 smg. 20 auto rifles 560 carbines 10 mortars 100 dead 300 wounded all st slavonski pozega. m.e. peter"

On May 6, 1943, Paul Pavlich reported that two German officers defected to the Partisans but were rejected until they received confirmation from Zagreb that they were pro-Partisan. Not reported was a disturbing visit to his sister in Debelo Brdo. Her village had been razed by Ustasi, the livestock slain and the people left destitute.

Alexander Simich requested uniforms, caps, coats, khaki drill slacks, ammo, boots, slippers size 8, six shirts, six vests, short pants, army socks, two tents, four beretta magazines, 150 pistol ammo, dubbin oil, sugar, tea, coffee, many tins of milk, pipe and cigarette tobacco, cigarettes and papers, soap and dental paste. They had landed with just the clothes on their backs.

FUNGUS received a response stating "Your messages very useful and encouraging. Destruction of railways at this time also very important for north African front," and they were to establish supply drop locations.

On May 9, 1943, Alex wired co-ordinates for a night drop at Dreznicki Lug. He noted that Partisan headquarters, not totally convinced of British sincerity, was unwilling to give full details of their maneuverings but intercepted German information indicated Partisans destroyed, on average, one locomotive and ten railcars daily. One unit destroyed 160 trains and 15 bridges! And would they send six tons of explosives.

Alex gleefully reported on May 17, 1943, that Yugoslav

GHQ agreed in principle to cooperate with British armed forces, would send proposals and would they send medical supplies to Montenegro. In return, he received instructions to light signal fires 100 feet apart forming an "M" on May 19, 1943, the night of Jones' arrival.

From Derna airfield, a plane thundered into the black sky carrying Major Bill Jones, Captain A. Hunter and Corporal Ronald Jepson, a wireless operator. The plane also carried three tons of explosives and a quantity of propaganda leaflets.

The flight was long; the passengers silent. From 10,000 feet, the plane dropped the leaflets over Zagreb, then continued on to the pinpoint of flaring bonfires.

Much later, above the valley of Krbavsko Palje in western Croatia, Captain Hunter jumped with three tons of explosives (half of Simich's request). He landed safely near a bridge. Jepson, then Jones jumped, drifting silently earthward. Jones wore his black watch beret and carried his New Testament in his pocket. He landed softly and the parachute dropped gently over him. After two years in the bleak desert, it was comforting to land amidst trees and hills.

He had barely cleared the parachute traces when a young man ran to him from the darkness. He greeted Jones with "*Zdravo,*" (Hello) embraced him warmly and Jones, at 47, began the greatest adventure of his life.

A reception party, including Sergeant Paul Pavlich, materialized, greetings were exchanged and they were led to a diesel truck where Partisans were already loading the explosives, equipment and stores dropped from above. The noisy truck drove along a main road for several kilometers, turned down a narrow road for many more and finally stopped at a burned out village.

Scattered among the ruined houses, Jones saw more trucks, a few cars and piles of supplies ranging from lumber to arms and ammunition. This was a transport/supply depot and he began taking mental notes.

They mounted saddle horses and climbed a long, rough mountain track deep in the dim woods. Two hours later, they dismounted in a clearing and followed their guide on foot along a black ravine.

Suddenly there was a sharp, *"Stojl!"* (Halt.)

The guide spoke a password and a sentry allowed them passage. They stopped at a long building with a wide verandah running its length. Another sentry stood at the doorway.

"Zdravo," the sentry said politely opening the door allowing warm light to leak into the night. He nodded and they entered a neatly carpeted room.

A man of about 30, in a neat uniform and shiny black leggings, said in perfect English, "How are you? Did you have a good journey?" He was Captain Drug Manola, adjutant of the Croatian command.

He led them to a long table in a room flooded with light. Electricity? Nice furniture? Bill learned it was captured from the enemy and he was in Croatian Command's secret headquarters no less!.

Manola apologized for the absence of senior officers who were on some night-time enterprise. They'd meet in the morning, but wondered: "Are you hungry?"

"We are," Jones responded. "We haven't eaten since we left Derna."

"We'll have something to eat then!"

Two blue-uniformed women promptly brought a tray of cold lamb, hot fried potatoes, cheese, corn bread, honey and tea. Unbelievably, there was sugar for the tea but not milk.

While eating, Jones turned to Captain Manola and said, "I can see we're going to pester you with questions. I'm quite bewildered at the moment."

They had expected to sleep in the woods and eat the meager rations stuffed into their pockets.

Manola smiled. "We'll be pleased to answer any questions you may ask."

Simich, Pavlov and Erdaljach had prepared the ground well.

"Where do you find provisions like this up here in this bush on a high hill?" Jonesy wondered.

"Yes, we're 7,000 feet up."

"Well how do you have lamb and potatoes up here?"

137

"Everything you see has come on the backs of mules. The food has been provided by the villagers. The equipment has been collected or made and carried up here."

"But where did you get the sugar?"

"Sometimes we're lucky and can capture it from the Italians. They are our commissariat!" He grinned. "It requires some effort but we generally get what we want."

"But what about the electric lights?"

"We generate this here. Alexander and Paul have been here nearly a month, and they have much to tell you. I don't think they have suffered, and now we're looking forward to a very happy association with you."

Unbelievable. Unexpected. So utterly civilized.

While drinking tea, Jones, still puzzled, asked: "Where did you get tea?"

"It's from a native plant and substitutes for tea."

"But what about milk?"

"Ahh, we don't always have milk, but the peasants provide what they can. Every night, women bring what food they've been able to muster. The Partisans look after transportation to whatever spot the troops are located. They carry it on their backs."

Hunger satisfied, Jones and his party were taken to a comfortable room with a stove, large desk, several iron bedsteads, blankets and sparkling white pressed sheets.

"Almost numb with bewilderment, we were quite prepared to resign ourselves to sleep, switched off the light, little daring to speculate as to what the morrow would bring forth, but not a little amused to find ourselves at last with the Partisans in Croatia." (*Twelve Months With Tito's Partisans* by Major William Jones)

Before sleeping, Jones asked Alexander, "Is this the kind of misery you've been putting up with for the last month?"

"Ah, we have lots more misery like this to show you."

In the wee hours, Alex Simich briefly telegraphed British HQ a "perfect landing."

Jones was beginning to realize that was not going to be like any war he had ever heard of.

138

CHAPTER 25 – AMAZING

It was a short night though they slept until 10:00 o'clock.

Poking their heads into the hallway, they were greeted by uniformed men and women who shook hands and wished them: "*Zdravo! Kako si?*" (Hello! How are you?).

A young woman brought hot water, soap, a basin and towel. Breakfast of corn meal porridge with milk, bread with honey and cheese was served and afterwards, Adjutant Manola, announced that the commandant and his staff would see them at 11:30.

Outside the building, Jones observed the changing of the guard. Six arrived; six left. They saluted formally with nothing careless in their manner despite the generally relaxed atmosphere.

After dispatching coded messages to Cairo headquarters, Bill looked around and found more cabins hidden among the trees. They had hand-split shingles, good doors, plenty of windows and electric lights. Telephone lines went to the largest cabins.

The main cabin, where Jones and his men stayed, was about 100 feet long by 25 feet wide, two stories high. This was the administrative building. Other cabins had various uses: guard rooms, records, stores, kitchens, sleeping quarters. Everything was carefully and effectively camouflaged, invisible from the air, barely visible through the trees and then only from close by.

Even more surprising, Bill found this whole enclave was just over the hill from an enemy encampment that had no idea they were there. Amazing!

He dashed off a wireless report to Cairo describing how well the Partisans were organized with an army of men and women and that half the territory was free of Germans and could he please have 50,000 changes of battle dress and detonators immediately!

Punctually at 11:30, Manola escorted him to the Commandant's large office at the end of the main building. It had two windows, a carpeted floor, polished desk, two lounges and three comfortable armchairs. He and Paul Pavlich would translate.

Adjutant Manola introduced Jones to Political Commissar, Dr. Vladimir Bakaric, the provisional president of Croatia, and camp Commandant Rukavana, who boldly asked: "Why is it that we Partisans have been fighting for two years, and this is the first recognition the Allies have seen fit to give us?"

A direct question deserved a direct answer.

"We had practically no information as to what was going on in Yugoslavia, except from prisoners of war who had escaped the Germans and Italians and made their way to Yugoslavia. They reported that the Yugoslav people were very helpful and were engaged in open resistance to the occupation forces."

Rukavana nodded.

Jones went on: "In the past two years we've been so busy preparing our defenses, expecting an invasion of Britain, that it was impossible for us to divert attention from the home area. Now we're ready to meet you, and the British Government's policy is to assist any force engaged in actual resistance to the enemy."

Their minds eased, a productive conference followed. Rukavana provided maps showing areas occupied by Italians, Germans and Partisans. Free areas appeared as islands in the storm.

The enemy wanted control of all communication, railways, main highways, large cities and important junctions clear to the Mediterranean. Jones recognized the impossibility as the enemy was engaged on too many fronts and lacked manpower.

Rukavana admitted to having 150,000 troops, with 10% being women. He added: "There is no standard in the weapons. The person carrying them had usually won them from an enemy he had killed or captured. Every recruit feels the challenge to obtain for himself a uniform and weapon, and you'll see the greatest medley in both–German uniforms, Italian uniforms, old Yugoslav Army uniforms, Austrian, or you'll see a combination of both, but," he added, "they all have a forage cap with a red star on the front that distinguishes them as members of the Partisan forces. They may have a pistol, a rifle or a sub-machine gun. The variety of ammunition is appalling and we have to save every round and it's up to every soldier to find enough ammunition to carry on–by whatever means."

140

"And what about your organization?" Jones asked.

General Rukavana said, "We're organized but loosely and flexibly. There's no one concentration of forces and no formal unit. We're organized in battalions, brigades and divisions. A whole area has a division and each village has a platoon under a local commander they have appointed.

"I might never meet the division or brigade commander, but he's a member of the local platoon. The variety of the platoons is determined by the nature of the countryside. Sometimes villages group together with 40 or 50 men and take up a position together in the hilltops under a common leader appointed by them."

"What is the motivation behind your organization?" Jones wondered.

"Well, suppose an enemy patrol comes to an unorganized village. If the villagers are determined to take a stand, they'll muster whatever means of killing, maybe an old scythe, a knife, an old shotgun, but they'll dispatch this patrol, take their weapons and uniforms and bury the bodies so there's no trace of them.

"But having done so, they expect an enemy follow-up with a heavier force, and take up positions along the roads into the village, but mainly up in the hills where they can hide. The older women and young children carry on in the village and maintain the fighters in the woods. Crops still have to be grown, clothing washed, socks knitted and mended. They take clean clothes to the men only at night. If the enemy comes, everyone chases the chickens and pigs away, hides whatever food they have, then vanishes.

"The enemy comes and burns all the buildings but can't find anyone or anything, so they leave. And we get to know the movements of the enemy through the children. They send us messages telling us where they are, how many, what kind of vehicles they have, and the information is constant.

"Should the enemy discover evidence of resistance measures, their brutality to the inhabitants is boundless.

"When a village decides to unite against the enemy, they appoint a committee which holds weekly meetings. These committees send representatives to larger centers which in turn send representatives to the higher command, either military or political.

141

Everything is coordinated and my job as Commissar, is keeping everyone informed. I am the liaison."

Fascinated by war fought on these terms, Jones explained: "I have instructions to report all information to my headquarters, and you've already given me more that I can ever hope to transmit. I doubt they'd believe it all.

"First of all, everything coming here to my mission automatically becomes your property. Any personnel we want to bring here will first have your approval. You will supply whatever information we request. I'd also like your assistance if we wish to move to any part of the country—as guides and protection. All messages we receive will also go to Partisan headquarters. You in turn will feed and protect us and help with any plan formulated by the Allies to liberate Yugoslavia."

The cards were on the table.

Dr. Bakaric responded: "You have been too generous. For instance, we don't want the material that is dropped by parachute to you personally, and we'll approve any personnel you wish to bring here and give you all the help and protection possible."

Relieved, Jones said, "We have no means of protecting any supplies we receive. You're in command of the country and we're only visitors. Any other basis might cause suspicion and difficulty in the future. I prefer it the way I've outlined."

After more consideration, they agreed and Bakarac sent their agreement to Tito and Jones to Cairo.

Lunch was served with a *"Dobar Tek"* (Good appetite.) Soup, stewed beef, potatoes and onions, jam tart, cheese, bread and wine were served by two young girls and the meal was followed by 15 minutes of singing!

Jones spent the afternoon exploring. Miles from anywhere, he wondered how the 20 horsepower generator was fueled and discovered a home-made still producing distilled wood alcohol.

In the foundry and machine shop, about 45 men were working with drills, lathes, a three-ton electric hammer and other equipment. They repaired bent rifle barrels, machined parts for breech blocks and springs. Bill found a sawmill, a building with a huge boiler and civilized shower baths, an armory, more repair

142

shops and a wireless station,

A German doctor greeted him at the 50-bed hospital. After being taken prisoner by the Partisans, he had asked permission to continue his profession and his devotion proved him trustworthy.

"These are admirable people," he told Jones. "They are fighting for a just cause. Caring for the sick and wounded is most difficult. The enemy has heavily bombed hospitals so we are organized into smaller units and hidden in the hills."

In an isolated cabin, three Partisans were filling grenade casings from their own foundry. Explosives were manufactured in a factory hidden in a small village several kilometers away. Fuses, detonators and caps were scavenged from the Italians. This job was extremely dangerous and only days earlier, an explosion blew up a hut, killing six workers and injuring several more. Every Partisan, by order, carried at least one hand grenade attached to his belt.

At the shoemaker's hut, Bill was asked: "Can you get us shoe thread? We're constantly short."

Another hut held a telephone exchange that could call headquarters 30 miles away. The operator said: "With wireless equipment we could reach all the military commands, but since we don't, we rely on couriers. It's very slow." Jones noted that.

Major Jones was captivated by this astonishing place and turned to his second-in-command: "Well, Hunter, certainly nobody in Allied command will believe this story. We must arrange a visit by General Harold Alexander or some other top general. It's impossible for them to accept my word for all this, especially sending it by wireless."

Next, he sent a message to British headquarters demanding to know why supply requests were not being met. He suspected this could be a problem and further recommended "that all sabotage of enemy targets such as railways be carried out by large-scale attacks on prominent and vital points with a view to permanent rather than temporary dislocation."

CHAPTER 26 – LET'S GET THE SHOW ON THE ROAD

A man of action, Jones organized his staff along proper military lines. He appointed Captain Hunter chief-of-staff, Sergeant Alexander Simich staff sergeant in charge of the orderly room, Sergeant Paul Pavelic the official interpreter, Corporal Ronald Jepson the wireless operator and Sergeant Petar Erdeljac was free for special duties. They met daily with corresponding members of the Partisan staff.

Major Jones (in the middle) and his team after parachuting into Yugoslavia. One member is missing from the photo. Photo courtesy of Bill Jones Jr.

Jones and his men immediately began reconnaissance trips throughout the surrounding area beginning with finding an area where a Lancaster bomber could land, perhaps carrying General Alexander.

After a hearty breakfast, horses were saddled and waiting by 8:00 a.m. They rode down the steep ravine with guides to the transport depot where a Fiat car was waiting. They were warmly welcomed in various towns and villages and regularly passed small armed Partisan units noting how well the countryside was protected. They found some villages heartbreakingly destroyed leaving the inhabitants destitute of crops and animals.

Young trainees were being taught wireless telegraphy at a partisan training centre. In the town of Otocac, they met members of the Anti-Fascist Committee of Liberation of Croatia and spent hours exchanging thoughts and plans. Dr. Gregorich, a small man of 50 or 60 wearing a corduroy jacket, spoke English and invited them to lunch where he introduced several people of interest.

Dr. Gregorich described the courier service: "Teenagers armed with bombs or grenades are responsible for certain areas. If they are caught they must use the bomb to kill themselves so that no secrets are given away. These children are clever and loyal and brave and the whole system depends on them. They distribute Party newspapers and pick up information about enemy movements and pass it to the command."

Dr. Gregorich explained the Yugoslav commitment to a unified country and the importance of Josep Tito. He named enemy collaborators, Mihailovic and Pavelic, who kowtowed to the enemy hoping an Axis victory would put them in power.

Of Draza Mihailovic he said: "When the enemy entered Yugoslavia, the regular army capitulated and the people were left to their own devices. Mihailovic took to the mountains with some of his soldiers to fight the enemy, calling themselves Chetniks. Then he was appointed Minister of War by the émigré government of Yugoslavia. He was to build a resistance force but to lie low and not openly resist until the Allies arrived. By 1941, Mihailovic saw the peasant organization as a threat to his own power and became a German ally diverting Allied supplies he received to the Germans."

This was what Jones intended to impress upon the British and it would take months of convincing that the Partisans were the only ones fighting the occupation forces. The others were quislings in the enemy camp.

Following lunch, they rose to find that landing spot. The choice was made, measurements were taken, the soil was tested, notes were made of trees and shrubs needing removal, but he

145

wondered how they would smooth the surface.

That night Jones had wireless operator, Corporal Jepson, send the landing strip location to MO4 who requested he check wind direction and speed at the location daily and acknowledged his request for General Alexander to make a firsthand visit.

Clearing the strip would need hundreds of people for eight to ten days and Jones had no idea how this could be accomplished.

Next morning, Manola informed Jones that: "There are 400 people ready to begin."

Thunderstruck, Jones wondered, "How did you get them so fast?"

Drug explained: "Every free town, village and district is organized locally by the people. Everything is assessed, recorded and regulated by an appointed people's committee and everybody cooperates with the committee. So the committee chairman called the town commandant and working through the committee, organized the labor, supplies and vehicles that are needed."

The workers came with horses and carts. Two young engineers arrived who fully understood what was needed.

Bill was enthralled. Nothing just happened. A lot of planning and organized effort went into everything.

He saw how meals at headquarters were served promptly and no one got more than another. To his amusement, he noted a much respected senior commander receiving a curt but apologetic, "No!" when he requested a second cup of coffee at breakfast before everyone had been served. The commandant gave a knowing wink and jerk of his head towards the young man.

As a military officer, Jones impressed the Partisans from the start. He got organized immediately, familiarized himself with the headquarters layout and acquainted himself with the necessary people. Understanding none of their language, however, he always worked through an interpreter and only mastered a few words.

He learned how information was systematically compiled from secret agents and couriers reporting on cities, factories, aerodromes, bridges, railway centers and fortifications. Architectural plans often accompanied the information and from all this

146

they produced high quality maps in their secret printing shops.

Bill personally astounded the Partisans. Every day this white-haired officer had a shirtless workout hoisting an enormous log over his head. Jones knew he had to stay fit to keep up with these younger men and women. In the evenings, he would sit by a bonfire with them listening to their accordion accompanied songs.

They didn't discover the artificial eye right away, but when they did, they were sure it had a camera built into it. Surely he was making photographs of everything and sending them to his people!

Jones had to persuade MO4 to provide a few more personnel and wireless equipment at strategic points though having these British in their territory presented the Partisans with a great responsibility. A British uniform was very conspicuous. If anything happened to them, they would be blamed. Then Jones discovered that London wanted to flood the country with personnel and succinctly reminded them he had only asked for a few and to please not send any more without Partisan authorization.

A May 26, 1943 telegraph confirmed that 12 fires were to be set in the form of a cross for the next supply drop-offs at Negodubsko Polje. FUNGUS supplies would include everything from ammunition to batteries, two pairs of pliers and one screwdriver. Instructions said: "On seeing fires aircraft will flash appropriate letter from air to ground phrase quote "Drink to me only" unquote. You will flash appropriate letter from ground to air phrase quote: "with thine eyes" unquote.

This was the routine. Dates, locations and times were absolutely secret. Correct codes, passwords and signals had to be given and a detailed memorandum dated March 27, 1943 directed Jones and his team exactly how to proceed. It included code words, instructions for signal fires etc., to be followed to the letter if everyone hoped to survive.

The parameters of Jones' work were taking shape. On May 27th he received this telegram in cipher that had to be decoded: "42 of 24. nr. 93. For Jones. Important for us to know details of railway
147

traffic over main lines in Croatia. Inform us if Partis. could arrange to obtain daily traffic returns at important railway junctions such as KARLOVAC, OGULIN, also shipping returns for SUSAK, FIUME, SPLIT, later we should like ask them try to extend this service to ZAGREB. You would then wireless these returns, if necessary and we would send another operator. Ends."

At a meeting with Commandant Rukavana, they discussed how information would be obtained and forwarded to the British. A day later on May 28th, using the Partisan network, Jones reported by telegraph the following:

"Enemy heavily guarding all vital points, Partiz. Using thousands of troops to capture and destroy and they know most vital points. Submit specific targets you have in mind, Partiz. have key men in Zagreb reporting facts, in April and May, 5 German divisions passed through Brod-Sarajevo-Dubrovnik, then by boat to Greece, example of Partiz raid on May 19, a troop train west of Ogulin attacked, 3 ½ hr. battle, 100 killed and wounded including 6 It. officers, took 26 It. and 15 Pavelic prisoners, one locomotive destroyed, 24 cars burned. Partiz are ready and able to destroy all lines in Croatia and Slovenia. Send anti-tank rifles and guns as ordered." He also confirmed 2 inches of rain in 3 days, don't use the landing field for a week, confirmed "reception" arrangements for June 1st for drops at Homoljac and Kejevica with signaling arrangements–letter of day is "D", rpt. "D", air to ground, and "W" rpt. "W" ground to air/to change daily, twelve fires lit 30 meters apart in form of letter "T" for first five days of month. And he recommended that all FUNGUS members be given medals for superb conduct in dropping blind into potentially hostile territory.

Jones' enthusiastic May 29th wireless described the out-standing Partisan organization. Food resources were under control. Local committees functioned in free towns and supplied the army, including beer and tobacco. Money was worthless. Everyone spontaneously submitted to organization and discipline to free their country. The old people continued farming; the young fought. A
148

boy of 16 could already boast two years on the front lines; many girls the same. Their biggest problem was a balanced diet. Huge stocks were not required as they slowed their ability to move quickly, but rather a steady supply worked better. Until new crops were harvested, they needed canned concentrates similar to those supplied to the British Army: milk, meat, vegetables, vitamins and salt.

Jones' May 31st transmission detailed a Partisan hospital he had visited deep in the woods. It was well organized but needed essentials and doctors and he included a list of pressing needs using Latin nomenclature.

By June 1st another air drop was organized and Jones' telegram described the landing ground, runway direction, prevailing winds and ground cover of the landing strip. He acknowledged the difficulties of providing supplies by air and their biggest priority was explosives, anti-tank guns, rifles and 200 gallons of petrol. "Remember," he added, "Even a mouse has freed a lion by constant nibbling."

In a second telegram that day, Jones reported that enemy attacks from Ogulin and Karlovac had petered out. Enemy troops advanced as far as Partisan lines, then withdrew. The Partisans followed them and blew up two bridges and two embankments at Ponori. Rail traffic had dried up for the moment and Partisans intended keeping it that way. British explosives were used in Croatia for the first time. Croatian headquarters recommended blowing up many small bridges between Zagreb and Brod as the countryside was very flat with no vital points.

Headquarters was pleased with Jones' speedy accumulation of intelligence and how quickly he set up supply drops. On June 2, 1943 they responded with: "Splendid work. Please pass our congratulations to partiz. HQ on their successes. Grateful for exact details of line destruction and difference this makes to Axis oil deliveries."

On June 3, 1943, Jones reported that thousands of Partisans wore captured Italian, Ustasi and German uniforms. Many wore partial uniforms and some wore only a Partisan cap with the definitive red star. "You meet a fine, soldierly, strong young man,

149

keen as mustard, in whole or part uniform, always with a rifle, frequently with only socks or barefooted. Boots, boots and still more boots are desperately needed."

This is the last existing telegram sent by Jones to British headquarters, though we know he became increasingly upset with the lack of response to his supply requests. From the start, his dispatches angered some but enthused and delighted the Partisans.

Mortar salvos, thuds from field guns and the occasional burst of machine-gun fire in the distance were commonly heard at Partisan headquarters. Bill had slept soundly in London through night-time air raids and did likewise in Croatia, although one night, persistent telephone ringing somewhere in their building awakened him. The Commandant spoke abruptly into the receiver, gave orders, hung up and issued instructions to the orderly who had wakened him. Minutes later Jones heard two horses cantering away from their hut. Something was afoot.

Next morning, Bill reported that two days earlier the enemy attacked north of headquarters, forcing their way through several kilometers of countryside before meeting Partisan resistance. The Germans pressed their attack the next day and night with little progress, and the Partisans retaliated by blowing up two railway bridges, two embankments, destroyed a train pulled by two loco-motives plus 32 wagons (train cars) including two armored units. All 200 train personnel were killed including seven Italian officers, Chetniks and Domobranci providing more evidence that Mihailovic's Chetniks were paying court to the enemy. The Germans withdrew and the Partisans rounded up their abandoned arms and ammunition.

At headquarters, Commandant Rukavana announced that everything was under control.

Major Jones met regularly with Commandant Rukavana and Commissar Dr. Bakaric, got to know many Partisans and heard stories of ambushes, close escapes, enemies captured, the glorious liberation of towns. With one or two of his team, he regularly forayed into the countryside with Partisan guides often venturing deep into German occupied territory.

Throughout the carnage, Jones observed that society's conventions were promptly restored when an area was freed. Courts were set up. Economic, industrial, educational and medical groups were appointed as advisory bodies to the state, and though Croatian administration was provisional, it met their needs.

Commissar Dr. Vladimir Bakaric remarked one day: "We (Partisans) are beating the enemy with organization," and this was becoming more apparent to the British Liaison Officer who was so delighted with this people's resourcefulness and ingenuity.

He wrote in *Twelve Months with Tito's Partisans*: "We know a young Partisan lad who spent ten days' leave in an Italian-occupied city just previous to their capitulation. It had been his second leave to that city in six months. In full Italian uniform he moved about and saw his friends at night, took his girlfriend to the theatre, avoided the military and the police by day, and after a week or so of what he called "rest," returned to his unit for duty. He brought with him many letters for other friends, including a few gifts from their relatives or loved ones, and official reports and information which he had obtained from underground organizations. This we were convinced from all accounts was quite an ordinary practice."

Farmers entered occupied areas with wagons, ostensibly going to market. They usually carried Partisan supply requisitions and presented them to a committee-man or directly to the 'safe' merchant himself. His wagon was loaded unquestioningly with no request for money. The local organization ensured the 'safe' merchant had blankets, clothing, tools, medical supplies, typewriters, paper and the myriad things needed by their comrades in the woods.

The Italians and Germans did not have the numbers to control the normal activities of life and quite blithely allowed them to carry on with little success at discovering what was going on among the people.

CHAPTER 27 – CHECKING OUT A VILLAGE

Despite idyllic fields, high hills, forests and splashing streams, there was an unrelenting awareness of war. Jones saw it all, heard the distant gunfire and hoped and prayed their secret hideaway was never discovered. Retribution would be grisly.

Such a large fighting force needed clothing, arms, heavy weapons, food and transportation and the British needed to drop copious supplies of just about everything and this became his foremost goal.

On another note, Jones pleasantly surprised that many Yugoslavians spoke some English and he discovered that many had worked in Canada and the United States for many years.

Jones needed to see what was happening throughout the countryside. With two team members, a Partisan commander and half a dozen Partisans, he spent a week at an unnamed village.

Friendly locals billeted them in farmhouses after they explained their purpose of organizing an intelligence gathering and reporting system and a supply drop.

Ever observant, Jones noted the village children tending sheep, the women and girls washing, mending and soil tilling. The men did the heavy work with horses and oxen, worked the fields, hauled logs from the forest, cut hay and all the other tasks of a rural community.

Curiously, the first evening, he saw about 75 women carrying beautifully knitted, colorful backpacks stuffed with food, clothing and clean laundry. Under the blanket of night, they were carrying these things into the hills to their men. They were the "army service corps" of the Partisans.

Local needs were assessed and Jones and his men set up a secret drop site, unknown even to the villagers. Spies were anywhere. He sent a telegraph in cipher, arrangements were made, code words and the bonfire figure were established.

The wily villagers figured it out and took their own precautions.

On the first possible evening for an air drop, the men crept from the hills to gather around small fires telling stories and singing. Their laughter filled the time as they listened for the drone of an airplane.

They heard the distant sound but no plane appeared. They returned, disappointed, to the hills and Jones impatiently wondered why they didn't get on with it!

This happened night after night. During the day, Jones and several others took long walks visiting sawmills, textile factories, tanneries, concealed boot factories and rooms where girls pieced the highly prized Partisan uniforms.

A reoccurring local problem was heavy fog blanketing the valleys after sundown. Jones received the message: "We were there last night. We couldn't see your messages. (meaning the fires) Is everything all right?" And he explained again about the fog and would they please try again.

From a high hill, while waiting, they watched a village through binoculars where German infantry was stationed, noting numbers and armaments.

And finally, on a dark, clear night, they heard the sound of two airplanes. Five hundred people collected for that night's vigil and a great shout went up followed by an immediate order to, "Hush up!" and move back so they wouldn't be injured by falling objects. Signal fires were lit and the drop was made on June 13th. Parachutes floated silently downward landing with quiet thumps in the long grass.

Tons of explosives were requested. They received a few hundred pounds and a few detonators. There were Italian boots salvaged from the desert, a few Italian muskets, thousands of rounds of small ammunition and other odds and ends. While not exactly what was requested, it was all useful. By morning, everything had been moved somewhere by truck and everyone finally got some sleep.

Wishing to thank his hostess, Jones gave her a green silk parachute to share with her neighbors. She was delighted, but the

153

next day came to him with a problem.

"My neighbours feel it would not be fair for our village alone to benefit in any way just because we are close to the drop area, so we think we had better give the parachute to the army or some other village."

Now what? Bill prayed for Solomon's wisdom and visited the local quartermaster in charge of supplies. He assured Jones that it was proper to keep the parachute in their own village, after all, a parachute can only be subdivided so many times. On another visit, Bill saw several tots running around in mottled green silk dresses.

They kept in constant touch with Partisan headquarters during this week. Team members either walked to the nearest telephone eight kilometers away, or 20 kilometers to headquarters.

In a larger town, Jones and his men saw faces peering through the barred basement windows of a large building.

"Who are they?" Jones asked the local Commissar.

"Prisoners: seven Italians, three Ustasi, four Chetniks and two Domobranci (another similar group). They were fighting together *under* Italian officers defending a section of railway we were attacking—another proof that the Chetniks are in cahoots with the enemy."

They met with them. The Ustasi and Domobranci claimed that Pavelic was their leader. The Chetniks declared themselves followers of Draja Mihailovic.

Since the Partisans could not keep large numbers of prisoners, those with bad records and guilty of atrocities were shot and those with clean records, were kept for a time, given a good tongue lashing, relieved of their uniforms and sent home in their underwear. Some chose to serve under the Partisans. Jones felt that, given the times, the Partisans treated prisoners fairly. Two of those prisoners were shot and the others freed minus their clothes.

Major Jones went on many similar trips, endearing himself to the people, enjoying their hospitality, food, music and culture, learning more about their wartime situation.

His wireless reporting system was expanding and he

eventually had 75 staff. Seven wireless reporting stations handled monumental quantities of information.

Rukavana cautioned Jones: "Don't forget, the enemy must know where you are and that there are so many here. You can only go so far before they'll consider it of such importance that they'll put on an overwhelming drive to catch you, and we cannot resist in terms of an opposing force. It is not our method. Our method is to let them in, wreck and damage everything and hope that they withdraw. When they come in, we take potshots at them without being seen, kill as many as possible, set mines to the limit of our ability and create as much opposition as we can but it's beyond us to block them, to stop them. We just have to withdraw and take shelter in hidden caves, conceal ourselves and wait until he withdraws. The less he sees and the less we can leave behind to give him any satisfaction in his effort, the sooner he goes.

"No so-called free territory is safe to the point that we can keep the enemy out. He can come in at will, but it's going to cost him every time and he'll get nothing. So he gives up and says there's nothing in that area."

"I understand," Jones responded. "In other words, if the enemy pinpointed the wireless transmission origins, the whole Croatian headquarters was in peril."

He was in a very dangerous position.

CHAPTER 28 - ZAVNOH

On Sunday morning after the airdrop, June 13, 1943, a car pulled up to the farmhouse where Jones was billeted. Dr. Vladimir Bakaric greeted Jones.

"Would you care to go to Otocac? There's an important meeting and we'd like to have you there."

Without hesitation, Jones replied, "I'd be delighted."

They piled into the car and nearing Otocac, the road became jammed with pedestrians and carts going somewhere.

In late afternoon, they pulled up to the same building where he had recently met Dr. Gregorich. On the second floor, they were greeted by an official committee and offered a meal at long tables. In fact, the whole building was set up like this with the women catering.

Exuberance and spirits soared, accompanied by rattling windows from bombs and mortars landing some miles away. The Partisans were diverting German attention from this gathering.

It was so real, yet so unreal—in the middle of war this tasty meal for hundreds as if nothing was happening!

Consumed with curiosity, but unable to understand a word, he eventually asked Dr. Gregorich: "What's this all about?"

Gregorich grinned. "This is the first elected parliamentary session in Croatia."

He handed Jones a program and translated the heading: "'June 13-14, 1943–The First Session of the Anti-Fascist Committee for the Territorial Liberation of Croatia'. ZAVNOH for short. We've dreamed about this for months. There are 640 elected delegates from all over Croatia, even Zagreb where the German command headquarters lie. We have eight or ten from there and they will present reports of conditions there. From every part of Croatia they've come! It's tremendous Jones!"

Next, everyone crowded into an old theatre decorated inside with flags and pictures of Churchill, Stalin and Roosevelt. A long table stood on the stage. Every seat was taken and people perched on window sills. Loudspeakers broadcast outside to the overflow.

Bill found a seat near the front and spotted Dr. Bakaric seated nearby, then General Rukavana a few seats further on.

Someone touched his uniformed shoulder and said in English. "Major Jones, would you go up to the head table."

"Ahh, certainly!" he responded wondering if he was dreaming. He was just the kid from Digby.

Dr. Gregorich invited him to sit at his left, and Jones realized there were a number of notables at the dais table. And-and he was sitting among them!

Dr. Gregorich, as acting chairman, called the meeting to order and they elected the Croatian council for that year.

Jones standing at the head table with Parliamentary leaders.
Photo courtesy of Bill Jones Jr.

Gregorich was elected Provisional President of Croatia. Any future national parliament would have to later approve these proceedings. This was such an exciting, hopeful occasion that everyone periodically broke into spontaneous song.

For hours, delegates reported and Dr. Gregorich translated for Jones. One man limping to the podium particularly stood out.

"Who's that speaker?" Jones asked Gregorich.

"That's Edvard Kardelj. He's a delegate from Slovenia.

157

He's come to wish us well and report with observations."

After Kardelj spoke, the Major noted, "Well, he's a very clever man, isn't he?"

"He's brilliant and still only a young man. He limps–lost his toes to frostbite two winters ago."

"May I meet him later?" Jones wondered.

"By all means."

The speeches continued. Dusk crept in, night settled. Finally at 1:00 a.m. they announced a break and suggested everyone visit the exhibition in the next room where many Partisan publications were displayed along with Croatian artwork, sketches, samples of homemade preserves and knitted goods.

More gripping speeches followed with Dr. Gregorich chairing and Drug Manola interpreting. Then the British Liaison Officer was asked to comment.

Jones addressing the delegates at the first parliamentary session.
Photo courtesy of Bill Jones Jr.

Surprised, but pleased, Major Jones made an off-the-cuff rousing speech on behalf of the British government that brought delegates to their feet when he stated: "He who has the love of freedom in his heart is not afraid to die for that which is deep-rooted in his soul." He added, "When I was parachuted into Yugoslavia, I found its people engaged, under German occupation, in unbelievable things to drive out the invaders. I learned a meaning of freedom I

158

had never realized before. It is this zest for liberty mixed with love and truth that drives you on."

Bill Jones undoubtedly ended with *Smrt fasizmu–svobodo naradu!*" (Death to fascism. Freedom for the people.)

The crowd roared approval and Major William Morris Jones was declared honorary vice-president of the first parliament.

The meeting broke up just before daylight and officials were billeted throughout Oticac for a few hours' sleep.

The second session was held next day at Plitvice Lakes, a lovely chain of 16 small lakes connected by waterfalls nestled in a valley between two mountain ranges, Gornja Pljeseva and Mala Kapela. Enemy bombers were expected over Oticac.

Protected by large pines overlooking the third lake, they sat on chairs and benches and continued until 4:00 p.m. with about 120 delegates present. Speeches were again recorded in shorthand and transcribed.

Meeting under the trees at Plitvice Lakes. Jones is in the middle.
Photo courtesy of Bill Jones Jr.

The seven-member Zagreb delegation particularly held Jones' attention. They reported on their well-organized under-ground, that they were busy knitting, sewing and getting the things needed to the Partisans by farm wagons arriving from the countryside. Right under German noses! As far as possible, goods were procured straight from the enemy! They had German firearms,

159

ammunition and some explosives. Whatever was needed: medical supplies, socks, clothing, underwear. Everything was shipped on to the fighting boys in the woods.

A Dalmatian woman smoking a cigarette and wearing a pair of breeches, leggings and a short-sleeved shirt, sauntered to the front, hands stuffed into her pockets. At that moment, the Germans were flying high overhead. She nonchalantly tossed the cigarette away, faced the audience and spit! The delegates roared approval and the gutsy woman painted a picture of conditions around her home, how they fought hand-to-hand in the passes of the Velebit Mountains, how they camped at 6,000 feet in the bitter cold.

The formal proceedings finally closed after thrashing out many important issues and Dr. Bakaric suggested they return to their mountain headquarters. Edvard Kardelj would be visiting there and Jones would have an opportunity to talk with him.

Back at headquarters, Jones conferred With Sergeant Alexander Simich, and replied to messages he had received, i.e. a Partisan unit attacked and captured Desinac Station, 'liquidated' the garrison and wrecked three trains loaded with war supplies heading south to Greece, destroyed 100 meters of track and burned the station house, shutting down the main Zagreb-Belgrade line for 68 hours, another unit put the Pozego-Nosice railway line out of commission for two months, an armored train was destroyed between Djulanes and Suho Polje and lacking explosives, they removed the rails for 350 meters on the Daruvar-Bijela line. Most garrisons attacked by the Partisans held a few Ustasi, Chetniks, Domobranci and Pavelic troops.

Now Jones experienced one of the anomalies of the secret service. He received messages from two different divisions in MO4. One said: "Excellent Jones. Your reports are excellent. Keep it up." From another source he received: "We can't accept your reports. Keep both feet on the ground. Keep to fact only."

Realizing that two rival factions were working in the higher echelons of the intelligence service–he simply carried on as he had been. He could play the game too.

CHAPTER 29 – AN INVITATION

By the end of June, 1943, Jones had 15 to 20 personnel under his command and wireless equipment at three or four points. Information was flowing seamlessly.

After long conversations, the brilliant, dark-haired Edvard Kardelj suggested: "Why don't you come to Slovenia for a visit."

"Well you know, Kardelj, I've studied maps of Slovenia and I have a decisive target in mind there."

The younger man leaned forward.

"It's the bridges at Zidani Most. You have two main railway lines and a main road coming south from Maribor through that village, crossing the Sava River. Those lines are vitally important to the Germans, cut them and you cut much of their access to Zagreb, Belgrade, Romania, right down to Greece. This is a most important railway point to dislocate."

Kardelj nodded.

"So if I do go, I'd like to find out what opportunity there is to get at these bridges."

"I don't personally know the military situation at Zidani Most but if I'm free here shortly, I'll accompany you northwest about ten kilometers and we'll pick up the trail of a man who will know exactly what's needed."

Days later, Jones, Kardelj and Simich headed off on foot. It was tough going, either through deep valleys or up sharp hills, climbing 3,000 to 4,000 feet, always in the sheltering woods.

There in the wilderness, they encountered a group travelling from Slovenia to Bosnia and had a discussion with a Franz Leskovsek (Code name 'Luka').

With Alexander interpreting, they discussed possibilities. Luka knew these important bridges were surrounded by 15,000 Germans protecting them from every angle.

Before they pursued that avenue, Luka insisted they had to liquidate the Italian garrison at Zuzemberk, a town about 10 kilometers southwest of Zidani Most. It was a centre for Italian mechanized, mobile forces and controlled the approaches to Zidani Most. A clerical centre, its lower town spread along the river bank and the upper walled town perched on a hill.

Jones concluded that a successful attack on Zuzemberk and Zidani Most would deal a monumental blow to the enemy and stop their southward trek of men and arms.

But the Partisans needed arms, and after consulting Luka, they agreed that a good quantity of mobile mortars, ammunition and two to three hundred rifles or more with small ammunition were needed and the only practical thing was for Jones to go to Slovenia where he could arrange for British supply drops there.

Giving his reasons, Jones sent a coded dispatch to Cairo requesting permission to proceed to Slovenia. He asked for the mortars, rifles and ammunition. Obviously the major's idea had merit and he was given orders to leave the Croatian outpost in the hands of his assistant, Captain Hunter and Corporal Jephson the wireless operator.

CHAPTER 30 – A DICEY TRIP TO SLOVENIA

Croatian local command organized a patrol to accompany several officials and others returning to Slovenia. Edvard Kardelj, Bill Jones and Alexander Simich joined them. Scouts would patrol the way ahead and troops armed with rifles and machine guns would protect them. Every traveler was armed.

Their commander introduced himself as: "Mrazovich. Viko Mrazovich. They call me 'Carlo' because I served in Spain in the Civil War."

In mid June, 1943, Jones and his small group left the safety of the Pljesivica Mountains by truck and met the rest of their party in Plaski. They were billeted in farm houses and Jones recalled a breakfast of bacon, polenta and porridge.

Eighty personnel were to move undetected through enemy territory. They started with four double-horse wagons, ten riding horses, enough equipment, arms, food and supplies to see them through the journey and deal with any skirmishes along the way.

They left in broad daylight for the next village. Most walked, but if anyone tired, he was free to ride.

Reaching the town by four o'clock, they were nicely settled at farm houses eating their evening meal, when word came they must leave promptly. It wasn't safe. Their next objective was two parallel rivers with a railway running between them that must be approached under cover of darkness. The scouts knew the enemy patrolled the rivers.

In fading daylight, they arrived at the first river, a tributary of the Sava. The wagons were abandoned and after crossing, they would continue on foot and horseback carrying their supplies.

It was a swift-flowing river about 125 feet wide studded with boulders, and white, foaming water curling in eddies and currents. Jones, the experienced canoeist, recognized a serious challenge.

Two impetuous young fellows, looking for the best way

163

across, urged their horses into the water. A few steps in, one horse was suddenly in deeper, swifter water. It panicked, reared and flung its rider into the turbulent, dark river.

From the bank, everyone watched, horrified, as man and horse were swept downstream. The other young Partisan leapt from his horse to rescue him. Mrazovich dived in after them, grabbed something, swam to shore and found he was holding an empty sweater.

Both men were carried to their deaths though the frightened horse climbed out downstream and was recovered.

The watchers were speechless. How could this have happened so fast, so unexpectedly? But it was too dangerous to linger. Enemy patrols lurked nearby.

Cautioned by the tragedy, one Partisan safely worked a zigzag course across the river towing a rope, secured it to a tree and by ten p.m. everyone had safely crossed.

The silent group hurried on. There was a railway and another river to cross before daylight and the railway was heavily guarded by pillboxes. (Pillboxes were stone and concrete and held about 50 men. The walls had slots for machine guns.)

After resting briefly, their guide led them down a faint trail for an hour. A dog barked half a mile beyond the river. Everyone caught their breath. A farmhouse appeared dimly and the commander held up his hand. Orders were whispered down the line to hunker down in deep shadow.

The commander moved cautiously to the house, tapped on the window three times and a voice responded from within. The door opened carefully. Code words were exchanged and the reassured farmer invited the commander, Jones, Kardelj, Simich and several others inside while the rest remained hidden.

A single candle was lit and they seated themselves at the kitchen table where the Mrazovich began writing. Curious, Jones asked Simich to ask what he was doing.

"I'm writing messages to the boys' mothers," the commander responded.

How different from Bill's military experience where nothing like this was done while they were on the move, and yet the man
164

took time to write personal letters to the parents.

"Is this the usual practice?" Jones asked.

"Yes, it is strictly our practice. Whenever possible, any commander aware of a death writes the victim's parents."

"Well that's excellent."

The farmer would carry the letters to the nearest courier post and after Mrazovich questioned him on recent enemy maneuvers, they left with the farmer's young son as their guide.

While travelling through enemy territory for the next five hours of darkness, they avoided settlements, zigzagged through pastures, slipped along sunken roads, moved like wraiths, not even disturbing the noisy farm dogs. The young guide was unerring.

They halted abruptly. Orders for silence and to take cover in the woods were whispered down the line. Scouts moved ahead to the nearby railway line hunting for a safe crossing. It would be by the switchman's house where a road crossed the railway line. The railway man, a trusted Partisan, instructed them to lie low until the Italian sentry returned from his beat.

The scouts finally reported the sentry had returned and gone inside. Feeling uncomfortably exposed, the group noiselessly hurried along the road for 100 yards, then easily crossed the railway and were swallowed by the night.

Jones learned that Yugoslavian trains were operated by Germans and Italians who mistakenly kept local crews who were as loyal Partisans as those fighting in their ranks. The underground in the cities received dispatches from train crews who had passed through other parts of the country. There were requests for socks, shoes, anything that was needed. Bundles were assembled, handed to the next train crew and much of it was distributed after Partisans held up the trains and killed the Germans or Italians.

Still in enemy territory, they safely crossed the second river on a bridge. The farm boy led them swiftly along a cow path until they finally reached safer territory. His job done, the young Partisan returned home.

Daylight was breaking when they came to the edge of a deep

165

woods and stopped for a short rest. Jones slept soundly, but briefly.

They sped through more towns. At one, there was a heart-stopping moment when several people dashed out to warn them of a small Ustasi unit asleep in their village. They hurried on.

The day was beautiful, the sky cerulean blue, as they hurried through more hamlets with white-walled homes and red-tiled roofs. After crossing several small rivers, they began climbing the wooded slopes of the Kapela Mountains.

It was a long day and everyone, including Commander Mrazovich, took turns riding. Various members veered off in their own directions and the party diminished to 20 including the 10 Partisan escorts who carried two light machine guns and eight rifles. Six horses remained.

A long, steady climb found them at 4,000 feet elevation looking down into a beautiful gorge with swift flowing water. On their trek downwards, they came to a village where a bridge spanned the ravine. It was an utterly picturesque crossing in broad daylight and though wishing to stay forever, this was war.

They pushed northwards to within five miles of the town of Bosiljevo, still in Croatia. The countryside was beautiful and the houses below were in compact clusters with fertile fields stretching outwards from them across a flat plain.

Exhausted after 12 hours of steady walking, they took a noontime rest and ate a substantial meal of hot soup, bread and cheese.

Somewhere near Lika, between the Velebit and Pljesiva mountain ranges, because of the constant danger, Jones buried a collection of classified documents that he carried. Some 25 years later, while visiting the country with Helen, he attempted to find the documents but was unable to locate the spot.

By late afternoon they reached Bosiljevo, in Karlovac County, found Partisan headquarters, were billeted in homes and given a good meal.

The travelers had seen an old castle on a hillside by a tumbling stream and asked Mrazovich questions about it. The
166

easiest answer was, "Let's go see it," and Jonesy and several others climbed the hill after dark to Bosiljevo Castle.

The keeper answered their knocks and Jones was pleased that he spoke English, acquired while living in Britain and Canada.

He ushered them in and made it clear that his loyalties lay with the Partisans, not the Italian owner, Baron Ante Cosulich de Pecine, who had abandoned the place at the onset of war.

The gregarious castle keeper explained how the wealthy old baron had restored the castle and filled it with treasures, most of which were locked in upper rooms that he never opened to visiting Italians because of their penchant for permanently "borrowing" things. He was pleased, however, to show the Partisans whatever they wished. Jones was particularly impressed by table tops and shiny floors all beautifully inlaid with different colored woods.

Finally, he led them to the echoing cellar to show off the baron's considerable collection of wines and preserves. He spread a table with fresh bread and preserves and popped the corks of several vintage bottles of fine wine.

Later, a pleasantly sated group wound its way to the village with Mrazovich cracking jokes that reduced everyone to laughter and for that moment in time they were simply tourists in a beautiful country.

Following the castle interlude, they met the local Karlovac corps commander and his staff. He updated them on the local military situation and how the Partisans were nightly reducing the number of trains passing through

The following evening, the party had the luxury of carts to continue their journey. At one point they comfortably crossed a main highway knowing Partisans were stationed every few hundred yards. It was Sunday, June 27, 1943.

Somewhere in the darkness, they crossed the border into Slovenia and their Croatian escorts were silently exchanged for waiting Slovenians. How did they know we were coming, Jones would wonder. At a broad, quiet river, they caught sight of the ferryman calmly rowing his small punt across the black water.

Mrazovich suggested they eat at the ferryman's house which

167

turned out to be a restaurant where he served his passengers before or after the river crossing. They reveled in fried eggs and potatoes and sampled the ferryman's fine Slovakian wine and this was the first time Jones saw actual money used to pay for a meal. It was captured Italian lira.

The ferryman, another trusted Partisan, regaled them with tales of rowing Partisans and Italians across the river within hours of each other and gathering information in the process.

The river crossing was uneventful. On full stomachs, they walked all night until reaching a burned-out village on a mountain slope. They reported to the local committee man who produced a tasty beef stew for breakfast and then everyone slept for hours.

A large Italian contingent was blocking their path so they remained hidden near the ruined village while Partisan troops cleared the way by their usual means.

Jones spent the afternoon with binoculars watching Italians drilling on a parade ground some four kilometers distant. They had rows of wooden huts arranged around the open area near a main road. He spotted a long viaduct (high railway bridge spanning a valley) to the west of the town and wondered why it was still standing. Closer inspection revealed pillboxes and barbed wire at either end. At least 140 Italians constantly guarded that bridge.

Word of their presence spread to that town, yet the enemy knew nothing. By late afternoon, three young women appeared. They talked about life under Italian rule and how the 3,000 village people were organized and supporting the Freedom Front. They had been allowed to leave by simply telling the guards they were visiting friends.

The local commander interrupted to say a Partisan brigade was clearing the road but they'd have to stay another day or two.

That evening an invitation came from the Partisan committee in a village four kilometers distant, asking them to a social in their local hall. Why not?

As darkness fell, Jones and the others crept down the hillside, ducked through grape vines and back alleys and found the village hall packed with Partisans and local people.

Two hours of entertainment included songs and skits. A girl

168

from the local battalion, dressed in blue tweed blouse, ski pants, Partisan cap with the red star and her rifle slung across her back, gave a spirited reading that brought the audience to their feet. She had dispatched five Italian soldiers. Bozidar Jakac, an internationally known Slovenian artist serving in the woods, immortalized her in oils.

Dancing to the inevitable accordion continued until early morning. Then everything was packed away, the citizens went home, the Partisan battalion left for somewhere and Jones and his party returned to their hillside fastness.

A local resident remarked: "Italian patrols visit this village nearly every day, but they never know about our night life."

The following afternoon guests visited again from the garrison town. The young women brought six friends, including children, and carried baskets of food. The guards understood they were going on a picnic. No lie at all.

Meanwhile, the Partisan battalion attacked the Italians blocking their path. Thirty were killed and many wounded. Six light machine-guns, many rifles and a lot of ammunition were liberated and several vehicles, including two armored cars, were destroyed. Their way was clear to continue.

They set out next morning and the party became smaller and smaller as individuals broke off, heading to their own destinations. Jones, Simich and their guides climbed to a high mountain ridge south of Crnomelj, crossed a small clearing and back into the surrounding woods where Jones spotted a camouflaged hut.

Major Jones and Sergeant Simich had arrived safely at Slovenian Headquarters.

169

CHAPTER 31 – BAZA 20

Dr. Metod Mikus the tough, popular chaplain of the Slovenian forces said later in a July, 1943 speech, "Since we are all human, we could not help wondering what kind of a person had been selected and sent by the British Empire and its centre in Cairo to us, the Slovene Partisans. . . . This was an important matter. Would this English representative understand what was going on here, and how would he appraise it? Could we, in talking to him, look him in the eye as befits honest and sincere men?"

Dr. Metod Mikus. Note the cross on his cap just above
the red star. Photo courtesy of Bill Jones Jr.

Major Jones and Sergeant Simich arrived at Slovenian Headquarters hidden deep in the forested hills of the Kocevski Rog region between Bela Krajina and Kocevja. It was late June, 1943.

Bill found an enclave of wooden huts similar to those in Croatia, yet different. They were smaller and more carefully concealed by the dense tree canopy.

They were warmly welcomed by Commandant Matya Matcec, a tall, dark-complexioned Partisan in full uniform. He introduced a smaller, uniformed man, about 35 years old, as Commissar Boris Kraigher and his chief secretary, Tvarisica Sveta, a beautiful young blond girl seated at a typewriter.

They were shown to bunks in the same hut. It had no partitions with one end being office, the other, sleeping quarters. Built of rough boards, about 14' x 18', it had windows on three sides and was roofed with dull red tile. They ate their meals there at a table and chairs.

Alex Simich immediately set up his wireless equipment and sent their first dispatches that night.

Jones naturally explored next morning and found more huts for personnel and soldiers and noted sentries and staff on duty. The headquarters was quite extensive but had no industrial setup as in Croatia. One building held about 30 men and women sewing uniforms. He found leather tanning, boot making and repair going on and a printing press with reams of newsprint ready for turning out periodicals.

Some of the well-hidden buildings at Baza 20, Slovenian Headquarters.
Postcard from Bill Jones Jr. collection.

Limestone caves are typical of this karst topography and the Partisans used them as hideouts that housed 25, 50 and even 100 people--or a hospital. Jones discovered its well-concealed trap-door, opened it and climbed down to an airy cave where a young Slovenian doctor and a number of nurses oversaw nearly 60 patients. He gave Jones the tour, cautioning him on the care they took to not let any other personnel near the hospital except on special occasions. Jones was a special occasion.

Jones learned from Commandant Matcec that Slovenia's 'Freedom Front' was identical in principal and purpose to the Anti-Fascist Committee for the Territorial Liberation of Croatia. They discussed Jones' proposal to destroy the Zidani Most bridges and the needed equipment and supplies. The manpower was there.

Jones began convincing London's MO4 and Cairo head-quarters of his plan. He said: "It took me two or three days again to get London and my other contact points thinking a bit our way. I was having great difficulty indeed with the Section (MO4). They weren't going to have anything to do with my reports, while others again were seeking more and more."

Within hours of arriving, Jones had been visited by President Josip Vidmar, Provisional President of Slovenia, who thankfully spoke fluent English, Peter Kidric, Secretary and several other government officials.

They sat on the bunks and talked, agreeing on many things, came to conclusions and asked difficult questions like: "Why do the Allies not understand us?"

Bill did his best, summarizing his findings and possibilities for the country. Slovenia needed more aid than Croatia. Their freed areas were mere islands in the enemy storm. South of the Sava River, a Danube tributary, the Italians held the lands between these "islands" and the Germans did likewise north of that river. Communication between the areas was by courier at night.

Jones concluded, "I have already had six weeks of very rich experience in Yugoslavia. I've made many observations and I am convinced that with proper recognition, the united front of this country is the answer to the problems here."

172

Slovenian officials nodded.

"If you like, I'll give you a written statement to that effect."

"We would be very pleased Jones," they responded.

He immediately composed the wording. Dated and translated, July 5, 1943, he gave it to the editor of a Slovene newspaper. It read in part:

"Major William Jones, representative of British Military with Supreme Headquarters of Peoples Liberation Army and Partisan formations of Slovenia:

We have orders as British representatives to get in contact with Partisans to overlook their action and movement and report to the British government. Under our observation we have found a well organized, efficient and democratically lead movement that represents all departments of political structure and that is voluntary and completely, unanimously supported by the people. They have only one goal–to free Yugoslavia of occupying forces and destroy all collaborators and to break the power of the Axis…. In the Partisan movement, we see the only hope for a united, free and democratic Yugoslavia. We believe that our beliefs are the same beliefs of their government."

This statement was printed on cards by the thousands. Artist Bozidar Jakac, did a pen sketch of Jones for the top corner.

Jakac's line sketch of Jones which was printed on the top corner of his statement. Bill Jones Jr. collection.

173

The cards migrated all over Yugoslavia, fell into enemy hands, traveled to Germany, Austria and Italy. British prisoners-of-war escaping Germany and Austria arrived in Yugoslavia with the cards requesting: "We want to meet Major Jones." Jones, typically, took no further notice of his statement. The startled Germans did.

Rumors spread of an English officer circulating among the Partisans. German High Command was outraged. How did he get there? Composite pictures bearing little resemblance to Jones were posted throughout occupied territories. A reward of 10,000 gold marks was placed on his head. Wanted dead or alive! They became coveted Partisan trophies and were carefully removed.

Dr. Mikus continued in his speech: "Rumours about his arrival spread through the country with such rapidity that even the White and Blue Guards heard of it; but they, claiming that "the English were on their side," were so furious at Major Jones that they disputed his English descent and accused the Partisans of rechristening some Janez from Kranjska into "Jones." May God forgive their silliness!"

Janez-Jones could only laugh.

Jones' charisma infected the people with hope as he spent the next months living and fighting with them.

At Baza 20, he found he share spaced with two medical doctors, a law professor, an economics professor, an internationally known literary critic, a mechanical engineer, a farmer, an artist, a judge, a returned soldier, an educator, a civil servant, a history professor, an ex-Cabinet Minister, an electrical engineer and many others. Some had been wounded, others had lost loved ones. They lived in constant fear lest their families, still in occupied territory, would be shot. They all wanted freedom for their homeland.

He began reconnaissance with his Partisan guides, often astonished at the intelligence they could obtain. He could discover the disposition of German aircraft, acquire maps and locations where munitions were made, details of the types and locations of labor in Germany, right down to workers' pay rates, factory addresses, details of products and quantities manufactured.

In Ljubljana, Slovenia, a stopping point for German trains,

174

underground workers at the station removed the third copy of cargo waybills and couriered them to Jones' headquarters where Alex coded and sent them by wireless to the Allies. It was so very easy, yet so terribly dangerous.

Meanwhile, British and American forces landed in Sicily on July 9-10, 1943. The Germans and Italians expected an invasion, but the date and landing points were a complete tactical surprise. The Italians surrendered but the Germans presented a spirited defense that temporarily put success in doubt.

On one foray, Jones spent ten intense days hiding with the Partisans in an underground hideout with the Germans, directly above, hunting them with tanks.

Partisan hideouts in the forest were often small shallow cup-like hollows about 300 to 400 feet across and 10 to 20 feet deep. Trees were cleared from the bottom, a false roof was built, sodded and trees planted. Entry was through a hatch. They were ventilated, had washroom facilities, a three month food supply and vast paper supplies for printing leaflets and newspapers. No trace of a path was allowed and the Germans were stymied to find them.

As in Croatia, the enemy in Slovenia was on the defensive. Their main goal was keeping the railways and main roads open. The Partisans were on the offensive, costing the enemy dearly in casualties and equipment. Italian morale hit rock bottom and they so dreaded Partisan attacks that they never ventured forth at night and only accompanied by tanks and armored vehicles by day. The Partisans were their worst nightmares.

What a different form of warfare this was for Bill. It was skirmishes involving gunfire, explosions and noise and then silence. There were no lengthy battles, no air thick with the smoke of a thousand bombs, poisonous gases and the cries of the dying. People died, yes, but it was not the slaughterhouse of WW I trenches. There was a lot of spying, creeping silently through the woods and hit-and-run tactics. Civilians were involved, children were involved. Women were involved.

175

Slovenian Partisan needs were great. Always short of ammunition and explosives, they had to be creative. Removing and hiding several hundred feet of track effectively derailed a train. Blowing up small bridges and culverts slowed traffic and did not use much explosive.

Partisan sappers usually planted the explosives. One well known squad was led by a young man expert in the use of explosives. If the usual explosives were unavailable, he improvised, emptying Italian and German shells, some dating back to World War I. He destroyed many small bridges, tore up stretches of track, blew up train stations and supply depots. He had already destroyed nine trains before Jones' arrival and invented an ingenious pressure switch from parts of two Italian hand grenades.

Jones, in his wireless messages, continued demanding supplies, explosives and munitions and finally on July 17, 1943 a supply plane appeared in the dead of night. Signal fires were lit, the plane signaled and Jones responded in Morse code with a flashlight. Cargo was dropped by parachutes and then the plane was gone. Three days later a second delivery brought dynamite, weapons and medicine.

Jones was outraged and embarrassed when that cargo was inspected. Short-changed again! The drop contained many rifles without parts and, of all things, a collection of shoes for left feet only!

Jones was exasperated. Who on earth got the right shoes!

CHAPTER 32 – SPY OR MOLE?

"I'm sorry Jones, but there's a rather unpleasant matter I want to discuss with you," President Vidmar said.

"Go ahead."

"London wants to flood the country with personnel and one who landed in Trieste has been arrested and brought here to Slovenian headquarters. He claims he is Captain John Leonard and British."

Jones nodded.

"Well, he's actually a native of Novo Mesto and well-known in these parts as Johannes Lenchek," Vidmar continued. "He's been secretary to a man named Crick, the editor of a Catholic publication originally in Rome and later in London. They turn out bitter propaganda against our country and the liberation process. Jones, we're uncomfortable that he's here being protected by that British uniform."

"I'll take immediate action sir," the major assured him. "I will order him to remain at my billet and will request information about him from London."

The president nodded thanks.

Jones outranked the man and minced no words: "Leonard, the whole command knows you as Johannes Lenchek."

"Ahh, yes. When I applied to British Intelligence, I asked to return to my native Slovenia and this is how they've sent me."

"You may be a British intelligence officer in a captain's uniform but you're among people fighting for liberation who have evidence that you haven't exactly been fighting that battle outside Slovenia. Explain."

He did and concluded with, "I got fed up working for Crick so I went to British Intelligence and asked to enlist."

"That's fine John, but will the Partisans accept that? Your position is dangerous and I'd advise you to strictly follow my instructions. You're staying right here. Don't get friendly with anybody. Go about your own affairs. I'll put you on an intelligence line and you will translate and encode reports from the Partisans for Alexander Simich to send to MO4. There'd be no objection to that, but that's all you're doing. Those are my orders."

Jones did not mention that he'd asked Simich to closely monitor the man and report any questionable behavior.

"Well," Leonard said slowly. "I'll certainly carry out those orders. I have no intention of upsetting anyone here."

Major Jones had Alex forward a message to London and promptly received a reply: "Please convey our apologies to the Partisan command. We did not know their authority extended to that part of the country."

He showed it to President Vidmar who said dubiously, "Well, the only thing is Jones, if he tries to go down on the plain into villages where he's known, it's hard to say what will happen to him."

"Yes, he could be shot as an enemy spy."

Both were truly puzzled that the British sent a man known and recognized as unsympathetic to the Partisans, whose life was in mortal danger if he strayed from camp. They could only assume the Intelligence Service was either playing both ends against the middle or that he was an unbiased observer who would not be influenced by with what was going on. Or maybe he was still connected with the enemy. A mole? Maybe.

I will never understand intelligence service methods, Jones concluded.

178

CHAPTER 33 – CHURCHILL SPEAKS

"Are you responsible for the following statement?" the wireless message demanded quoting a line from Jones' declaration of British support written for President Vidmar to spread throughout the land. "If so, you have shipwrecked his Britannic Majesty's foreign policy. You are guilty of the most serious military offence."

Jones looked up absolutely furious though pleased he'd caught someone's attention very high up. The wording had that Churchillian air about it.

After thinking for a moment, he instructed Sergeant Simich: "Do not, under any circumstances, receive any messages over the wireless. Keep it open for dispatches that I will send and we'll start tonight."

By this time, Alexander would put nothing past Jones who took himself off to a quiet place to write a complete argument for the Yugoslav situation based on facts as he had gathered them. He explained plans for subduing Zuzemberk and the destruction of the Zidani Most bridges, how vital they were to the Germans, and characteristically demanded arms and ammunition. For the next week, Simich coded and sent sections of this argument each night with frequent interruptions of: "You must take our messages."

"Accept no messages until we are through," he reminded Alexander.

On Friday night, he wired the last installment ending with: "If you cannot accept this argument, my services are of no further value in this field," and told Simich he could receive messages again.

Only one arrived.

"Carry on," it said.

Jones always felt that only Churchill himself would have sent something so brief, so succinct, so clear and so direct.

"Well, Simich, success! Zuzemberk next!"

CHAPTER 34 – THE BATTLE OF ZUZEMBERK

Though destroying the Zidani Most bridges was vital, Slovenian headquarters put this in abeyance while waiting to see what guns and supplies arrived from the Allies. But first they could deal with Zuzemberk lying square in their path to the bridges.

Located in the Bela Krajina region on the banks of the Krka River, Zuzemberk was a two-level town with the lower business area strung along the bank where a bridge crossed. High above, on the crown of a hill, lay the residential area and an ancient compound containing a twin-spired church, convent and rectory surrounded by nine-foot stone walls, four feet thick.

A large Italian garrison commanded by Captain Rafael Rosano had commandeered the church compound and reinforced the church and buildings until they resembled their blockhouses in the lower town. Machine gunners and snipers occupied the spires and other vantage points. The church was surrounded by barb wire and protected by six 105 mm. guns and ten 80 mm. mortars.

The upper and lower garrisons held 500 Italians and 80 White Guards, locals recruited by the Italians. More forces were billeted in several nearby towns.

All this data was studied, plans were made, arms were accumulated and soldiers gathered. Days before the attack, Allied planes dropped six big guns at a Croatian landing point that Jones had arranged before leaving. These were sped to Slovenia along with 200 ammunition rounds, 5,000 rifle rounds and 300 muskets.

Commandant Stanei had a fine reputation as a fighter and as Supreme Commander of the Slovenian forces, would direct the attack. He was a 40-year old Spanish Civil War veteran, and would lead despite a broken arm in a sling.

To Jones he said, "Would you like to come along?"

"Certainly," he said without hesitation.

To capture Zuzemberk, 5,000 troops were ordered to Toplitz, five kilometers from Zuzemberk and seldom visited by the enemy.

In late afternoon, Jones, Simich, the local commander 'Rudy' and several brigade commanders rode on horseback to a local roadhouse in a small village west of Toplitz. Over wine and bread, they reviewed the plan of attack.

Jones then inspected the 3,000 troops already lined up in the field in broad daylight. Armed with machine guns and rifles, they felt fairly safe but could quickly take cover in the surrounding woods.

During inspection, one troop, knowing the major's background, stopped him, "Sir, I have an English rifle. How do I operate it?"

Jones quickly demonstrated.

A little further on, an officer nabbed him, "Major, sir, the mortars. How do we operate them?"

They too were British and his thorough training emerged as Jones carefully demonstrated how to load and fire the mortars.

The soldiers were impressed. Major Jones knew his stuff.

This was such a frustrating problem. Their arms were scrounged, ancient, or captured from the enemy and the leaders were hard-pressed to educate the men on the various types.

The commanders addressed the troops, infecting them with the spirit of the moment. Though the target was still undisclosed, they sensed something big afoot. This was the first time such a large troop gathering had happened in Slovenia and they were conscious of their strength. This people's army was going to war and many were barefoot and unarmed.

Commandant Stanei finally disclosed the target was Zuzemberk and wished them success. Loud cheering erupted with an appropriate battle song.

Jones wished them good luck knowing the British government was backing him on this one. He joined a group heading to the northern approaches of Zuzemberk.

Hundreds were armed with carefully cleaned and oiled rifles and machine-guns, but many were unarmed and carried the equipment. A few men carried large balls of high explosives in their bare hands and everyone had at least one grenade.

The engineering section carried cross-cut saws, ropes

sledgehammers, ladders, long poles and sheaves of straw to be tied to the poles, lit and either held high in the darkness to draw enemy fire or used for setting fires.

They moved silently through rough, hilly country. Suddenly, heart-stopping enemy mortar shells screamed overhead and thudded into a nearby hill. Likely random Italian target practice, as no more came.

In pitch blackness, Jones/ group forded a river between two bridges guarded by enemy garrisons stationed a measly few hundred yards in either direction. By morning they reached a tiny village, were billeted in barns and houses, and the women produced a breakfast of milk and polenta for so many. Then everyone waited until the order came.

Sunday evening the units moved to encircle Zuzemberk. From their vantage point, Jones and the officers in charge viewed the upper town through binoculars, particularly noting the fortified church. The lower town lay hidden below the hill.

At dusk, Jones and his group headed to a distant farmhouse they'd spotted through binoculars and took up positions there. By ten o'clock that evening, Zuzemberk was invisibly surrounded and the Italians were none the wiser.

The lower town was to be captured first and the power station disabled immediately to draw the Italians from the fort.

The commandant, Jones and a few others at the farm were served cornbread and ham while they waited. Couriers arrived. Their brigades were in position. All was silent.

Zero hour came. Ten interminable minutes crept by.

Suddenly! A loud report! Mortar fire! Rifle shots! A machine gun rattled and the noise increased. The whine and crack of shells solidly filled the air. It was July 24, 1943.

Only momentarily stunned, the fort sprang to life.

Fires lit in the lower town became crackling, orange infernos. The noise deepened as the big guns came into action.

Eleven o'clock inched nearer. If all went well, the power-house would be blown up then. More fires erupted followed by a deafening machine gun barrage and bombing.

Suddenly, there was a shattering explosion so loud it

182

drowned out all the mortars, machine-guns and rifles.

Sweet success! The power plant was gone; all went dark.

The next hour was bedlam in the lower town with mortars from the fort above landing helter-skelter amid the din of Partisan return fire. Couriers to the temporary headquarters, reported stubborn resistance, one blockhouse had been captured and the partisans were trying to surround others and blow them up. Other units were working up the steep hill to the fort and the commandant ordered the artillery to concentrate covering the advancing troops, a familiar move to Jones and quite possibly instigated by him.

Another courier reported that two small towns, several kilometers distant, were in Partisan hands and German troops stationed some kilometers further were helplessly blockaded.

By 1:30 a.m., the lower town had been captured. Three machine-gun posts at the fort were destroyed and the Partisans had reached the barb-wire below the high wall. Resistance was strong and showed few signs of weakening. Dawn was approaching

Commandant Stanei had two options: he could call off the attack altogether, or he could leave some troops holding the lower town and withdraw the rest to nearby villages until the following night. His biggest concern was ammunition. Each troop had been allotted 30 rounds and cautioned to take careful, deliberate aim. Could they continue? Always that problem.

More couriers reported. Stanei's commanders unanimously supported the second plan. They had captured enormous quantities of ammunition and food in the lower town.

Major Jones slept late on a straw bed in a barn. At noon, a beef stew dinner materialized only to be interrupted by the drone of approaching airplanes. Everyone scattered. Four light Italian bombers swept low over the rooftops but saw nobody. They rattled their machine guns, still saw no one and left.

Another courier from a town 10 kilometers to the north reported that an Italian force of 11 tanks, 500 men and a battery of 75 mm. guns approaching by rail had been stopped five kilometers north of Zuzemberk.

This Italian column took to the roads and would pass through the village where Jones and the others were holed up. They hid an artillery gun at a sharp bend in the road and felled several trees as roadblocks.

Airplanes reappeared, observed the road block and flew up and down the road strafing anything they imagined they saw.

By 4:00 p.m., the enemy column approached. Planes furiously bombed the village to clear their path. Typically, Jonesy stood casually leaning against a tree watching.

Suddenly, Bill heard a woman screaming as she frantically tried to chase the pigs from her burning barn. He and several others restrained the poor woman and moments later the roof dropped to the ground sending up a firestorm of flame and cinders.

Around 6:00 p.m., Partisan troops moved from the village and relaxed hidden in a copse by the road waiting. They were startled bolt upright by gunfire from a tank just a few hundred yards away. A heavy, earth-shaking explosion followed. Then all was still. What happened?

An hour later, a lone wooden wagon appeared pulled by a clip-clopping horse. On it was the turret and quick firing gun of an Italian tank. The tank had been destroyed by a Partisan mine.

The Italians hastily backed off, tried again and lost another tank. They retreated to a town 10 kilometers away.

The nervous enemy in the fort expected aid and their periodic mortar and machine gun fire did little. Meanwhile, the local committee in the lower town greeted the Partisans, fed them and cared for the wounded. An armored car that broke from the fort was destroyed and the personnel captured. After some persuasion, they admitted that those in the fort were in rough shape. Many had been killed the previous night and the wounded were demoralizing those remaining. Rosano, the fort's commander had requested aid several times, was told it was coming, but it never did. He ordered his men to fight to the last man.

The attack continued through the next night. Fire after fire broke out within the walls, yet the Italians resisted.

Around midnight everything suddenly went dead silent. Jones, now in the lower town, heard loud shouting and realized someone was delivering a speech! In the middle of a battle! What on earth!

184

Unbelievably, the Partisans were broadcasting to the Italian garrison that their leader, Mussolini, had fallen! So they might as well surrender. Partisan originality was boundless.

While in the lower town, Jones checked out a dressing-station and found several women attending the wounded Partisans. Many were so young, in such pain, and some would not live. They had fought well.

Finding everything to be under control, Jones, Simich and the other leaders returned to headquarters to deal with the startling events in Italy and their effect on Slovenia.

The Partisans maintained the siege for five more days but never captured the fort. Shortages of ammunition and explosives forced them to withdraw.

Two days later Jones attended a memorial service on a hillside near headquarters for a fallen brigade commander and three of his staff. They were given a Partisan burial on their favorite hill.

CHAPTER 35 – THE BRIDGES AT ZIDANI MOST

Zuzemberk was deemed a success. The second half of the plan was the destruction of the Zidani Most bridges. This was on hold, however, until they saw what guns and ammunition would be forthcoming and what troops Commander Matea Matchec could produce to deal with the 15,000 German troops stationed there

Jones needed the actual layout and construction of the bridges and asked the Partisan commander who replied: "If you can wait three or four days, I should be able to give you the actual bridge plans."

"Well," Jones responded a little dubiously, "would there be any doubt about that? Can we really get them?"

"Oh, we can get them. They're in the Ljubliana archives."

The actual architectural road and railway bridge drawings arrived as promised and were studied in detail along with maps.

He planned to assign Simich the dangerous task of chief sapper, to be lowered by ropes to place plastic explosives on the bridge structures while Partisan troops occupied the Germans.

Meanwhile Jones sent regular messages to Cairo and Britain demanding supplies, guns, ammunition, and everything necessary for an attack. Couldn't the British, the Allies, MO4, SOC, the prime minister see how strategic this was!

Disappointingly, the operation was called off. It was just too dangerous without proper fire power.

On August 6, 1943, an outraged Jones treated the higher-ups in Cairo to a blistering communication:

"8 of 5, nr. 14. Hunter to relay to Cairo at once, "From Major Jones to whom it may concern. I have never seen such weak-kneed, white-livered, spineless efforts made to achieve anything of importance as that which you have made since I have been here. We have carried out implicitly your instructions to the letter. You have failed us in every point. . . . Conts.

Pt. 2.nr 15. We asked for a few miles of telephone wire. None came. . . six 47.32 guns asked for. None came. A first-class landing ground was provided. It was ignored. Croatian HQ expressly asked for a few hundred gallons of petrol, anti-tank guns. None came.. . boots were asked for. Perhaps 100 pairs arrived. Z.M. (Zuzemberk) operation was laid on fortnight ago. 4 guns, explosives asked for. None here yet. Conts.

Pt.3.nr.16. Rifles, 40 L.M.G.s, S.A.A. asked for. No sign of it yet. Admittedly change of drop area upset one sortie. We cannot control Italian activity, such minor hitches bound to crop up. Why did plane not return next night? We would have intercepted it at Ribnik en route. From 9th to 20th we showed fires at Homoljac for one arrival. Some personnel walked 40 km. daily during this period. Conts.

Pt.4.nr.17. You think us pro-partisan, you do not believe our statements, you will not understand the magnitude of this field... Three old liberators are no damned use for this job. Partisan mentality is not to be played with. Conts.

Pt.5,nr.18. Serious all-out effort. Difficulties must be overcome. No hypocrisy tolerated here. We are pro-Partisan to the extent that we are pro-British. For God's sake, be British! Ends."

Over a year later on Saturday, November 18, 1944, U.S. Tactical Operations (Twelfth Air Force) comprised of medium-sized bombers dropped their payloads on bridges at Pizzighettone, Romano di Lombardia, Castelnuovo di Garfagnana, Migazzone, Casarsa della Delizia, Casale Monferrato, Italy. Continuing north, they bombed the Zidani Most bridges and pounded the Brod-Ljubljana railway line, the principal German escape route in the Balkans.

It was a strategic idea, but more manageable from above.

187

CHAPTER 36 – MAJOR WILLIAM JONES VS GENERAL GUIDO CERRUTI

Back from Zuzemberk, President Vidmar came to Jones' barracks with Tida, his 17-year-old son.

"Major Jones, my son will be here for a few days. Perhaps you could teach him a little English?"

"I wouldn't mind at all in my spare time."

So Tida and Jones had several English sessions.

Four days later, President Vidmar visited again, "We've learned that General Cerruti, the commander of the Isonzo Italian division lives in the same house where Tida lives in Novo Mesto. We've talked among ourselves and we want you to be involved. We think it is time to contact Cerruti as he's heard of a British officer with us. He seems willing to meet you. Would you agree?"

"Certainly I would."

What was Cerruti up to? Jones had already been told by his military headquarters that, in light of Mussolini's fall, he should take over the Italian troops in the area. By himself? Sure!

His answer to that communiqué was that the Partisans had the matter in hand and would take over the Italian troops themselves.

Headquarters agreed but maintained he should be on the alert. Jones didn't bother reporting that they were making contact with General Cerruti.

Tida was instructed to return to Novo Mesto, this town of 6,000 inhabitants lying 20 kilometers from Slovenian headquarters.

Days later he reported: "General Cerruti is prepared to meet Major Jones here," and pinpointed the spot on a map 25 miles west of Novo Mesto. "There's a thicket of woods beside the road, no settlement nearby and if Major Jones agrees, he will meet him there at a time and date to be determined."

Tida returned to Nova Mesto with Jones's reply.

August 17th was the chosen date and Jones took along an interpreter named Alsalnik, a Croatian who had accompanied him to Slovenia as a guide.

They cautiously approached the spot not knowing what Cerruti was up to. Hidden Partisans already surrounded the area.

Jones and Alsalnik sat down to wait. Cerruti was late but they finally heard a car and watched it pull up slowly and stop.

An Italian officer dressed in his finest gray uniform, gold braid, medals and shiny black boots stepped out. He was short, stout, though appeared energetic and agile despite his rotundity.

Jones and Alsalnik cautiously moved from the sheltering trees. Cerruti saw them and advanced enthusiastically, arms out-stretched. He saluted and Jones, in his plain khaki field uniform, returned the salute.

"I'm General Cerruti. I am a friend of Britain. We are allies. There's the military cross," he said touching his medals. He had received the cross from the British during World War I.

"I'm glad to meet you sir," Jones replied and pointed to chairs placed under a tree. "Won't you sit down."

The General did, and, with only his staff officer and driver present, seemed quite transparent with no hidden agenda.

He reiterated his statement: "Yes, I've always been a friend of Britain."

"You don't approve of the setup in Rome then?" the Major asked.

"No. I don't go along with the fascist regime."

"So you're speaking for yourself right now?"

"Yes. That is it."

"Well, let's analyze your position." Jones rose and paced. "Right now you're a trespasser. You're in this country and you have no right to be here whatsoever. You're in arms against the people here and that makes you a trespasser! Let me remind you that we've already stood against each other in Africa."

Cerruti looked at him scornfully. "You're no soldier. You're intelligence service."

Jones ignored the comment and not mincing words to a man who was his superior in rank, continued: "Your only course now is to place yourself under the command of the Partisans in this part of

189

the country."

Cerruti considered that, remembering that El Duce, their fascist leader, was in prison. Beads of sweat ran down his round face. "We won't lay down our arms but we'll work with the Partisans," he hastily reassured Jones.

"Not good enough. You must submit to Partisan authority. If they allow you to keep your arms, that's up to them. If they say you are to disarm, you must do so," and he read a list of 13 points provided by Slovenian headquarters.

"We shall not disarm," Cerruti declared adamantly.

"You are defeated General Cerruti."

The chubby General, incensed, leaped up and shouted in English, "Italia never defeated! Never defeated! This is no way to speak to an Italian General! I'd rather die for my beloved Italy!"

"Never mind," said Jones, his temper rising a fraction. "You are defeated on this occasion. You know better than I do that the Germans are just north of you. Aren't they?"

The general's silence answered the question and Jones had shrewdly gained information.

"If you want protection, you'd better take this opportunity to place yourself in Partisan hands. And in case you don't know it, the British and Americans moved in on Messina today. Sicily has fallen. Tomorrow it will be Rome. Italy is defeated and the Partisans are part of the Allied army!"

"No! Italy is not defeated!"

Jones stopped pacing directly in front of the Italian, pointed at him and said curtly, "Very well then. Good day."

Cerruti was speechless. They parted wordlessly.

Back at headquarters, Jones reported to President Vidmar and his commanders.

He said to Jones with a twinkle in his eye, "Jones, you did the right thing. You didn't know exactly how it would work out, but you took the right stand."

Major Jones chuckled. "I'd give him a few days before we hear from him again."

Not two days later, Partisan brigade commanders in the field

190

began sending word to headquarters: "Italians surrendering locally to our personnel. What should we do with the prisoners?"

They were told to collect them at the foothills below Baza 20, feed them and take their weapons. They needed to think this through as these prisoners would be a severe drain on the supply system.

London responded with yet another wire to Jones: "Proceed to take over Italians in your area." Uh hu.

Jones met with President Vidmar, Kidric and Kardelj. Grinning, he told them that London wanted him to take over the Italians in the area, "And it looks as if we'd better get right at it."

"We're thinking of going into Novo Mesto."

"Good. Take over the city hall, establish your authority and order the Italians to surrender. I'll go along."

Jones, General Ausnic, Commander Aselmik, Krasovic and one other leader, backs ramrod straight, boldly rode on horseback down the main road to the municipal building and confronted General Cerruti and his staff. He knew why they had come but had no idea whether they were surrounded by Partisans or not. It was Thursday, September 9, 1943.

"Could I have a conference with you?" Cerruti asked Jones specifically.

"Alright," Jones agreed, knowing he was stalling.

He beckoned Ausnic to follow as he spoke German and Italian.

So while the President of Slovenia waited at headquarters, Jones, Ausnic and Aselmik followed Cerruti inside and were seated at the board room table.

The place was bedlam. Telephones rang continuously throughout their negotiations and Cerruti constantly shouted orders into the phone giving them time to have quiet whispered conversations. To some degree they had to play ball with the general as he had the numbers and firepower advantage.

Cerruti was stalling and they would do likewise because, in the meantime, Ivan Macek and his troops were taking over Italian positions all around the countryside.

191

The phone kept ringing with reports that unit after unit had surrendered and Cerruti became more and more furious as his entire command melted under Commander Macek's ministrations.

"You'd better hand over your arms," the delegation told him.

"I am not handing them over! We're going back to Italy armed." It would be less humiliating.

"You must be sensible and reasonable," Jones reasoned. "If you give over say five or ten thousand, no, how many rifles have you got anyway? And how many machine guns have you got? And how many armored cars have you got? How many vehicles have you got altogether? Trucks and so on?"

They peppered Cerruti for figures to keep him off balance.

"We'll take 15 percent of the machine guns and we'll take 25 percent of your armored cars."

They kept changing the numbers and by late afternoon reduced him to keeping a small percentage of arms with the Partisans getting most of the cars, trucks and other things so badly needed.

"Then," Jones told the sweating General, "you'll order your troops here to Novo Mesto."

Word came that all Italian troops were in Partisan hands and somewhere a clock chimed 5:00 p.m.

"Now are these terms satisfactory?" Jones demanded.

"Yes they are," the defeated general responded.

The terms of surrender were quickly drafted and signed by General Cerruti.

"Fine,' Jones said, "And don't you leave this city and don't let any of your personnel. Got it?"

"Well, what if other troops arrive?"

"You will disarm them and their arms will be put in the park and they will remain here in the square until you're given instructions to move. Got it?"

Cerruti nodded.

"Now I want a car and chauffeur immediately," Major Jones curtly ordered the general.

Cerruti produced the car, Ausnic, Krasovic and Jones leapt in and instructed the driver that they had to quickly reach Commander

Macek who was near a place called Sutjeska.

The countryside was agog. Abandoned vehicles cluttered the roads. Italian troops wandered aimlessly, and after a lot of racing around, they found Macek.

"Call a conference of your military command immediately," Jones told him. "We have things to report."

Macek did so and Jones and Ausnic reported the events in Novo Mesto.

"What's the next move?" Macek asked.

"You go right in and take Novo Mesto and put it under military law. Accept all who come in, but don't let anybody out."

Macek quickly assembled a unit and marched into Novo Mesto and the takeover was done by daybreak. The park was piled high with arms and vehicles were simply stopped there. Italian soldiers were on foot everywhere.

The Partisans reclaiming Novo Mesto from Italians.
Photo courtesy of Bill Jones Jr.

Over half of Yugoslavia was now free, though they still had to contend with the Germans.

193

CHAPTER 37 - PLANS

The following day, a gathering was held in Novo Mesto in the town square, with the actual meeting in the town hall. The newly liberated regions had to be organized, people had to be fed, injured and sick looked after, schools continued and the danger always lurked that the Germans might retaliate.

John Leonard (Lenchek), who had quietly followed Jones' orders, asked him the evening prior: "Could I be your interpreter?"

"Well John, I'd be pleased to have you be my interpreter, but I'll have to consult the command here."

Jones buttonholed President Vidmar, Boris Kidric and Edvard Kardelj: "Gentlemen, do you have any objection to Lenchek accompanying me as my interpreter in Novo Mesto?"

"No," they said after a brief consultation, "so long as he stays with you. He's a good linguist and he'll serve you well."

It was a short night for Jones as he put notes together for the speech he'd inevitably be asked to make.

September 10, 1943 was an auspicious day.

After lunch, he and President Vidmar drove by car towards Novo Mesto and passed many two-wheeled donkey carts with unarmed Italian troops heading west to Trieste.

This disturbed Jones and he turned to him, "This is all wrong President Vidmar."

"I don't know Jones. We want to get rid of them."

"But, this is all wrong. They've got to walk."

"No, no Jones," he replied.

"Yes!" Jones insisted. "These animals and vehicles belong to your people. They can walk to Trieste."

The distance was about 75 miles as the crow flies, but much longer winding through the rugged coastal mountain range.

"Do you think so?"

"It's war. They're your captives. You've got to do it."

194

"I'll ask Kidric," and they found him about 20 miles away.

After a quick discussion, Kidric saw Jones' logic and agreed: "Of course, but we should put up roadblocks. Take the vehicles and make them walk."

It was enough that the Partisans were feeding them. Why should they ride to Trieste using Slovenian equipment? The Italians just wanted to get home unscathed.

Partisan soldiers immediately set up roadblocks, took the vehicles off the road and ordered the fleeing Italians to walk.

That taken care of, they drove into Novo Mesto. Delayed over the 'ride vs walk' business, they arrived as proceedings were about to begin.

Astonishingly, 8,000 Slovenians were packed into the square, up on the balconies, in the windows, on the roof tops. Happy shouts of "*Sloboda!*" (freedom), "*Demokracia!*" (democracy) and "*Osvobodilna Fronta!*" (Freedom Front) rang through the air. Flags flapped and horns honked.

A large wooden dais decorated with bunting and pictures of Stalin, Roosevelt, Tito and Churchill had been erected in front of the town hall. Loudspeaker equipment was hooked up. Various dignitaries had arrived on short notice.

President Vidmar spoke, followed by Peter Kidric, then the rest of the executive. Speaker after speaker clarified the huge responsibility that lay ahead, that organization was essential, that the price for a free life was great. The crowd applauded noisily following each speaker.

Jones spoke as the British representative and found he'd never had a better interpreter than John Leonard. He was barely aware of the man as he spoke.

Later Vidmar told him, "Jones, Lenchek did a simply marvelous job."

During the speeches, the women prepared a tremendous banquet in the municipal hall. It was decorated with drawings by artist Bozidor Jakac of every place the Partisans had occupied.

Afterwards, long tables were set up in the second story of the municipal building. Candles were lit and they sat in semi-darkness,

195

able to see only the faces of those sitting around the table.

Peter Kidric rose and everyone took out notebooks. He gave careful directions from the very minute services required in Novo Mesto to more complicated responsibilities. They had to find food for thousands of people. People from bombed out villages had to be relocated. Food rationing had to be established. Schools had to be kept open. These were immediate needs. Then he gave details of how other areas could contribute to Novo Mesto's needs. He talked for three hours and copious notes were taken.

Afterwards Jones said to him, "Peter, I knew you were a great man, but I wish to God that the British people could have seen you in action tonight. It was absolutely wonderful."

The following day, General Cerruti, signed the formal papers of capitulation.

Around midnight Macek received a report that Cerruti and his staff had escaped Novo Mesto by car and were heading to Trieste. At the roadblock, armed Partisans ordered them from the vehicle.

"Walk," they said.

"Can't we take the car?" Cerruti asked.

The soldiers contacted Partisan command wondering what they should do. He was a general after all. Partisan command answered that they should follow Cerruti and his staff, make sure they had enough to eat and not to abuse them but they were to walk.

By the second day of walking Cerruti decided to join the Partisans who obligingly added him to a Partisan work party.

During the Italian capitulation, Jones was heading along the road to Cronomelj and saw a small howitzer manned by Partisans.

"Where are you going with that?" he wondered.

"To the repair shop near Zagreb," they replied.

"That's a long way away."

"Yes, and it's also German headquarters, but still we're taking the howitzer there to be repaired."

"But you're all Yugoslavs!"

They laughed. "And we all speak German!"

196

That howitzer went to Zagreb alright, the turret was fixed, the tank was filled with petrol including some spare tanks. It was loaded with a good supply of ammunition and boldly driven away!

Shortly after that momentous day, John Leonard came to Jones' cabin wanting to discuss a serious matter.

"Very well John. I'd be glad to hear you out."

"I've been here for many weeks. I feel terrible seeing my countrymen engaged in this struggle and doing nothing. It's embarrassing and I want to be with them."

"You mean you'd join them John?"

"Yes," he said, "if they'll have me. I will do anything they want me to do."

"John, this is the finest thing you could say and I'll see about it right away."

Jones went straight to the commanding officers, Vidmar, Kidric and Kardelj, and said, "Gentlemen, John Lenchek has expressed what I think is an honest desire to join his countrymen in a first rank capacity, ready to do anything and make any sacrifice. I don't know what your reaction will be, but I'm happy to think that he, voluntarily, has taken this stand. From the day he landed, I thought if he is a man, sooner or later there would be an intimation of this kind. I'm happy that he has made it."

No one objected.

Immediately after the Novo Mesto meeting, the *Izvrsnj Odbor* contacted committees all over Slovenia and assisted in conducting local affairs. Food and relief commissions were appointed, thousands of refugees were looked after, clothing was distributed, workers were sent to areas short of laborers and many industries were brought back into production.

Local elections were held in each town, village and city and people nominated their choices for this Freedom Front Provisional Government. Candidates were elected by secret ballot and any man or woman over 18 or serving in the army could vote. Every single eligible voter did.

197

CHAPTER 38 – THE BRITISH PROBLEM

As the British liaison officer, Jones directed endless information to the Allies, yet his requests for aid fell largely on deaf ears. On September 21, 1943 he sent yet another missive.

"Nr. 57 of 21.Sept.

There is a strong feeling of disappointment and criticism of Br. Policy towards Yugoslavia setting in and spreading rapidly. The people frankly question Br. relationship with traitor collaborator Mihailovic and his government in London. It is very difficult for them to understand why it is that one of the Allies can be serving two masters.

Turjak–That last stronghold of Mihailovic white and blue guards fell to Partisans Sept. 19 but not before the encircled garrison had threatened to hold out until their German friends should arrive on the one hand and until they should receive word from Cairo to surrender on the other. . . .

These elements of Mihailovic followers numbering six hundred strong had been left to continue the struggle by their former Italian masters. They were trapped before they could get away to join their foster parent–the Germans, as a few of them from other parts succeeded in doing.

The fear inspired by such Br. attitude has aroused suspicion that, God forbid, that so called Yugoslav government in London may be brought here and forced upon a united indignant people under protection of British forces. It is our military duty to point out that such a policy, if pursued, would, we believe, entail most bloody consequences. The injustice of which would redound to the dishonor of Britain. . . .

They have asked for Allied assistance to which they have right and just claim. This assistance, they begun to believe, is being deliberately denied them. . . .

As Britishers we pray that honesty, truth and justice be

accorded this country, and strongly recommend that action in the nature of immediate help and relief be taken to allay and destroy this cancerous fear.   Jones"

The response came a month later in September:

"Following guidance H.M.G. policy may be passed to Partisans. Reference your 2 of August 1st.

A.   British policy is to give material and propaganda to all Yugoslav resistance movements wherever they may be, who can and will operate against the Axis provided they will not fight against each other except in self-defense.

B.   Scale of material support will rapidly increase.

C.   Chetniks who persist in attacking Partisans, and vice-versa, will lose this support, and are acting as enemies of the British.

D.   Although Mihailovic is war minister, British do not expect Partisans to put themselves under his command. They still desire, however, to bring about ultimate cooperation between Chetniks and Partisans with us against Axis. British do not wish Yugoslavs to remain passive until Allies arrive. British wish to increase active resistance against enemy, only reservation being that they do not wish resistance forces to risk crippling loss.

E.   Before we are able to give them maximum help.

F.   Dissolution Comintern irrelevant our relations with Partisans as military resistance movements.

G.   British Gov. has adopted no official attitude towards Anti-fascist Council.

H.   British favour Yugoslavia and not Greater Serbia. Chetniks have no right speaking in the name of King Peter of Greater Serbia."

At least they were showing signs of recognizing that the Partisans were a legitimate force, but still fence-sat regarding Mihailovic as war minister for Yugoslavia and assumed both the Chetniks and Partisans were against the Germans.

199

CHAPTER 39 – AUTUMN IN SLOVENIA

On a sunny morning in late September, President Vidmar invited Jones to accompany him and his executive to the first session of the Provisional Parliament of Slovenia in Kocevje in south central Slovenia.

They left on September 30th in five shiny cars removed from the Italians but the grandeur of their transportation was deeply contrasted by blackened piles of rubble and ruin along the way. Each portrayed shattered lives.

Reaching Kocevje, they drove straight to the meeting hall–a movie theatre.

The hall was decorated with the national colors of red, white and blue. Allied flags were displayed in the front corners. Artistic signs warmed the bare walls: "Long live the Freedom Front of Yugoslavia," "Long Live the Allies," "Long life AVNOJ," (the provisional parliament of Yugoslavia). The names of Tito, Stalin, Churchill and Roosevelt were boldly displayed. Comfortable seats were set on the stage in a horseshoe with a small speaker's table in the middle. A long table for interpreters, recorders and clerks stood to one side.

The hall was overflowing. A block of 140 seats was reserved for the recently elected representatives from free Slovenia who would form the parliament. The remaining seats and standing room were for visitors and local citizens.

A brass band sounded a chord, everybody rose to attention, soldiers saluted and a standard-bearer ceremoniously unfurled the flag. Everyone heartily sang *Zdravljica*, the national anthem: "God's blessing on all nations who long and work for that bright day when o'er earth's habitations no war, no strife shall hold its sway"

The honor guard retired, leaving a motionless sentry at the corner of the stage. President Vidmar rose to thunderous applause, welcomed delegates, then paid high tribute to his spirited people. He praised their successful efforts against the enemy, then outlined the work to be accomplished in this session.

Dr. Ribar, a popular veteran lawyer from Belgrade, followed and he congratulated the Slovenians on behalf of AVNOJ on the opening of their first parliament. He encouraged them, reiterated the progress of the Freedom Front Movement and read a formal message from Tito himself. The applause was deafening.

After more speeches, Peter Kidric, secretary of the *Izvrsni Odbor* (Executive Committee) submitted his report. He held his audience captive for two hours, then wearily retired to his seat. More speeches followed. A peasant woman from Stajerska appealed for greater efforts against the enemy. Her husband, a farmer, had been tortured and murdered by the Germans. She had lost three of four sons fighting with the Partisans. The crowd cheered, demanded she be given a seat of honor beside President Vidmar and two Executive members escorted her to the front.

The British Liaison Officer was called to the microphone and Major Jones rose to wild cheering.

"Citizens of the World Democracy and Freedom, I am indeed honored to be invited to address you on this occasion. It is with humility in my heart, that I stand here as British representative and attempt to convey the expression of friendship and goodwill which I know my countrymen would voice were they here this day. I know what place the love of freedom and democracy has in the hearts of British people and I assure you your joy this day will be truly shared by them when they hear these glad tidings .

"Today, I believe, marks the day of a new era in the history of your country. We witness here today, a gathering of representatives from all parts of Slovenia. . . . What is most significant to me is that here, surrounded as we are, by a ruthless enemy, the courage of the Slovenian people gives fame to their determination for freedom and that the enemy cannot prevail against it. . . . You have done it alone by your indomitable spirit, by your fearlessness in battle, by your tenacity of purpose. No sacrifice could be more horrible or sacred, and no efforts greater than that which you have made for freedom. By the will of God, it is your bout to rejoice today. . . .

201

"This is truly a memorable day. With all freedom must go responsibility, discipline and hard work. It will be your task to solve many difficult problems; to lead and assist your people through yet trying times will require courage, patience, unity and co-operation. Your task is hard, but a people who have fought so gallantly, who have endured hardship beyond description and who have overcome difficulties of the greatest magnitude, are not the people to fail in such a task. With the will to endure and a sense of responsibility tempered with love, truth, justice, good will and a burning faith in the Almighty, you shall not fail. . . .

"As British representative I take this opportunity to thank the people of Slovenia for their whole-hearted, unselfish cooperation in our common effort to defeat the enemy. You have made it impossible for the enemy to move his trains across your country, you have unceasingly harassed his line of communication. Yours has been a great and valued contribution to the Allied cause.

"If it is so that Allied help has been slow in reaching you, I ask you to be patient and liberal in your judgment. It is a tremendous distance to overcome and the technical difficulties are great. I believe it will not be long before the assistance you have asked for will be forthcoming.

"In the meantime let us stand on guard and seek to the best of our ability, to destroy the enemy wherever he is found.

"I congratulate you on your great achievements and wish you strength and success in bringing security and happiness to your people.

"DEATH TO FASCISM! FREEDOM TO THE PEOPLE!"

The people roared with applause. Jones was one of theirs.

The new Izvrsni Odbor was appointed to hold office for the duration of the war and as dawn crept across the sky, they adjourned until the following night, when, after more decisions and speeches, Dr. Rebar and President Vidmar spoke in closing, the national anthem was sung to the furling of the flag. The first session of the Slovenian democratic parliament was history.

CHAPTER 40 – THE BATTLE HEATS UP

The Germans could not ignore the threats of the resistance. The Italians had been ignominiously ousted, their territories lost. The Germans had to either ignore that fact or regain control of those areas knowing the Partisans would not give in easily.

In late September, they brought in extra divisions to begin large-scale offensives against various parts of Yugoslavia. The Partisans, knowing they'd pay for turfing the Italians, prepared themselves. Despite acquiring arms and munitions from the departing Italians, they were still no match for a mechanized army in open battle. They would stick to what they did best–guerilla warfare and pure, sheer strategy.

Slovenian Partisans lying in ambush for the enemy.
Photo courtesy of Bill Jones Jr.

Long columns of Germans descended from all directions to squeeze the country, but their weakness was in following only main roads leading into the heart of Slovenia. The Partisans, knowing their geography, watched every move from hidden lairs and put sufficient obstacles in their way to constantly delay them until they moved in their own troops.

They destroyed small bridges and culverts, planted roadblocks and mines, constantly ambushed advancing enemy forces, and all the while sent their own men around to the rear of the enemy to pick off stragglers. They never stopped harassing them, while putting themselves into as little danger as possible.

When German tanks actually reached the hilltops from which mortar shells and machinegun fire emanated, the Partisans had vanished like ghosts, a completely unnerving maneuver.

Always conserving their munitions and protecting their manpower, the Partisans fought only when they had the advantage.

Jones regularly participated in these skirmishes, always in the forefront, and when he got close enough to the Germans, he was often seen dashing up, pulling the grenade pin and lobbing it into their midst.

The price on his head rose to 50,000 gold marks. Nazis contended that he was not English but a man named Janes from Kransjska operating under the 'Jones' alias. Stories circulated everywhere and posters reading "the capture, dead or alive" of "The Notorious General Jones" were nailed to trees and walls as far north as Vienna. German radio stations ranted against him, speculating that he was some leading British general undercover in Yugoslavia, whose appearances coincided with daring autumn raids and military thrusts in a dozen different directions.

The Partisans were on the offensive. German soldiers were increasingly agitated with their inability to hold their territory. Local commanders, frightened victims of their own propaganda, withdrew into garrisoned towns for protection, afraid of the sudden onslaughts of this mysterious phantom general. Jones was a magnificent hero to the Partisans and a specter of terror to the Germans.

While the Germans stepped up their predations, the Anti-Fascist Women's Congress met in Crnomelj, in the Bela Krajina region on October 16th and 17th, 1943. Bill attended and spoke as usual, saying: "It was my privilege last week to attend your nomination meeting at Crnomelj. May I take this opportunity of expressing the deep satisfaction and pride which I felt as I sat in your midst and followed the proceedings of your meeting. I say **your** meeting emphatically because it was in the fullest sense a

204

peoples' meeting–a public forum. In the same indomitable spirit of unity which you have so admirably demonstrated to the world in the united front movement and which has won freedom for a very large part of your country, you assembled yourselves to select leaders–servants–whose duty it shall be to carry out your desires and aims–the desires and aims of a free, responsible people. . . ."

Throughout, cries erupted of "Second front, war supplies!" "Open the third front, we have already opened the second!" This only made Bill more enthusiastic and he spoke of victory and freedom, and his conviction that the British would help.

The British 'back at the office' got wind of his passionate speech and took exception to it. He had spoken on his own behalf again! Allied officers were only observers and were not to become involved in local politics. Jones told his superiors that he had been overwhelmed by the events and plight of this beleaguered country.

Meanwhile, the Partisans, positive that the Germans would come and wreck havoc on the Crnomelj area, targeted a long

Crnomelj viaduct after it was blown up by the Partisans. Note the Train engine. Photo courtesy of Bill Jones Jr.

viaduct spanning a shallow valley. They planted explosives high in the stonework, waited until a German train was crossing, then blasted out the bridge, the train plus its contents and personnel. The result was decisive, though they sorrowfully destroyed a piece of their own beautiful stone architecture.

The Germans tightened their hold by placing larger garrisons in the bigger towns and keeping a few railway lines open in Northern Slovenia. By sheer force and numbers they replaced the defeated Italians along the entire Adriatic coastline from Istria to Montenegro.

In November, 1943, they punished Novo Mesto by blasting the town to smithereens as retaliation for the brazen way President Vidmar and his troops took over, ousted the Italians and made them walk to the coast. The town was a shambles of bullet pock-marked walls, roofless, windowless, once white buildings burned to blackness. The Partisans resisted strongly.

Bombed out Novo Mesto after the German retaliation.
Photo courtesy of Bill Jones Jr.

This German offensive raged for six weeks. Jones and the Baza 20 inhabitants spent a suspenseful time hidden in caves and secret hideouts, their camp and government headquarters being too close to German activity. They maintained their activities and reporting.

Jones still arranged supply airdrops. On November 28th, three planes parachuted their cargos. This was a highly satisfying result to his requests and Jones responded with: "Your efforts are laudable. Three flights are in order. The Partisans highly value your help which gives them courage and accelerates all the efforts in the area."

He reported a new innovation they had devised. Ground crews would further assist planes in finding their location by using hand-held reflectors. "Even if the pilot doesn't notice the fires, he can start dropping. Send us 10 airplanes of explosives and bazookas with mines, 16 radio stations, oil for guns, Vaseline and some glycerin."

Toward late November, they felt safe enough to return to headquarters and were barely back when Jones observed members of the *Izvrsni Odbor* heading out at midnight on the snowy trail. Mostly on foot, they were going on a long, hard journey of 300 to 400 kilometers to somewhere. Something was afoot.

He learned that 250 delegates from all over Yugoslavia had assembled in Jajce, Bosnia on November 29, 1943 at the second session of the national provisional parliament with Dr. Ivar Ribar as president. (The first session met a year earlier at Bihac, Croatia.)

This second session captured the world's attention. Despite the enemy incursions, the unity of the various nationalities of Yugoslavia became their sovereignty. The world heard this for the first time and learned of the nation's suffering.

This parliament resolved that the Anti-Fascist Council of National Liberation of Yugoslavia would assume all legislative and executive power for the remainder of the war, and when the Council was not in session, authority rested with the Presidium of the Council consisting of president, five vice-presidents, two secretaries and a minimum of 40 members.

After two and a half years of isolated struggle, a new Yugoslavia was emerging with over half of its territory already liberated. The people were more united than ever before in history.

The Presidium appointed the National Liberation Committee with Josip Broz Tito as Chairman and Commissioner for National Defence. He was given the title "Marshal". Jones' much-admired acquaintance, Edvard Kardelj became Vice-president.

This session was a political success and the will of the people crystallized as the proceedings of the meeting spread throughout the countryside. Long-standing racial jealousies were put to rest. Morale climbed even higher with everyone focused on exerting even greater effort against the enemy.

Young King Peter II was forbidden to return to the country and was to be dealt with after it was liberated.

With little progress, the Germans discontinued their offensive and moved their Panzer divisions elsewhere. The Partisans returned to offensive operations, slipping deeper and deeper into occupied territory, eventually crossing the Austrian frontier.

The colored leaves of fall fluttered down and winter's chill swept down the mountain slopes. People pulled their threadbare coats tighter and chipped ice from water buckets in the mornings. The war wove its weary way through the countryside and everyone dreaded the deep snows and cold and hunger of winter.

CHAPTER 41 – THE MONTH OF CHRISTMAS

December. Another Christmas away from Canada, from Helen, from their cozy home beside Lake Ontario with its blazing fireplace.

Political and psychological warfare continued. It caused no physical pain and deprivation, but it demoralized the enemy's mind and encouraged the Partisans. Pamphlets were printed and distributed, radio transmissions and newsreels were circulated.

Jones and his Baza 20 team regularly supplied such information as: location and recent movements of enemy troops, German troop behavior, information on prisoners of war, effectiveness of Allied propaganda consisting of radio transmissions in the Balkan languages, effectiveness of the leaflet campaign, which enemy newspapers circulated, the effectiveness of this 'campaign of rumors', availability of printing equipment and paper for Allied use– and this was considered very SECRET!

Back in London, the British Parliamentary Debates continued in response to the November 29th second session of the National Provisional Parliament at Jajce, Bosnia.

Foreign Secretary, Robert Anthony Eden took the floor and spoke: "As the House is aware, a Supreme Legislative Committee and an Executive National Committee of Liberation have recently been set up under the auspices of the Commander-in-Chief (Tito) of the Partisan forces. So far as I am aware, this National Committee does not claim authority outside the borders of the area in which it operates. It has certainly not claimed any form of recognition from His Majesty's Government. As I understand the position and as it has been reported to me by our officers, the Partisans emphasize the provisional nature of this administration, and they hold that it is for the Yugoslav people, as soon as their country is liberated, freely to choose the form of government they prefer. If that is the position, this, too, is the view of His Majesty's Government. It is also, as I know, because he has told us so, the desire of King Peter himself and the policy of his Government."

Members of Parliament responded with a collective: "Oh!"

Eden continued: "They have publicly declared it as their policy. We must be fair in all this. A public statement was made by the Government that the moment the war was over they would lay down their portfolios and the country would choose what Government they preferred."

One member asked if the radio pronouncements of the Yugoslav Government from Cairo confirmed that statement.

"Certainly. I am not trying to say that the Government in Cairo agrees on all points with the Partisans. Clearly that is not so. I am trying to make a fair approach to this very difficult question, and what I am saying is that all, including the Government in Cairo, have declared that the moment their country is liberated they will lay down their offices and it will be for the country to choose its Government. This is a point on which all are agreed–the King (Peter), General Tito and the Yugoslav Government. I feel myself the greatest sympathy for this young king. He came to his responsibilities at a most critical hour in his country's history. He did his best to rally his country to the Allied cause and is now faced with the most difficult problems that any young monarch could be faced with."

Honorable Member Riley wondered if the government was supporting Marshal Tito and his forces fighting for liberation AND General Mihailovic and what were the conditions of support?

He had hit the nail on the head. Who exactly was Britain supporting? Tito, Mihailovic and his crew, King Peter?

The member continued: "It is common knowledge that during the last two and a half years General Mihailovic has been in collaboration, first, with the Italians before the fall of Italy, receiving arms from them, and within recent months, it is rumored that he has tried to contact the Puppet Government set up in Yugoslavia by the Germans under Prime Minister Nedic. It is very important that the Allied Governments make it perfectly clear that we cannot play a double game by giving support to those who have shown, by their actual fighting, that they are fighting against the aggressor and on behalf of the people, and also that section of the military direction which has alliances with the enemy. We have to make it clear to the world that we are not playing in this war the role of restoring fallen Kings to their thrones. It is the right of the people to choose their own way of government."

Christmas was coming and hopefully all would lay down their arms for a brief respite and the various departments at Baza 20 were billeted in three small villages in a triangle of about nine square miles.

Marija, with two small boys and active in the underground, and her young husband Albin, a lawyer and brilliant linguist, invited Bill Jones, several of his group and some Partisans to spend Christmas with them.

Just before dark on Christmas Eve, Bill found the couple in a tiny attic above a carpenter's workshop. Dana (with whom he had traveled to Slovenia) and Lado, newly married were there, and President Vidmar and others of his executive.

In one corner, a tiny, decorated spruce tree sat on a small table with a home-made Nativity scene at its base. Tinsel sparkled in the candle light and Christmas so far from home suddenly became real--the celebration of the birth of Jesus, the Son of God.

And poor Lado waded miles through deep snow that afternoon ferreting out apples and walnuts from various farmhouses and begging a litre or two of wine.

They feasted on these goodies and delicious Slovenian cake called *potica* (a yeast dough rolled flat, covered with filling of butter, sugar, raisins and nuts) made by the carpenter's wife. It lacked sugar, but was still quite wonderful.

President Vidmar, relaxed and casual for once, entertained them with his lively wit. They sang and talked until midnight

Some then went off for carol singing at the church and after they returned, everyone lay down on the wood floor and slept soundly.

No turkey for Jones' Christmas dinner, but at noon, he dined on a delicious soup of roast pork prepared by a famous cook and her 14 year-old daughter, Diana. She'd been cooking for a group of

211

lucky Partisans for over three years.

Later that day, they all returned to their more serious duties but it was a Christmas to be remembered, though so lonely without Helen.

CHAPTER 42 – JOHN DENVIR

"2-1-44

Hello Sweetheart,

It is just possible that this letter will reach you though it will be more or less a miracle if it does.

Your last letter dated Oct. reached me in November. It was a treat to hear from you. The snaps also were most interesting though it would require a magnifying glass to make out your features. But I'm glad to have them nonetheless. . . .

My life during the past six or seven months has been shut off from everyone and everything except the new friends I have made here in the course of my duties. I have little or no contact with outside except your letters and official messages. It is intensely interesting work and I admit I like it very well. If only I could have the usual contact with you it wouldn't be so bad. I have enjoyed excellent health and there is little danger of enemy harm during the coming months. . . . The general scenery of this country resembles that of Slovenia. Hills, trees, small villages etc., just the sort of country that Partisans like. It is delightful in any respect and the people are marvelous. You will never rest until we come back here after the war and see for yourself how beautiful a country it is and to experience the friendships I have made while here.

Corp. John Denvir, who will take this letter with him escaped from a prison camp in Germany and is well known to me. He is a prince of a chap and will become a very famous character when the truth is known. I hope you contact him by letter. His address: No. 8028 Corp John Denvir. Maori Point, Maramea, West Coast. S.I., New Zealand.

Heaps & heaps of love Sweetheart. My thoughts and prayers are ever with you. Give my love to all the family and keep brave.
As ever Nurtz"

213

Should the letter fall into the wrong hands, his 'Nurtz' left no clue as to the writer.

Curiously, as an Allied soldier, John Denvir remained a Corporal, but as a Partisan, known as Frenki Rabel, a.k.a. "Frank," he was a Battalion Commander. Jones set out to rectify this with the following commendation dated February 1, 1944:

"TO WHOM IT MAY CONCERN:
The bearer, No 8029, Cpl. John Denvir., 20th Battn., 4th. Inf. Brigade, 2nd N.Z.E.F., after serving with his unit a year and a half in Africa went to Greece where he was captured by the Germans in Dec., 1941. He was taken to Maribor, Yugoslavia when he escaped (19/20 Sept. 41. He was recaptured by Ustasi on 25 Sept. 41 at Zagreb but escaped again in Dec. 41 and made his way to Ljubljana where he was befriended by townspeople in touch with the Partisans.) He had the choice of making his way to the coast or of joining a small band of Partisans, 120 strong, who, he had learned, were conducting guerilla warfare against the Axis occupier of Slovenia. He joined the Partisans and continued to fight.

Cpl. Denvir served with the Partisans from Dec., 1941 to Dec., 1943, having been promoted to Company, then Battalion Commander and in Dec., 1943 to Brigade Commander, though he was not active in this last capacity due to effects from wounds.

Cpl. Denvir was wounded three times during his service with the Partisans. He took part in many operations against the Italians and Germans and performed all his duties with outstanding courage, tenacity and a conscientious sense of duty.

For most conspicuous bravery in an action in August, 1943, when his unit attacked a German Maintenance Unit while en route by train to Italy in which the train and all equipment was destroyed and 15 German soldiers killed in hand-to-hand fighting, I recommended to the British C-in-C that Denvir be awarded the D.C.M.

Denvir enjoys the full confidence and esteem of the Partisan Command and is recognized as a hero of the highest order. His conduct since his escape from the Germans has done much to enhance the respect of the British soldier through Yugoslavia.

Cpl. Denvir was badly wounded in the arm in Sept., 1943 and because of lack of local facilities is being sent to rejoin the British Forces in Italy for hospital treatment. *

The veracity of the facts in this statement is vouched for by me as I have had the opportunity of personal contact with Denvir and his commanders during my term of duty as British Liaison Officer to Slovenia.

Signed: "W. Jones" Major"

Jones added a handwritten note: "*Denvir was wounded on this occasion during action against the Germans near Ljubljana. He was taken to a field hospital which was later raided by the Germans but was able to escape. He later took part in actions near Novo Mesto and finally, having contacted the British Liaison Officer at Partisan HQ Slovenia, was given the task of organizing supply dropping areas. He started his journey to the coast on 3 Jan. 44, was evacuated from Senj to Vis in a Partisan schooner and then to Bari by a British Vessel.

W.M. Jones, British Liaison Officer, Slovenia"

Helen received the letter!

The train attack mentioned in Jones' letter was initiated by the Middle East Command and brilliantly carried out by Denvir with his Partisan shock brigade who destroyed the armored train carrying four valuable and much-needed German repair shops to the Italian front.

The D.C.M. (Distinguished Conduct Medal) was awarded to Corporal Denvir, the escape artist, for his outstanding service. During his 1955 visit to Yugoslavia, Marshal Tito recognized his work with the Partisans by presenting him with a Mauser sporting rifle.

CHAPTER 43 – THE CAT IS OUT OF THE BAG

Jones' job was getting supplies to the Partisans and forwarding intelligence to the Allies, but he specialized in being a nuisance to the enemy, participating in skirmishes, destroying tracks and trains and seemingly impervious to bullets. He issued proclamations and urged the people to beat the tar out of them.

Jones sitting in front of a camouflaged cabin at Baza 20.
Tatjana the secretary is to his right and Bozidar Jakac, the
artist, to his left. Photo courtesy of Bill Jones Jr.

Radio Berlin was regularly calling down hellfire on a certain Jones insisting he was a disguised British general and that his name had been published in the Nazi "White Book" for liquidation. His involvement in loathsome incidents against *der Faterland* was embellished along with the price on his head.

The British picked up the broadcasts and Parliamentarians in early January, 1944 demanded: "Who is he? What Britisher is

216

causing so much distress to the Germans?"

Foreign Secretary Anthony Eden responded reluctantly: "Jones is a Canadian attached to our Black Watch Regiment–you know "the ladies from hell." He's on loan by them to Marshal Tito."

"Ahh," Parliament responded remembering those "ladies" from World War I, but missing how Eden had passed the buck to the Black Watch Regiment.

The news hit the front pages of British and Canadian newspapers, but no one could make head or tail of it.

In a Long Branch munitions plant, a pint-sized woman read one of the puzzling newspaper dispatches and laughed gleefully: "That's my Bill!" Then she added to the coworkers crowding around her, "I had no idea where my husband was, but I read an exciting account of General Tito's adventures the other night, and I remarked that Bill was likely with him. He always manages to go where things are hottest."

This was Helen who had not yet received Bill's letter sent via John Denvir. Rejected as an army vehicle driver because of her small stature, she was acceptable to the munitions plant.

On January 17, 1944, *The Star*, tracked down Bill's mother in Digby. When told of the price on her son's head, the 86-year old Mrs. Jones responded dryly: "Oh, they have, have they?"

The following day, the *Toronto Daily Star*, captioned an article "In Distinguished Service" noting Jones' distinction serving with the Yugoslav Partisans and a brief history of their situation.

Not to be left out, *The Advertiser,* a paper geared to outlying areas of Toronto, shouted in bold headlines on January 21, 1944: "New Toronto Hero Aids Guerilla Fight." In slightly smaller print: "Hun Price on Head of New Toronto Major Daring Aide to Tito," and then wrote: "Hero of Last War, Major William Jones Dropped By Parachute Into Guerilla Hideout–Known To Friends As "Man Without Fear"." Photos captioned "Huns Seek New Toronto Major" featured the uniformed Major and Helen. They added: "Liaison Officer with the Yugoslav Partisans, Major William Jones, Lakeshore Drive, New Toronto, on whose head the Huns have placed a price, is shown above. Pictured with him is his wife, the former Helen Scott, of Hamilton, a war worker on the staff of the

217

Small Arms plant. Major Jones is a veteran of the last war. For some time he taught a Boys' Bible Class at Century United Sunday School and has met some of these boys overseas."

A Hamilton paper proclaimed: "Major Wm. Jones, Hero of Partisans, British Liaison Officer Serving With Tito's Forces," and noted: "Married Hamiltonian–Frequent Visitor in City."

The Montreal Gazette, on February 3, 1944 declared: "Maj. W. Jones, Now in Tito's Army, Once Served with Black Watch Here," and a Toronto paper got in on the act with: "Allies' Officer With Tito Is Toronto Last-War Hero."

Newspapers loved the story; their readership adored it.

The whole Allied world became enamored with the Major Jones story, making him a larger-than-life, inscrutable figure who engaged in wild escapades, some based on fact and some pure speculation. He was proclaimed the "Lawrence of Yugoslavia!"

One newspaper said he was a nasty *little* man, but on the other hand stood six feet, five inches tall. (His Attestation Papers dated September 27, 1914, say he was five feet, seven inches.) Apparently he was tough and muscular and wore quaint disguises including a very wide moustache and used the name "Major William Jones." The media wasn't sure of his real name.

Newspapers reported he had been dropped into Yugoslavia in German-occupied territory, that he'd gathered a lot of people around him who hated Hitler and, despite his towering height, he passed unnoticed through very dangerous territory. He did most of his useful work before the Nazis even realized it and was so useful to Tito that this famous guerilla could not get along without him.

One reporter claimed a lot of Partisan troops landed secretly in the capital (We assume he meant Belgrade.) and were planning a coup. The Nazis did a house-to- house search with orders to shoot on sight anyone who looked suspicious. Of course, at Tito's secret headquarters up in the hills, they immediately found out about this. He informed Allied headquarters in Italy and R.A.F. bombers were dispatched to bomb the city and the Nazis were prevented from searching for Partisans who exited quietly to nearby hills.

Papers claimed Anthony Eden told the British House of Commons that Bill Jones was actually "the gallant member for

218

Lancaster," and not a Canadian. Toronto papers claimed he was a Nova Scotian living in Toronto, and therefore Canadian. But if Eden was right, then Jones was actually Brigadier Hew Royle Maclean of the Cameron Highlanders, Conservative M.P. for Lancaster, England. If Toronto papers were right, he was a gallant war veteran of the First World War whose wife knew only that he left on a secret, dangerous mission a year earlier.

They claimed he had led a suicide column on a flank movement in Africa that ended just behind Rommel's rear during the withdrawal of the Nazis. And if Jones was really this Maclean, then he'd been given the Croix de Guerre for that little escapade.

He was called "The Notorious General Jones," and "The Mysterious Canadian."

The *New York Mirror*, on January 17th reported "Hitler Can't Keep Up With Tito's Canadian, Maj. Jones. A middle-aged Canadian, serving as an allied liaison officer with Marshal Tito's Yugoslav Partisans, was described today as an almost legendary figure, feared by the Germans and loved by the guerillas... Gen. Wilson, Allied Commander in the Mediterranean, appointed "Maj. Jones"–believed to be a pseudonym–to the post."

A Toronto newspaper refuted this, stating "Maj. William Jones" was his actual name.

Amidst the carnage of war, it was so exciting to have this baffling hero emerge.

The Evening Telegram in Toronto began getting the facts right. They interviewed Helen and quoted her on January 17, 1944 saying: "In the last letter I received from him in February, 1943, he told me that so dangerous was the mission on which he was being sent that only the importance of the struggle had induced him to accept. Naturally I have been terribly worried during the last year," she confessed to the reporter, "and while it is reassuring to know where he is and that he is well, the fact that the Nazis have placed a price on his head is not easy to overlook.... I am not surprised to hear that my husband was chosen for the job. He makes friends easily and is able to get along well with people. He has a keen sense of humor. He was a Greek and Latin scholar at Dalhousie University and speaks Greek, French and German well. Besides he

219

always likes to be in the thick of things…. He joined the Royal Air Force and then transferred to the Black Watch in which he holds his commission. He was then sent to Egypt and the last letter I had came from the Island of Cyprus."

Bill's brother, Doug, in Edmonton, dashed off a telegram to Helen:

"CONGRATULATIONS YOUR BILL STOP CANADIAN PRESS WANTS HUMAN INTEREST STORY BUT I HAVE DECLINED GIVING INFORMATION BECAUSE FEEL THAT BILL WOULD NOT WANT PUBLICITY AND TOO MUCH PUBLICITY MIGHT INJURE HIM STOP HOPE YOU WILL AGREE WITH ME AND TAKE SAME ATTITUDE WITH PRESS SHOULD THEY APPROACH YOU LOVE DOUG JONES"

Her husband's notoriety was exciting, the requests for interviews enticing, but a second letter dated January 23, 1944 came to Helen while the story was still fresh news in the papers. Signed by an "A.D. Kean" it also cautioned her to say no more to the media as she could jeopardize his security in Yugoslavia.

"2067 Bleury Street, Montreal.
19th January, 1944

Mrs. William Jones (Wife of Major Jones of Yugoslav Partisan Forces),
Longbranch,
Toronto, Ontario.

Dear Mrs. Jones:

In my Regiment here we have been most interested in the recent press references to your husband's activities with the Yugoslav Partisans, and have wondered whether he is the same William Jones who had a distinguished career with one of our Battalions in the last war. Press references here have referred to the fact that he lost an eye in the last war, was a theological student
220

before the war, was wounded five times and was awarded the Distinguished Service Order and Bar, but these press dispatches have not mentioned the regiment with which he served during the First World War.

Our William Jones, according to records at our Regimental headquarters, served with one of our Battalions in the last war in the ranks, was wounded <u>three</u> times, was awarded the Distinguished Conduct Medal and Bar, won his commission and in recent years carried on a real estate business in Toronto.

Could you let me know whether your husband is our William Jones, and with what regiments he served during the First World War?

We have been endeavoring to keep as accurate a record as possible of the service of our officers past and present, but of course do not wish to claim credit for your husband's wonderful recent service in our list if he is not the same William Jones.

Is there some address in England through which one could write him?

Yours very truly,
'P.P. Hutchison' Colonel
Commanding The Black Watch
(RHR) of Canada"

"45 Lakeshore Drive,
New Toronto, Ont.
Jan 20th, 1944

Col. P.P. Hutchison
The Black Watch of Can.

Dear Sir:

Your letter of Jan. 20th to hand, I wish to advise you that your William Jones is one and the same William Jones with the Yugoslav Partisans. I believe you will also be glad to hear that he is once again identified as a Major of the Black Watch Reg't., but from

221

the scanty bits of information that we have, I am sure it is the Imperial Black Watch.

It was rather annoying to me that the Press made so many errors but it seems that one has to accept them. Perhaps by now, you have noticed that the DSO & Bar has been corrected to DCM & Bar.

The following address is the one I have been using for the past year:

> Major Wm. M. Jones
> Black Watch Regiment
> MO4 HQME
> Middle East.

A cable received from him Jan. 2nd, 1944 informed me that he received my letters.

If there is any other information concerning my husband that you think I might be able to furnish you with, let me know and I shall do my best to oblige.

> Yours very truly,
> 'Helen L. Jones'"

Several letters went back and forth between Helen and Colonel Hutchison including a resume of Bill's activities to that point. The Regiment was thrilled that one of their own had been assigned such a noteworthy task and was doing such a spectacular job. The Colonel was prompted to immediately write the following with a copy to Helen:

> "2067 Bleury Street, Montreal.
> 26th January, 1944

Major W.M. Jones, D.C.M.,
The Black Watch,
M.O. 4, H.Q. M.E.,
Middle East Forces,
OVERSEAS

Dear Jonesy:

If this ever reaches you I know you will be interested to know that all of us in the Regiment were very thrilled when we saw by the daily press news of your recent exploits. The first reports were somewhat garbled and did not indicate your former Regiment, but all who knew you were practically certain that they did refer to you. I wrote your wife who was good enough to confirm the situation.

At the annual dinner of the Sergts. of the Regiment last week I identified in my address the press dispatches with you, and so many of your old friends among the old Sergts. were mightily interested, i.e. Bob Haxton, George Morrison (now R.S.M. of the Regiment) etc.

No one of course was more interested than "Major Mac", who incidentally for the past two years has been the O.C. of our 3rd Bn. In the non-permanent Army. The other Reserve Army Bn. is commanded by Lieut.-Col. Hugh Johnson, whom you will also remember.

Incidentally Lieut.-Col. George Cantlie has just sent me a collection of press clippings about you which had been sent on to him by Jim Lovett.

We were all greatly intrigued, particularly at the news from your wife that you were back in our uniform (it is not quite clear whether with Canadian or Imperial badges), and I am simply sending you this line in the hope that it may reach you to say how much we all admire what you have been doing, and to wish you the very best of luck.

Many of us envy you very much, particularly those of us who have been told by the Authorities that we were too old for more active service. I have been commanding the Regiment here since war broke out, but unfortunately they will not let me do more active service. The Regiment, however, has done extremely well and I am sure that you will see many of our lads before you return to us. When you do return be sure to come to see us at the old Armory.

With very best wishes, I am,

223

Yours sincerely,
'P.P. Hutchison'
Colonel Commanding
The Black Watch (RHR) of Canada"

Completely unaware of the excitement he was causing, Bill somehow got the following telegram to her through Canadian Pacific on January 29, 1944:

"MRS JONES
45 LAKESHORE DRIVE NEW TORONTO
AM WELL AND FIT MY THOUGHTS AND PRAYERS ARE EVER WITH YOU
ALL MY LOVE
W JONES"

We do not know whether he ever received Hutchison's letter. If he did, he would have known that the cat was out of the bag.

CHAPTER 44 – BLEAK WINTER, EMPTY CUPBOARDS

The winter was bleak. People were starving and cold, but the intelligence gathering only became heavier.

To Major Jones' surprise on January 4, 1944, a Lieutenant Colonel Moore had appeared unannounced at Slovene headquarters claiming he was taking responsibility for activities in three supply delivery areas.

He brought signal apparatus, reflectors and lights to aid supply drops, though during the dark winter months airplanes seldom came because of the harsh conditions and the British were still supporting the Chetniks, dividing supplies between the two.

It was soon apparent that Jones and Moore would never see eye-to-eye on running things. Moore, the observer, the by-the-book military man did not get personally involved with the Partisans and found it impossible to work with the major. Jones was totally involved and regularly accompanied sorties into the countryside.

Meanwhile, reports flowed in, were summarized for head-quarters by Jones, including enemy movements, personnel and equipment losses, the destruction of a bridge over the river Dobro.

The Germans were blocked in Novo Mesto but periodically broke out to attack points in the countryside but were constantly repelled by the Partisans. An attempt on January 25th left 13 dead and several wounded and they dreaded being ordered out knowing the inevitable cost.

A typical report dated January 10, 1944 noted at Dolenjsko: "The German units blockaded in Novo Mesto constantly tried to break out. Partisan units keep them in check. Partisan units attacked a WG patrol with heavy mortar until it fled. Partisan units impede Hun traffic on the road Ljubljana-Kocevje. It came to a fight on the Jasnica-Star Cerkev. The Huns wanted to clear the road of our tank blocks and fill in tank ditches which are mined as well.

Several mines exploded while the Huns tried to clear the road. Our units attacked the enemy with mortar fire. Enemy losses unknown."

Despite harsh winter conditions, the Partisans remained active and Jones kept busy reporting to headquarters.

"14 Jan 44.
My dear Jones (The salutation is handwritten, the rest typed.)

Brigadier MACLEAN has asked me to arrange for his various Missions to receive a regular supply of publicity material so that the PARTISANS may be more fully informed of the War Effort of the United Nations and in particular of that of Great Britain and the United States.

I am enclosing to you herewith a first installment of photographs and literature. It is intended to send you further regular supplies as often as occasion offers.

It is suggested that where it is possible you should display the photographs in your Headquarters and should encourage Partisan HQs to arrange similar displays with the extra copies provided.

The first installment is not very varied, nor have we been able to supply many copies of each photograph or magazine. Would you please communicate as soon as possible with CHILLBLAIN, letting them know how many copies of each photograph and magazine you can usefully employ. Please also let them have any suggestion that may occur to you as to other types of material which might be of use.

Beginning on 11 Jan 44 Radio BARI are transmitting nightly at 2330 hrs a News Bulletin read at dictation speed in English. The transmission is on 283.3 metres, 1059 K/cs. This bulletin is specially intended for JUGOSLAVIA. I would be grateful if you could listen to it and have the news circulated in your district. Perhaps you will also let us have your comments and suggestions as to the contents of the bulletin.

Yours sincerely,
(Signed) "R.S. Churchill"
Major G2 Allied Military Mission

To the N.A.L."

At the bottom, Jones handwrote his dutiful order but must have wondered who had nothing better to do.

And that was Randolph Churchill, Winston's son, and he was attempting to keep the Yugoslavs informed of what was going on elsewhere perhaps accounting for the puny supply shipments.

January air drops were meager indeed– some guns, machine guns and ammunition, a radio station and some other goods. The final drop of guns and munitions landed on a rocky outcrop that damaged the guns beyond repair. The Partisans and Jones felt this was deliberate. The British were only giving the appearance of support. Even Tito received no deliveries for a month and a half.

Many Slovenians considered their Allied relationship broken. For three years, they had fought a desperate war and felt they deserved better recognition. They supplied the Allies with invaluable reports, yet in recent months, received only 20 air deliveries, some 30 tons of goods that were mostly explosives of direct benefit to the Allies. Surely their information was worth more than that.

Jones' dander reached stratospheric proportions. The British could send posters, photographs and magazines but what use were they when you needed arms, ammunition and food! People were starving.

On January 14, 1944 he sent the following telegram:

"Nr. 44 of 14 Jan. DDDD
Allied relationships with Partisan verge on complete breakdown in Slovenia due inadequate, clumsy, indifferent handling policy and supplies here resulting in mistrust, resentment and complete lack of good faith.

People who honestly fight common cause for three years through improbable difficulties, persecution and hardship believe themselves worthy of better treatment from their Allies. They have denied enemy use of valuable Lines of Communication at great cost of life. Have practically freed this country. Held many enemy divs. from other fronts. Have given every possible assistance and valuable intelligence service to the Allies.

Slovenians have in six months received but 20 sorties–approx. 20 tons. Chiefly explosives used in direct service to Allies. They are gratefully mindful of accrued benefits Italian collapse, though just appraisal must award much to their own efforts. These benefits were not however, in themselves sufficient.

We have endeavored from the beginning to report facts and pressing requirements. It is obvious from this end the fundamental importance of this field is not yet appreciated. There has been grave lack of determined policy and honest, frank relationship in Allied attitude throughout our term here. We have been given little or no encouragement much less support in our effort to build up mutual confidence and friendship. There is a deep-rooted affection and friendship in the hearts of these people for the British people.

As a result of this most incredible bungling the value of the Partisan Army to the Allies has been greatly cut and many possibilities lost.

It is our duty to suggest that unless a change in policy implemented by immediate delivery of adequate urgent supplies by air and sea is effected, further cooperation between this HQ and the Allies ...."

He carried out his threat. On January 20, 1944 he and John Lenchek wired a second notice to London: "It was decided that we don't send any information anywhere any longer until the Allies change the politicking to the Slovenian Partisans and that they show this indeed, in particular with the delivery of goods. The Allied relationship with the Partisans has reached the point of a complete break."

That got their attention. Even Churchill recognized that Allied supplies were inadequate to really help the Partisans and in a telegram he said: "I mean that the opening of the coast (Yugoslavian) and the supply of the Partisans is one of the most important secondary objectives."

Astonished by his audacity, the actual response to Jones' wire took a month to formulate and arrived with a long schedule of demands and it is not known whether transmissions actually ceased during that time. Slovenian H.Q. staff took matters in hand and responded with: "We demanded a loan of 100 Millions and a complete outfit, weapons and clothing for 50,000 men that we can mobilize anew etc." Poor Bill was caught in the middle. Sometimes they made him feel that British shortcomings were his responsibility as well.

On a late January Saturday, Bill and several others were invited by a Slovenian farm couple to their vineyard some four or five kilometers away. Crisp snow, almost four feet deep, sparkled with diamonds and there was no distant thud of mortars or crack of rifle fire that day.

Dressed in their Sunday best, the farmer carried a knapsack filled with liter flasks, in one hand a five liter oak cask and in the other an alder stick to help them through the drifts. His wife carried a knapsack filled with more liter flasks.

They walked single file on a barely broken track winding through silent woods and finally topped out on a cleared mountain slope overlooking a broad valley.

Trudging to a nearby farmhouse, the farmer tapped on the window with his stick. It was raised, friendly words were spoken and three large iron keys were passed out.

What's going on, Jones wondered as they followed the couple several hundred feet downwards to the door of a tiny stone and plaster building half buried in snow.

The farmer turned the key, walked in with everyone following. Inside was a pocket-sized winery consisting of two rooms. In the outer room stood a huge press operated by a wooden screw. A large vat filled with mash was gently fermenting, kept to the correct temperature by a typical Slovene wood-fired heater (*pec*).

The inner room contained a large wooden bed made up with snow-white sheets and woolen blankets, a cherry-topped table with seats on two sides and another *pec*. A crucifix and picture of Christ still trimmed with Christmas bits of spruce hung in the corner. A wall calendar from Cobalt, Ontario showed a view of a Colorado mine.

Logs were laid in the stove and lit. The farmer disappeared

229

down stone stairs to the cellar with the keys and an empty liter flask. They heard a gentle gurgling and he reappeared with a flagon of amber-colored wine.

From the table drawer, the woman removed three long ham sausages, a local delicacy. She cut thin slices to eat while sipping the amber ambrosia.

During the next hours, four visitors dropped by: an elderly weeping lady, a man of about 60 and two young Partisans with red stars on their caps. They whiled away the time, all friends, somehow mysteriously knowing the couple would be there.

Jones learned that the elderly lady was the lone survivor of a family murdered by the Italians. The elderly old man had two sons serving with the Partisans and managed the farm with his wife and daughter. The young Partisans sipped small amounts of wine, rationed the butt of a cigarette between them, chatted and then continued on their way.

This was a Slovenian open house for anyone passing by. According to custom, only one glass was used. After taking a swallow or two, the drinker refilled the glass and placed it in front of the next person and when the flask was empty, someone went downstairs for a refill. Spirits were refreshed and news was passed on.

By six o'clock the shadows had lengthened and the night chill crept through the walls.

"We've got to get back," Jones told his hosts.

Through his translator, the host said: "Stay Major for the night. You can sleep on the table."

They ate supper of boiled ham and cabbage by the pale light of a carbide lamp. Quite innocently, the farm wife suggested they all sleep crowded in the big bed rather than on the hard table.

The couple crept away around five a.m. to attend church some two kilometers away, returned by 10 o'clock and five more visitors dropped by shortly after. Then it really was time to head home. The small oak barrel was filled and the keys left at the neighbor's house.

What a wonderfully dreamlike weekend, and Lieutenant-Colonel Moore deemed it quite inappropriate for a British officer!

230

Imagine! Everybody sleeping in the same bed! Really!

Back on the political scene, members of the National Committee (the new government) visited Slovenia and Croatia in January reporting to great crowds on the state of affairs. Jones attended one meeting where a huge grandstand trimmed with evergreens and bunting had been set up. The stage was filled with officials and delegates including President Ribar. The crowd waved streamers and flags as a full, armed battalion of Partisans proudly marched past. The cheering drowned out the band.

Dr. Ribar held the crowd riveted for over an hour. Speeches went on until dusk, though dancing and singing in the streets carried on until daybreak. For a people deep in the dregs of war and winter, this represented hope.

This summarized situation report from these times is attributed to Jones and marked "Top Secret":

- Enemy forces sent to guard railways and roads across Slovenia, including the important Maribor-Zidani Most-Ljubljana-Trieste line connecting Germany with Italy. In Zidani Most, it branches to Zagreb and Belgrade. In St. Peter, it branches to Fiume. The enemy transports most of its troops along railways and roads. The railways are guarded by a double line of German garrisons, the first close to the railway, the second further inland.
- From Zagreb-Zidani Most-Maribor there are 10,000 German soldiers, from Zagreb-Zidani Most, there are 2,500 soldiers near the railway. Larger garrisons at Brezice (500 men), Krsko (500) men, Zidani Most (500 men) and small garrisons. Inland this sector is guarded mainly by Novo Mesto garrison (750 White Guards–Yugoslav royal guards–and 250 Germans). Small garrisons along the Novo Mesto road. Territory between Novo Mesto and Brezice, except for the road itself, is firmly in Partisan hands. Germans keep more than 10 tanks and several armored cars in Novo Mesto to ensure

231

use of road.

- Sector Zidani Most-Maribor is guarded by 6,000 men, with garrisons at Celje (2,000 men) and Maribor (3,000 men) and smaller places along the way.
- Composition of garrisons for above sectors is mixed– German troops consisting of SS troops, railway police, gendarmes and customs guards. "The treacherous White Guard troops are only used at Novo Mesto and Brezice, under the command of Captain Vuk Rupnik.
- 1000 SS troops, police, railway police and customs guards guard railway line Zidani Most-Ljubljana.
- In Ljubljana, estimate only, 1,000 Germans and 3,000 to 5,000 White Guards, under HQ command at Bled, "Der Hohere SS und Polizeifuhrer im XVIII Wkhrkreis, Stab fur Bandehekampfung" headed by Captain Schumacher (German) and Colonel Peterlin (Slovene).
- Jones reported on areas still held by Germans and areas liberated by the Partisans and noted that in liberated areas, military, political and administrative organizations of the Freedom Front are at work.
- The Slovene Freedom Army has pinned down 50,000 Germans, including 7,000 White Guards among them.
- The Ljubljana-Karlovac railway lines are completely destroyed."

In Jones' opinion: "In the former "Province of Ljubljana" we could get hold of German strong points by concentrated attacks on Kocevje, Novo Mesto and Lasce. We attacked these centers with small units, trying to entice the enemy to fight in the open. We would not sacrifice our men by attempting to storm enemy positions, our basic principle being to annihilate Germans while preserving as many of our own as possible. Isolated towns and strongholds are unimportant: our objective is to maintain our national existence, to destroy the maximum enemy lives and material. The Partisan army could take all of Slovenia as soon as the enemy is unable to use motorized armored units, i.e. destroy the railways, take the roads."

From September 7, 1943 to February 1, 1944, Jones reported that Partisans used 15,363 kg of explosives (11,442 kg. were supplied by the English and the balance captured from the Germans and Italians). They used 1,125 meters of Primer-cord and 823 detonator units, blew up 137 bridges, destroyed high tension line pylons, mined a railway tunnel or two, sabotaged trains, destroyed tracks, set booby traps, laid mine fields and did all kinds of other damage such as blowing up a mercury mine.

On February 10, 1944 Jones received this disturbing letter from Boris Kraigher on behalf of the GHQ of the National Liberation Army and Partisan Detachments of Slovenia.

"To Major W. Jones,
Senior British representative with the National Liberation Army and Partisan Detachments of Slovenia.

We have the pleasure to inform you that the conditions on the neighboring territory, controlled by the units of the National Liberation Army of Croatia, now make possible the departure of Major Neville Darewski, British representative with the units of the Slovene National Liberation Army of Primorsko area.

On this occasion we once more give you the reasons which induced us to ask your HQ to recall Major Darewski.

At the end of October 1943 a Gestapo spy ring was discovered in Cerkno, Primorsko, then headquarters of the IXth corps of the Yugoslav Liberation Army. Its chief organizer was Ranzinger, an engineer, from Trbovlje, a Kocevje German, a mine manager who lived in Cerkno. This Gestapo spy ring was directly inspired by the representatives of the treacherous organization of General Draza Mihailovic in Ljubljana. This spy ring based its activities on declarations and slogans of the treacherous general and the refugee Yugoslav government in Cairo. On one hand, Ranzinger had direct connections with the Mihailovic group in Ljubljana and on the other with the Gestapo centres in Skofha Loks and Bled, Gorenjsko.

Some members of this Gestapo organization, especially Ranzinger, declared during the investigation that they had

233

connections with Major Darewski, stating he sympathized with them as far as connections with Draza Mihailovic and the refugee Yugoslav government were concerned.

We know the methods of the Gestapo who try by all means to disrupt relations between the National Liberation Army of Yugoslavia and the Allied representatives with our units and we consider that the Gestapo tried by means of the above mentioned declarations to sow suspicion and doubt in our mutual allied relationship. That is why we refused to investigate any further the declarations of the Gestapo agents. In the same time we requested the GHQ of the National Liberation Army of Yugoslavia and the Commander in Chief, Marshall Josip Broz Tito to ask for Major Darewski's recall.

We repeat that only our wish to assure sincerest collaboration between our army and the allied armies induced us to undertake this measure. We ask you to express to Major Darewski our acknowledgement for his efforts and his self-sacrifice which he showed in organizing the Allied help for the National Liberation Army and the Partisan Detachments of Slovenia in Primorsko.

Death to Fascism – Freedom to the People."

So, let's get him out of Yugoslavia immediately. He either misunderstood the situation or was a traitor. Jones recommended to Slovene headquarters that Major Darewski be removed and he was.

Along came a Military Directive dated February 29, 1944 from Brigadier F.H.R. Maclean, commander of the Anglo-American Military Mission to the National Liberation Army of Yugoslavia who reminded Major Jones: "As I command all Anglo-American Submissions with the NLA you are under my command and will be guided by this directive at present. For technical reasons the channel of communication is through CAIRO. If conflicting orders are received you will comply with CAIRO's orders and communicate with me at once, if necessary through CAIRO."

All right! Ignore conflicting wireless messages from Britain and report only to Cairo.

The Brigadier added that Captain James Goodwin is posted to him as his second in command with the sole purpose of increasing

234

efficiency in decentralizing, i.e., work with sorties and drop areas, routine administration of his sub-mission and any other work he wished to delegate.

Brigadier MacLean suggested that Goodwin act as his deputy to enable Jones to be more involved in operations. Perhaps he understood that Jones liked being in the thick of things.

With respect to Anglo-Partisan relations, he was to explain to the Partisans at Slovene HQ that the bottleneck for supplies was the availability of aircraft and difficult weather conditions.

MacLean, was totally responsible for advising the War Cabinet on sorties required for Yugoslavia and he ordered: "You will stop bringing pressure to bear on CAIRO by making impassioned appeals and larger demands than they appear likely to fulfill, as these have no effect, waste signal time, and raise unnecessarily the hopes of the Partisans when they read copies of your signals. If you consider that Slovenians are NOT getting their fair share of sorties, HQ Slovenia should communicate with Marshal Tito."

Next MacLean directed Jones to refrain from expressions of personal opinion about Allied conduct in the war and to not overstate his case.

The Brigadier reassured him: "As sea supplies to Croatia and Bosnia increase, I am impressing on Marshal Tito the necessity of increasing the allotment of sorties to your area. **Your needs are well known**. It is therefore essential that your reception arrangements should be perfect."

Intelligence concerning local enemy divisions, or those passing through, was of utmost importance and Jones was to use every bit of influence he had on the Partisans to ensure it was obtained.

Jones' wireless set had been confiscated for some unknown reason and the Brigadier, having discussed the matter with Tito, was assured this would not happen again.

As to railway interruptions he said: "Your urgent need of explosives for this is appreciated. This will become more important as spring approaches and the Italian Campaign progresses. At present a large proportion of the little you receive is being used for

235

defensive measures. This is understandable in view of conditions in your area, but I hope to have sufficient sorties sent to you to enable a reserve to be built up for offensive operations later."

He promised the British anti-tank mines being used with outstanding success in Croatia and finished off with instructions regarding air targets.

Jones undoubtedly read this directive many times, alternating between hope that the Allies were "getting it", to the ignominious wrist slapping.

His following requests were brief and circumspect. On March 7, 1944 he wrote:

"From: Brit. Military Liaison officer, Slovenia
TO: C.O., M.O. 4, Cairo

The need of explosives here is most grave. The Partisans report they have used the last kilogram of the balance shown in the enclosed report of Feb. 4, 1944 and are intensely worried as to how to carry on.

Many splendid opportunities of damaging the enemy are reluctantly passed up, and in many cases the Partisan positions are rendered precarious because of the lack of explosives.

We enclose here with a comprehensive list of explosive requirements submitted by Partisan HQ, Slovenia. Included in this list are items of components and essentials required to condition a quantity of Iti shells and mortars which the Partisans are anxious to make serviceable.

Signed: "W. Jones" D.C.M. & Bar, Major,
Brit. Liaison Officer, Slovenia"

This was followed by locations for two new landing sites.

The war drama was unending. On March 8, 1944, the Allies informed Jones that they wanted to establish an airport for the Partisans on liberated land. Was it possible to land large aircraft of the Lancaster type in the area?

236

He discussed the request with the Partisan commanders and their reaction was not enthusiastic: "We've recently heard rumors of an Allied invasion of our country," they said wearily, and we don't want yet another inundation of armies."

"Well," said Jones, "Churchill and some of the British strategists are considering landing on the Istria Peninsula from the Adriatic. From there they'll push through to Ljubljana right into the belly of the Germans."

"We can't make this decision ourselves given the implications. You must ask Tito."

Jones had his wireless operator sent a coded message saying: "This information indicates the possibility of an English invasion. How should we answer? We've answered that we will study the possibilities."

Marshall Tito responded: "Give them the description of the airport and its capability."

Jones supplied a potential location and by mid-June, construction was begun in the Loska Dolina valley.

On March 22, 1944, Captain Goodwin arrived at Baza 20. Apparently Brigadier General Maclean was not entirely satisfied with the Allied mission and wanted him to assume Jones' position. Like Moore, he found it impossible to work with Jones or to improve the mission's well-oiled machine. He discussed the situation with Lieutenant Colonel Moore who agreed to put Goodwin in Jones' place.

The reasons could be numerous, including the recent international newspaper publicity, or Jones brashly confronting the powers with demands, threats to cut off communication until they complied with his supply requests, that he unconventionally took things into his own hands, that he personally took part in Partisan raids, and there was the German price on his head. The reasons were never clear. The British were in the ungainly position of having backed the wrong people and it would be embarrassing to admit this.

The Partisans were livid when they heard of his impending departure as Jones' greatest task had been convincing the Allies of where their loyalties should lie. The Partisans loved him but whether the actual orders came is not known.

On a brighter note, he received this letter from the British Intelligence agent who had earlier given them so much concern:

"7th April, 1944

Dear Major Jones,

I am very sorry indeed that I did not meet you in the HQ yesterday afternoon. As I had urgent work to do at home I had to return without seeing you again. I would like to take this opportunity to express to you how deeply I have appreciated and loved you not only for your outstanding qualities as a sincere worker for the Allied cause but also as human being as such. I thank you for all and assure you that you will always live in my memory even if we shall not meet again.

And now I have a job for you: Please, take the letter addressed ISLD Bari with you to the Vrhovni Stab and urge it to be dispatched soonest possible to Bari. I will be very thankful to you for that.

With hope to see you again in our Slovenia. I greet you from all my heart and wish you a good travel across Yugoslavia. Same from Lojze.

Sincerely yours,
Signed: "John Leonard""

Jones was saddened to hear later that Johannes (John) Lenchek, a.k.a. Captain John Leonard, was killed in a confrontation with the Germans, but he was pleased to hear that the man had given an excellent account of himself and served the Partisans well for months. His assessment had been correct.

On Easter morning, April 9th, in a nameless village, he and several others were soundly asleep on the second floor of a Catholic school next to a twin-spired church. The windows were wide open catching the night breezes.

Suddenly, at 4:30, the stillness was shattered by six large

bells tolling in the adjacent towers. Shocked into wakefulness, they leaped to their feet shaking.

What on earth was going on?

"Happy Easter!" someone exclaimed and throughout the day, a steady stream of people visited the church as the bells tolled. At eight o'clock, a formal procession neared and a Partisan battalion formed an honor guard, presented arms as the procession passed, then followed them into the church.

Bill tucked the day away in his mind for later recall.

CHAPTER 45 – A VERY LONG WALK

Days earlier, on Palm Sunday, April 2, 1944, Jones and the Baza 20 people were startled by a formation of 33 American bombers rumbling high overhead.

After dropping their payloads over Steyr, Austria, they were suddenly faced by nine German Junker Ju-88's firing rockets at them from below. Several planes were hit, including *Maggies Drawers*. Her pilot, Fred Streicher, determined they could not reach safety and prayed they would at least make it to free territory rather than falling into treacherous German hands.

But the B-24J was losing altitude and he had to order the crew to bail out over enemy territory, Novo Mesto in fact.

They leaped, their parachutes snapped open and the Germans waited below like circling wolves. Partisans also saw the bailout, regretting the inevitable outcome, but as the airmen drifted helplessly downward, the wind miraculously shifted and wafted them over free territory.

Nineteen year-old Joseph (Joe) Leo Maloney, the rear gunner, was rescued by the Partisans and later provided background for the following events.

The entire crew was safely rounded up with no idea who their rescuers were. Friend or foe? After being given a meal, they were taken to Podgrad for a day or two until finally an English speaking person appeared. Janez Ambrozic explained that they were in Slovenia, that Marshal Tito was their leader, that they were Partisans and they would get them out of Yugoslavia. They must trust them implicitly and NOT learn the names of anyone or the places they passed through. There were two airports in the vicinity (Podzemlju and Krasincu). Though close to the Germans, an attempt would be made.

When the time came to move, they walked mostly at night, sleeping in the woods, in homes, in barns and never far from German troops or White Guards.

The days blended into sameness, but around April 10th (the day after Jones' enjoyable Easter Sunday), near the villages of Metlike and Crnomelj, they joined a large group of Allied men and now numbered 80.

On April 12th two important looking strangers appeared. They were shaved, dressed in pressed uniforms and polished shoes contrasting sharply with the Partisans' ragged uniforms.

The shorter of the two, mustached, white-haired, with a black patch over one eye said, "I'm Major Jones," then pointed to his cohort. "This is Lieutenant Colonel Moore. We are British liaison officers with the Partisans." He continued, "We will travel with you for the next few days but you must follow Partisan orders implicitly. They will get us through. They know the country and where the enemy's positions are. You can trust them."

The men nodded.

"The Partisans," Jones continued, "will arrange for supplies and security to get you to the airport so you can be flown out," and then he enthusiastically explained who the Partisans were. "Trust them. They'll watch out for your safety and return you to your own lines. I am travelling with them and at some point radio contact will be made with the 15th Air Force at Bari, Italy. Let me remind you that it is at great personal sacrifice and risk of their lives that these Partisans are leading you to safety."

"But why are they protecting us?" a flyer wondered.

"We share a common enemy," Jones answered. "The Yugoslavs are fighting for a better life and have put together this amazing fighting force and support system among the villages. And don't ask any further questions," he ordered curtly wagging his finger.

The provisional governments of Slovenia and Croatia were reluctant to remove these men from a local airstrip lest the Germans find out and retaliate with excruciating payback. They discussed the matter with Jones.

"Then we will take them to an airport in Bosnia," Jones concluded and they nodded in worried agreement knowing the 200 mile distance.

To keep from attracting attention, they were broken into

smaller groups, moving parallel but not within sight of each other, and the servicemen never knew where they were going. Major Jones traveled with one group or another. When they faltered, he tirelessly plowed on, and Joe Maloney often wondered about this fascinating man.

Meals were mostly corn meal (polenta) or barley soup with bits of meat added and the Partisans graciously ensured that the servicemen were fed first.

Danger and dread were constant.

Nearing a major Croatian railway crossing, the Partisans nabbed a young White Guard who certainly would have reported them to the Germans.

As Joe wrote: "The Partisans walked the man beside our column all afternoon, beating him and knocking him down with their rifle butts. They encouraged us to do the same, but we didn't have the heart."

Nearing the railroad they shoved him aside, someone took out a long knife and slit the young man's throat. He sank to the ground and died at their feet.

"I will never forget that sound and to this day when I hear a certain sort of gurgle, I'm reminded of it again," says Joe.

Shocking? Yes. But necessary. This was war.

While crossing the tracks, two women with machine guns protected them.

Joe Maloney studied that baffling Major Jones with the wonderful rapport with the Partisans. They laughed and joked but showed the man great respect. Even more curious were German posters nailed to telephone poles and billboards. When he heard the translation, Joe was thunderstruck. Reward? Dead or Alive! Ten thousand gold marks! What on earth had Jones done to the Germans? But Joe never learned more than that he worked for British Intelligence and the Partisans claimed his reports went straight to Winston Churchill. Young Joe was awestruck.

On April 18th, after walking all night, they neared a village. Word was whispered that pancakes and eggs awaited them. Their anticipation was short lived as they approached the village from one side, because a German patrol entered from the opposite. Everyone

242

melted into the nearby woods, but they had been spotted.

Soon several small German planes (similar to Piper Cubs) skimmed low over the area, firing randomly and tossing hand grenades.

The noisy little planes retreated and by mid-afternoon they skirted the village, regrouped and were walking down a long straight road when they heard it, then saw it. A twin-engined Junkers Ju-88 was heading straight for them, strafing the road; the shells kicking up bits of dirt and gravel as they pockmarked lines down the road.

Everyone dived for cover. As the throbbing engines faded into the distance, they slowly rose to their feet, hearts still pounding. Miraculously nobody was injured.

They stayed under cover until nightfall, then continued in carts, safely crossing a major highway where Partisan troops were stationed every few hundred yards.

Beside a river, they crammed into a farmhouse that served as a restaurant for boat passengers during peacetime. Fried eggs and potatoes and a sampling of Slovenian wine were provided.

The farmer/ferryman explained that a small plane regularly patrolled the river and the Partisans began timing the intervals.

After the timing was down, the ferryman loaded three men into his little rowboat and rowed them across the dark river. Back again, he beached the boat, turned it over and scurried into the house so the plane would find nothing amiss. He repeated this until everyone was safely across with Jones likely on the last trip.

Now they were in Bosnia, home of the vicious Ustasi and a whole new dread entered the picture.

Next afternoon, they climbed into three army trucks for an hour's ride, the only ride on their journey. Again they walked all night and at dawn arrived at a burned-out village on the mountain slopes. The Partisan courier system had efficiently notified the local committeeman who produced a beef stew, their first food and rest in 24 hours. Everyone slept like the dead.

Joe Maloney observed how everyone knew and utterly respected this Jones, a man with no airs who slept on the ground like they did on beds of leaves and twigs.

April 19th, they set out after midnight. After silently trudging

243

up one side of a mountain and down the other, a German held railway track barred their path. The moon was shining brightly and Germans patrolled the area with hand cars and shot flares that hung in the air on little parachutes. Gunfire rattled in the valley ahead and they were silently halted by their guides. Everyone took cover. Two dim shadows were moving up the mountainside. Who was it? Rifles were cocked and aimed. Ahh, relief! They were Partisans reporting that it was too dangerous to proceed. They wearily turned back to the burned-out village on the other side of the mountain.

All the next day, Jones and the Partisans kept watch with binoculars, and he spent considerable time reassuring the refugees that they would be alright.

They finally moved on to a new village. Next morning, before finishing breakfast, there was a sudden thundering din. Machine gun fire! Everyone dashed willy-nilly for cover. The smell of spent ammunition and smoke filled the air, accompanied by machine-gun fire and flying shrapnel.

Unfortunately this village, Mazin, lay in a horse-shoe shaped valley and they were at the closed end.

Everyone, villagers included, ran across the closed end of the valley to the woods, only to be met by German and Ustasi troops viciously firing at them. One option remained--a dash to the open end of the valley some two or three miles distant.

Villagers, refugees, Partisans, Jones, ran for their lives.

A man driving a wagon hitched to a pair of snorting horses and filled with people hit a bump that pitched him to the ground. The driverless wagon had not gone a hundred feet when a mortar shell landed between the horses and the wagon. The explosion lifted people and animals into the air in a fiery mangled death.

Bullets and mortar shells landed everywhere. Panicked, screaming, blood-spattered people and animals blanketed the freshly ploughed fields.

"I'm hit!" screamed Fred Streicher, the pilot of *Maggies Drawers*.

The impact of the shot through his right calf tossed him headfirst into a ditch with his legs in the air, and like some avenging angel, Major Jones charged up through the smoke. He sized up the situation, whipped off his belt and applied it as a tourniquet to the pilot's profusely bleeding leg. It was the best he could do given the situation.

George Morrell, the co-pilot dashed up to help.

"Go, go," Fred insisted. "There's nothing you can do. I can't keep up to you."

Reluctantly George began running but had gone only a few feet when he was struck in the back and died instantly.

German troops found Fred, beat him with their gun butts until he passed out, then hauled him off in a covered wagon. He finished the war in a POW camp.

Typical of Jones. In the midst of all the smoke, explosions, blood and guts, oblivious and seemingly impervious to personal danger, he calmly urged over and over again, "Keep moving. Move along. Get moving. Just keep walking."

Many villagers were killed, their houses and barns burned and George Morrell was buried in an unmarked grave in the Bosnian woods.

Having escaped Mazin, they walked and ran until evening covering some five miles. They finally stopped in the woods, regrouped and counted heads. Dead tired, they'd had six hours rest in the last 48 and one real meal in the past three days.

Jones encouraged the haggard men and Joe felt he was the one who was really watching over them and guiding them to safety, but with Partisan help of course.

After several more days, including one 50-hour walking stretch, they arrived at Drvar, Bosnia on April 23rd where Marshal Tito's headquarters were located. The group was turned over to Colonel Randolph Churchill and U.S. Captain Lynn Farish.

And sometime during the last day or two of travel, Jones had silently, mysteriously disappeared.

The following day, April 24th, they walked to a Partisan airstrip at Bos Petrovac and waited there until April 28th when the first plane could safely land. Joe Maloney, because of severely infected feet, was on the first flight out.

On May 1st three planes evacuated the rest of the group.

On May 2nd, German paratroopers slaughtered the villagers

of Bos Petrovac for aiding the Allies.

Joe Maloney spent four days in the army hospital being treated for his feet and was eventually shipped back to the United States.

For decades he wondered who this remarkable Jones was, and through a surprising set of circumstances, met a former Partisan in Nova Scotia who had known of him and filled in many missing details.

Statistics show that of every 100 members of a heavy-bomber crew, only one who was shot down managed to evade capture. And these Partisans and Major William Jones saved 80 from capture, though two were lost along the way.

CHAPTER 46 – TEN DAYS WITH TITO

Artist Bozidar Jakac's drawing of Tito.
Bill Jones Jr. collection.

After arriving clandestinely in the village of Drvar, Bosnia, Major Bill Jones was escorted at dusk by armed guards to a goat path disappearing into deep shadows. Passwords were exchanged and a different guard escorted him steeply upward beside a roaring waterfall. Mist hung in the air and the cascades drowned out all other sounds.

He was led deep into a black rock fissure in a towering crag. Slipping through the narrow darkness, they entered an unbelievably vast, cool grotto with a mountain lake glinting in the dim light.

Just weeks earlier, 15 German Stukas had brazenly dive-bombed this crag with no more effect than a flea attempting to puncture a bull. As long as Tito's men kept foot soldiers off the slopes, they were safe in this rocky fastness.

Tito welcomed Jones into a pleasant paneled room carved from the living rock. They sized each other up, this Yugoslav leader and Jones, the British representative. They had communicated previously only by wireless. Both were larger than life.

The people's leader wore a simple gray-green uniform with gold laurel leaves on the lapels and cuffs indicating his rank as Marshal of Yugoslavia. He had thick, dark blond hair and a smile regularly flickered across his face. A prodigious smoker, he used a pipe-shaped cigarette holder. At his side, was "Tiger," a calf-sized German Shepherd. People idolized him for his honesty, frankness and strategic genius.

Tito spoke calmly and deliberately, allowing himself to be interrupted at will. He spoke German, Russian, some French, read English fluently but hesitated to speak it lest he made mistakes.

Jones and Tito had long conversations. They admired each other's accomplishments. Tito fighting for his own, and Jones for a people he had known but a short time. Tito understood Jones' disgust with British support and knew he often fought side-by-side with the Partisans.

But there was tension in the air.

On May 22, 1944, Lieutenant-Colonel Vivian Street, acting chief of the British Mission with Tito's headquarters, spotted a Luftwaffe reconnaissance aircraft flying over Drvar.

"Marshal Tito," he said, "I've concluded that a massive enemy attack is imminent. The time is ripe, and I'd suggest you evacuate your headquarters."

"I will consider this and take the necessary action."

Not knowing when the assault would come, he ordered Partisan units to block roads leading from Bosanski Petrovac and Kljuc to Drvar and to slow or stall any Axis movement in those areas. Partisan brigades and divisions were moved from north-western Krajina to this area leaving one Partisan company of Tito's personal Escort Battalion defending the cave.

248

Three days later at 5:00 a.m., May 25th the Germans, under Field Marshall Rommel, launched their Seventh Offensive code named *"Rösselsprung"* (Knights Move). Fifty bombers "softened" the terrain, then Junkers transport planes dropped paratroopers and glider SS landed. Tito, Street and others, including Bill Jones, watched from the cave, knowing the Germans would fight their way to the cave at all costs. Their main goal was capturing Tito.

Bitter fighting raged all day. More Germans poured in with field pieces and supplies. The Partisans regained much ground the first night, but on the second day, the enemy pushed an armored column into Drvar and took the airport at Petrovac from which Joe Maloney and the others had been evacuated just days earlier.

The RAF and US 15th Airforce supported Tito. Flying Fortresses pounded the German supply operations center of Bihac on May 26th. Liberators charged across the Adriatic twice on May 27th and plastered troop concentrations at nine locations. Simultaneously, P-38s and Spitfires attacked motor transports, troops and the airfields that had spawned the paratroopers.

Four divisions of German ground troops were assigned to surround the Partisan high command and members of the Allied mission. About 40 gliders landed in the area in one phase of a well-planned operation.

The Germans struggled towards Tito's cave, exchanging heavy gunfire with many casualties. Those in the cave knew what was inevitable. Tito quietly gave the word and he, his men, their guests, including Major William Jones and Colonel Randolph Churchill, quickly vanished through a trapdoor in the floor of the platform at the cave's entrance.

A harrowing, dangerous scramble up a water course cut by a dry waterfall followed and they had many close escapes along the way as they avoided the enemy.

Scarcely an hour later, the Germans arrived, certain of success. There was no one there! Tito was gone and they also missed capturing Jones with the enormous price on his head. The commandos did seize Marshal Tito's uniform. They fired their rifles at it in frustrated anger and later displayed it in Vienna—a puny trophy of war.

249

Fierce fighting continued in Drvar but the Yugoslav leader was safely away though suffering pangs of regret that he had abandoned his country.

Sergeant Ian McGregor, aka "Parachute Pimpernel", was one of those James Bond types. He dashed from place to place organizing clandestine airfields and rescuing downed airmen. (A lethal item he carried was a special safety razor supplied by SOE (Special Operations). It contained a single .22-calibre round in the handle which, when pulled back and given a half turn counter-clockwise, would fire.) He was with the British Mission in Drvar and his expertise cleared the way for Tito, his staff, Street, Churchill and Jones to safely reach Italy.

For nearly a week, Tito and his party were safely escorted on foot by Partisans who knew every goat trail between Drvar and the region of Kupresko Polje. They finally hunkered down in the woods to wait near a landing strip.

At nightfall, June 3, 1944 they heard the sound of a DC-3 two hours earlier than expected. Who was it? They were shocked to see the Partisan Red Star insignia painted on the side. The plane was signaled in and as *Dakota* taxied down the runway, Tito, his dog Tiger, his bodyguards and aides left the sheltering woods. Behind them came Lieutenant-Colonel Vivian Street, members of the British Mission and of course Major Jones. The plane barely stopped to load passengers before the twin engines throttled up and it turned and roared back down the runway.

The passengers discovered the crew was Russian! The plane, supplied by the British, was operated by the Russians from Bari.

The dark colored DC-3 swung into the night sky towards Bari, Italy, and Tito was then transported by the British destroyer, *Blackmore,* to the island of Vis in the Adriatic. It was securely held by Allied and Partisan forces.

Bill Jones immediately flew from Bari to headquarters in Algiers, Algeria to meet with General Wilson.

He wondered, a little apprehensively, what his reception would be, having pulled no punches as he bearded the highest echelons in British command with demands for supplies and aid for the beleaguered Yugoslavs.

General Wilson came towards him grinning, hand extended for a handshake.

"I congratulate you Jones," he exclaimed, "on having done a damn good job and a damn hard one!"

Bill breathed an inward sign of relief. Job well done!

The General continued: "Now what do you want to do?"

Well, he hadn't had time to think about that what with the fighting, narrow escapes, the events of the past months including the past few days. And for a general to ask a major what he wanted to do next! Incredible!

"But first we need a full report on your experiences in Yugoslavia."

"For publication sir?" asked Jones.

"Yes, by all means," replied the General. "The British public must be brought up to date." And perhaps the general had a twinkle in his eye, having heard tales of this major's escapades, the German price on his head, that he was a great hero of the Yugoslav people.

"It will not be possible to mention place names or names of individuals or to divulge Partisan strategy."

"Right," agreed General Wilson, "but go back to Bari where the records are and do the best you can."

Jones took the first plane back and worked prodigiously while the memories were fresh. By the end of June, 1944, his report was complete.

A year later it was published by Bedford Books Limited as *Twelve Months With Tito's Partisans*.

CHAPTER 47 – BACK TO ENGLAND

"45 Lakeshore Drive
New Toronto, Ont.
June 2, 1944

Dear Col. Hutchison: (Of the Royal Black Watch)

I can think of no good reason why I should not pass the following news of Bill on to you.

Letter written April 30th, somewhere on the shores of the Mediterranean, informed me that Bill was temporarily relieved of his duties in Yugoslavia, was writing his reports, proceeding to England, and, if all goes well, he hoped to be in Canada by June 15th. What means of travel he will use and the route he will take still remains a question. I hope to hear from him from England.

To say I am delighted at the prospect of his home-coming would be expressing my feelings rather mildly. I feel that you, Col. MacFarlane and other friends will rejoice with me on receipt of this latest news.

Yours very truly,
Helen L. Jones"

Even before he reached England, word leaked out that the "Lawrence of Yugoslavia" made a daring escape with Marshal Tito and it wasn't long before newspaper reporters tracked him down.

On Tuesday, June 13, 1944, *The Maple Leaf*, a Canadian army newspaper wrote "Partisans' Footwork Too Much for Nazis." Staff writer, Lieutenant, J.L. McKenna reported: "The marchingest army in the world today–exceeding even the record set by the Canadians in Sicily–is the Partisan Army of Yugoslavia, according to Major William J. Jones, Canadian officer who recently left Yugoslavia after more than a year's attachment to Marshal Tito's headquarters."

The article's main intent was to explain equality of the sexes during the war, in fact Jones declared he'd never even seen men and women holding hands. This was not the time. He admitted: "Women often seem to stand up to the rugged life better than the men," and he reassured the reporter that these women were not Amazons who delighted in killing, but were fighting magnificently for something they cherished.

Bill returned to England in July, 1944, and though it was a familiar place, it took time to adjust after the rigors of the previous 14 months. He had to lose the habit of looking over his shoulder and ducking flying ammunition. Even the diet was different. Unlike World War I, he returned physically unscathed. Though finished in Yugoslavia, he was still enlisted with the Black Watch and he discovered he would not be going home any time soon.

Soon after returning, he sat down with Yugoslavia's King Peter, now sequestered in England. Fresh from that country, Jones reviewed the situation with him in no uncertain terms.

Finally the young king asked, "What should I do?"

Jones responded bluntly, king or not: "Since you didn't see fit to return to your country during the past two years of struggle, you had better stay away until the people decide what they want."

King Peter declared, "Well I wanted to parachute back into Yugoslavia more than anything."

"But you didn't."

The king reluctantly agreed to a regency, meaning other people would rule the country. Newspapers like the *Montreal Daily Herald* on March 29, 1946, reported that Jones was responsible for convincing the defeated man to accept this stance.

And Jones, in a new Black Watch uniform bright with decorations of two wars, continued fighting to gain recognition in Britain for the Partisans at a time when many officials still repudiated his views.

Since his popularity preceded him, he was in demand as a guest lecturer all over England. People wanted to hear about his amazing adventures and this platform became his "One man

253

campaign" to indoctrinate the British on the plight of the Yugoslavs. He spoke to groups and organizations all over the country. Youngsters wrote in broad, round letters asking him to speak to their classes. His military duties were not onerous as he gave 167 lectures over the coming months and throughout, he was ever mindful of what he could not say so as not to jeopardize the war efforts there.

On August 20, 1944, Monica Person recapped his life in the British *Reynolds Newspaper*. In the "The Amazing Major Jones," she described him as having a "quiet bearing and silver hair, as packed with energy as a coiled spring, shrewd, direct, passionately sincere, filled with mental and physical resilience.

"'Supplies, particularly medical supplies, have become an acute problem, says Major Jones. This is because the Partisans have blown up all the major railways and main lines of communications. They knew that in striking this heavy blow at the enemy they would be inflicting grave hardship on themselves. That consideration did not deter them'."

She added that Jones looked forward to getting out of the limelight, returning to his wife in Canada and going fishing.

Bold as brass, on October 18, 1944, he sent a letter to N.R. Tillett, Esq., M.P., House of Commons, London setting out the desolation of the country, the sickness, death and cold. He commended the Yugoslavs on their superb efforts, and reminded him of the Yugoslav affection for the British. He said Britain owed them a duty to hurry supplies to them, that air transportation was inadequate but that sea transportation was available.

Bill sent 50 copies to members of Parliament, irrespective of party. One return missive from Black Watch Lt. Col. F.C. Caillard, A.A.AG warned him "against making political use of any information gained in his capacity as a Military Officer." Added to the bottom of this particular declaration was a handwritten note by the Black Watch Captain saying: "Sorry to create a fuss. They must be afraid you say too much!! We are trying to hasten your trip to Canada."

Jones received many positive acknowledgements from parliamentary members saying that they appreciated his stance.

254

The February 21, 1945 telegram below requests a lecture:

"LEWIS 3 HALSEY HOUSE REDLION SQUARE LONDON WOULD MAJOR JONES BE PREPARED TO GIVE THREE LECTURES FOR REGIONAL COMMITTEE ADULT EDUCATION HM FORCES AND ONE PUBLIC LECTURE IN TENBY MONDAY TO WEDNESDAY WIRE REPLY TO BOWEN CLIFTON HOUSE TUDOR SQUARE TENBY,"

and a typical handwritten 'thank you' dated February 19, 1945 from Northgate School for Girls, Ipswich:

"Major Jones,

Dear Sir,

I am writing on behalf of the girls of the school to thank you very much for so kindly coming to speak to us on Friday about Yugoslavia. I know that all the girls enjoyed your talk immensely, and we all deeply appreciated the chance to learn more about one of our allies and to see so many wonderful photographs.

We really are very much indebted to you for giving up so much of your valuable time.

> Thank you once again,
> Yours faithfully,
> (Sgd) Joy Brown (6A)"

Still concerned, the higher powers sent him a further direction regarding security and requesting that he refrain from giving public lectures. It cautioned him about making any personal pronouncements which could be contrary to official policy or saying anything that might endanger the safety of any other liaison officers because of the difficult elements in Yugoslavia.

Jones understood full well that he was bound by secrecy and disclosed nothing, even shared next to nothing with Helen. And he continued right on with his lectures and personal pronouncements

255

regarding the difficulties in Yugoslavia.

Major William Jones back in England wearing his new
Black Watch Uniform.   Photo dated Dec. 31, 1944.
Courtesy of Bill Jones Jr.

The Second World War ended with a complete and unconditional surrender.   May 8, 1945 was declared V-E Day. Partisan loses amounted to 245,549 killed, 399,880 wounded.

Meanwhile, Jonesy renewed friendships, visited Rev. and Mrs. Glidden (the invalid), Betty Glidden, the teacher and her two associates, Miss Day and Miss Sendamore and others.

But when was he ever getting back to Canada? To Helen? To Sweetheart? He was back dealing with questions of pay and bureaucratic red tape.   It was a conflicting time.   He wanted to go home but he also wanted to promote the Yugoslav cause.   Would he ever be demobilized!!   He marked time with his lectures.

CHAPTER 48 – HOME AT LAST

Bill's demobilization papers finally materialized and this time he did not have to work his way across the ocean.

Assuming he would land in Halifax, telegrams began arriving at his mother's place in Digby. One dated January 31, 1946 read:

'WELCOME HOME BILL I ENVY YOU FOR YOUR ACCOMPLISHMENTS YOU KNOW I ALWAYS ADMIRED YOU FOR YOUR CAPABILITIES I AM GLAD THAT NOW THE FIELD OF ADMIRERS ARE SO NUMEROUS. A MERKUR"

A February 3, 1946 telegram from his brother Doug read:

'MAJOR WILLIAM JONES CARE OF MRS FRANK JONES DIBGY NS WELCOME HOME AND ALL OUR LOVE ANITA DOUG BONNIE AND FRANK"

Helen was anxiously waiting on the wharf in Halifax on February 1, 1946 and they had eyes only for each other. After visiting briefly with his mother and family, they hurried home to 45 Lakeshore Drive, New Toronto.

Home at last with his wife in their house by the lake, home to get reacquainted with Helen and the concept of a normal life after being absent for nearly six astonishing years. What would life be like now? What would he do?

Of course Bill's fame preceded him and he was barely acclimatized and reacquainted with Helen when he received a letter dated February 28, 1946 from the Canadian Broadcasting Corporation. It was signed by Dorothea Cox, Maritime Talks

Producer, Halifax. She confirmed a telephone conversation they had when he was still in Nova Scotia concerning a live broadcast in April, the subject being "When I Was Overseas." Could he please do this in the style of a "yarn," in a simple conversational manner in just under fourteen minutes.

Fourteen months into 14 minutes? Well, he'd work it out.

His alma mater was deliriously proud of him and Bill and Helen received a copy of *The Alumni News* from Dalhousie University in their mailbox. Dated April 1946 it reported: "Major William Morris Jones (Arts 1919-23), native of Digby County, N.S., on February 1st returned to Halifax, after more than five years overseas, 12 months of it spent behind enemy lines in Yugoslavia as the first, and for some time, the only British liaison officer, serving with Marshal Tito's Partisans."

Speaking engagements rolled in, but all Bill wanted was peace and quiet and time to come to terms with the recent past, then to quietly get on with life.

"DON'T MISS . . .
MAJOR BILL JONES, D.C.M. and Bar
British Liaison Officer with Tito 1943-44
WILL SPEAK
At Elks' Hall, Sunday, May 12th, at 8:30 p.m.
SUBJECT:
"Soviet Influence in the Balkans"
"I heard Major Jones speak in Edmonton. He is a dynamite and thrilling speaker and has a great story to tell. I recommend him enthusiastically." - Alexander Calhoun.
AUSPICES
Canadian-Soviet Friendship Council
Silver Collection"

This appeared in *The Albertan, Calgary, May 10, 1946.* Just back to Toronto, his next engagement was already being advertised.

"Is Gen. Draza Mihailovich a traitor?
Should Yugoslavia get Trieste?
MAJOR WILLIAM JONES
Will speak on these and other questions
Concerning new Yugoslavia
At MASSEY HALL
June 2nd, 8:00 p.m.
Major Jones spent 12 months in Yugoslavia as a
Member of a British Military Mission, and is well
informed on up-to-date facts on Yugoslavia.

Yugoslav songs and music will be provided by
DUQUESNE TAMBURITZA ORCHESTRA
Of Pittsburg, PA
Admission: Silver Collection
Auspices: Council of Canadian South Slavs"

There were lectures, debates and radio interviews. Jones soon tired of it all, yet his work was appreciated as indicated in this letter dated October 29, 1946 from the Yugoslav Legation, Ottawa:

"My dear Major Jones,
        I listened to the debate dealing with a book "Ally Betrayed." Your stand on it was truly indicative of your great objectivity and it proves once again that you are a really great democratic man.
        My first contact with you in Otocac in 1943, at the inauguration of ZAVNOH, gave me a justified belief that I had seen a man, a noble and splendid democratic allied fighter and leader. Such was the impression left upon us, partisan fighters and our leaders, and it was in such a way that we always thought of you. It was a great pleasure to discover that we were never disappointed in that belief, even though there were some disappointments in regard to the others. With you the contrary was the case. Every stand of yours, your daily work, has always met with ever increasing admiration, and our hearts beat cheerfully as we know that our

dearest comrade during the last war, and now a great friend in the peace, is at the same time a fair defender of our people in his own country. All of our fighters and our leaders who know you and who have heard of you, with all the rest of our heroic nation, will be full of joy when they hear of your courageous and democratic attitude.

In their name I want to thank you most heartily and congratulate you with a desire of shaking your courageous and friendly hand.

Please convey my warmest greetings to Mrs. Jones.

I remain, Mr. Jones,

Very truly yours,

Signed: "Branko Vukelic"

Attaché of Legation of R.P.R. of Yugoslavia."

CHAPTER 49 – JONES THE FARMER

What should they do? He was over 50 years old and did not care to return to the real estate business, a career he had never particularly liked.

As Bill Jones Jr. says of his father: *"He wasn't a business-man. He was too honest. He took up real estate between the wars but his heart wasn't in it. He had access to a lot of industrial properties and could have made a lot of money, but that just wasn't his priority. After World War II, Dad just wanted to relax and write his book. He was born and raised on a farm in Bear River so why not go back to farming."*

They put their house at 45 Lakeshore Drive, New Toronto up for sale in 1946 and the search began. They chose 150 acres on a wide bend of the meandering Welland River on the Niagara Peninsula near the hamlet of Wellandport. Though the barn had recently burned, this was the best they could buy from the house proceeds and there was that lovely white clapboard house facing the gentle river. He named it Belgrade Farms.

Belgrade Farms, named after the Yugoslav capital, as seen from the air.
Photo courtesy of Bill Jones Jr.

The work was endless. He was up at 5:00 every morning, eventually milking 50-60 head of cattle and only later realized what drudgery this would become. He was constantly tied down, instead of writing his book to get the facts down while fresh in his mind. By the time the 25 years' enforced secrecy (1973) passed, it was to be ready for publication.

A letter from his mother expressed her concern that they were working too hard:

"Digby, N.S. April 16th/48

My dear Helen and Will:

I very much enjoyed your letter this afternoon. Please don't work too hard and try to do too much. If you do there will be no gain in the end... Louise will finish this for me. Tons of love to you both.

"Mother"

Dears:

Your building-bee sounded mighty inviting. How would you like to have that many 'hands' to cook for all the time Helen?

I am so glad that I sent the cheque along this week. You should have it by now. Let me know that you have received it, so I can get rid of this horrible feeling that I was a heel to be so slow in getting it off....

Best love to you both.

"Babe" (Louise was Bill's sister.)

Bill and Helen had help from Toronto friends for their old-fashioned barn-raising—a pole barn for storing hay. Financing had been difficult.

Several months later they received another letter:

"Digby,
Aug. 3rd, 1948

Dearest Helen and Bill:

You will find the cheque for five hundred enclosed, <u>I hope</u>.

We were so glad to receive your letters. It is all very well for me to check Mother's worry by constant reminders of your business, but it is much better not to have the worry to check.

"Putting the hay in the barn" sounds pretty good to us. Will you be able to get the roof on before winter? And will you keep the stock there too? When it is completed, how about sending a floor plan. I refer to the plan you sent of the farm quite frequently.

We are delighted too that your grain crop is better this year. All in all it sounds as though you were beginning to see the improvement that your labor deserves. . . .

And how we are looking forward to your visit this fall. Please don't let anything interfere with it.

I hope that you enjoy every minute of your Yugoslavia trip. It will be a wonderful experience. I don't expect to have to say a word when you are here. Just a key question at breakfast and a goodnight kiss.

Best love from both Mum and me. Don't work yourselves too hard.

Your sister
"Babe"

In 1950, the second biggest event of Bill's life occurred after marrying Helen. That summer Bill Jr. was born at St. Joseph's Hospital in Hamilton. The son they had promised themselves should he survive the war had arrived. Now Jonesy's biggest goal was building up the somewhat run-down farm as a legacy for Billy.

That summer, he hired 16 year-old Earl Rutherford to help with the dairy herd. The young man found the company congenial and later continued working there on weekends.

Says Earl of Bill Jones: "He was one of those 100 percent people. He said what he thought, wouldn't back down and was very honest and generous."

Earl and Ann, his wife, have many happy memories of the Jones family.

"When Billy was about four or five years old, we'd be doing the haying, and being a little kid, he regularly got in the way. We'd

263

send him to fetch water to keep him out of the way. When he wasn't looking, we'd pour it out and send him for more.

"And Bill was as strong as an ox. If two guys were unable to pick up something, why he'd come along and just pick it up and say: "I must have got the light end. He worked harder and faster than anybody. We grew sugar beets for the cattle and he could hoe a row as fast as you could walk.

"We used to skate up the river from Wellandport and would stop in. There was always so much food there. Helen was an excellent cook. At Christmas, she'd make Bill's favorite mince meat pie soaked in a cup of rum and delicious. After dinner he'd invite me into another room and we'd enjoy a cigar and a shot of cherry brandy–but only one shot. That was his limit and he rarely smoked cigars.

"Bill was behind the times with his farming methods and neighbors sometimes laughed at him, but he didn't care. He was generous to a fault. When a Wellandport drover bought some pigs and failed to pay him, I bugged him to talk to the man. Bill said: "He needs the money more than I do and he's got to live with his conscience." The man never paid, yet Bill always spoke to him.

"We often used his birch bark canoe and he'd loan us a teepee he'd acquired from somewhere. I took my family camping in Effingham with it and it caused quite a stir.

"Bill Jones had such a sense of humor. One day we were hunting rabbits, not knowing he'd shot a couple of cottontails the day before. We shot a rabbit sitting upright in the grass and went to collect it. It was as stiff as a board! He had 'planted' several for our benefit."

The neighbors felt there was some mystery about him. Who was he anyway? He never talked about himself and they did not connect old newspapers stories to this particular Jones.

They wondered about the foreigners who came by speaking little English. It was rumored that they were Yugoslavian and wasn`t Tito a communist? This was the cold war. Gossip flowed throughout the countryside. They talked about his friendly wife, Helen, and their little boy, Billy, who Bill dropped off for Cubs at the Wellandport church. Even the birch bark canoe was noteworthy. (The canoe survived into the 1960s before being retired for good to the shed rafters.)

When Bill and Helen took in two teenaged foster boys, the neighbors had even more to talk about.

Bill Jones, the farmer. Photo courtesy of Bill Jones Jr.

On October 15, 1954, the Dominion Weather Office announced that Hurricane Hazel had moved onto the North Carolina coast and was heading northward. By 9:00 p.m. it was centered between Buffalo and Rochester. Winds of 40 to 50 mph were conservatively predicted but were much stronger, gusting to 100 mph. It rained torrentially.

Bill and Helen watched the Welland River rising higher than they had ever seen it do so before. It crept up the broad lawn, inched toward the house. Trees whipped in the wind. Timber by timber, the pole barn was collapsing. The water reached the basement windows, trickled down the cellar walls and became a deluge.

Bill took off his shoes and went to the basement to rescue the water pump. Sloshing through murky water, he stepped on a spike that went right through his foot.

Meanwhile four-year old Billy reported from the living room window that water was creeping up the wall of the clapboard house. By the time the carnage ended, the basement was filled to the rafters, and Bill Sr. had a very sore foot.

For this family struggling to be self-sufficient, the loss of the barn and the flood damage was devastating.

The total cost of the destruction in Canada was estimated at $100 million in the currency of the day.

Bill Jr. recalls: *"We were away for the day at the Exhibition in Toronto–my mother, my two foster brothers and me. We came home and found Dad crawling around. He'd been attacked by the bull, though he wouldn't admit it, and Mother didn't know what to do so she called Dr. MacLean who was basically a horse doctor. He'd broken 6 or 7 ribs on either side–almost all of them. So the doctor looked at my mother and said: "I don't know what he told you but he didn't just fall off the hay wagon like he said." He'd told her that because he didn't want to sell the bull. He did sell that bull in the spring. My mother got suspicious and so did Larry and Gary, my foster brothers. Dad warned Gary not to go anywhere near the animal, so Gary carried a big 4 x 4 with a spike on the end when-ever he went near it."*

That story sufficed until years later when Bill and Bill were leaning on the pasture gate watching a different bull.

"Don't go near that animal," Jones told his son.

"Why?"

"You know what happened to me."

"Well, what did happen?" Billy persisted.

Bill wagged his finger, "OK, but don't tell your mother."

Billy nodded in agreement.

"When bulls mature they get more aggressive. I was working out in the first field, repairing the electric fence. I noticed the bull was being aggressive and straying from the cattle. The cattle were heading down the field towards the far end, when the bull turned and headed toward me. He stopped a few feet off,

266

started pawing the ground and snorting. This was not looking good.

"I took a swing at him with the sledge hammer. Missed. The sledge hammer flew out of my hands and the bull attacked. For five minutes, that seemed like five hours, all I saw was horns and hoofs. He tossed me around like a rag doll, nearly killed me. When it was over, I was lying on the ground and watching that darned bull casually saunter over to the other cattle as if nothing had happened.

"I didn't want your mother to know because she would have wanted me to sell that bull and we couldn't afford another one. So I just carried on with the milking with those broken ribs. MacLean taped me up good but it was excruciating. This was before there was hydro in the barn and I did it all by hand. We only about 15 or 20 head then."

CHAPTER 50 - BESIDES FARMING

Bill Jones maintained his interest in Yugoslavia and visited there in 1948 and several subsequent times.

In November, 1951, he attended the Zagreb Conference for Peace and International Cooperation and spent seven weeks traveling throughout the country. Afterwards, Bill contacted many agencies requesting assistance for the still troubled country.

From London, he wrote on another trip:

"West London Air Terminal
5 a.m., Fri. 27th/June (1958)

Hello Sweetheart,

We were late in arriving at London yesterday. It was 5:30 p.m. before we were free of the airport and on our way to London city. The airport is twenty odd miles from Trafalgar Square. I booked a room at Waverly Hotel, Southampton Row and prepared to settle down to do some telephoning. I tried to find out who is at the Yugoslav Embassy whom I might know. The one who answered had a faint notion who I was but knew nobody there who did know me. She wished me a happy journey and let it go at that. I then put in a call for the Gliddons at Chippenham. Mrs. G. came to the phone and was so surprised. She called Betty at once. She was so excited she could scarcely talk. However, she got her wits together and would not hear of anything but that I should go at once to Chippenham–a matter of an hour and a half by train. My first train out was at 7:15 p.m. but I couldn't get to Paddington Station to catch it, so had to take the next one at 8:05 which got me to Chips at 9:15. Betty and Arnold were there to meet me. And what do you think had happened? Betty had telephoned to Dorothea and her hubby and also to Olive and Douglas. They were all at Betty's home to meet us. What an evening we had! Gee, I would have given anything could you have been there! Helen, it seemed that no time had passed since I saw them last. They have all kept so well and youthful. Even Mrs. G. was just as I had seen her last. Arnold has aged a bit but looks much better than I could have expected.

Betty, Olive, Douglas & Dorothea are exactly as they ever were. We chatted until 1:20 a.m. at which time I had to leave to arrive back at London in time for my flight at 7 a.m. The only train to London that would put me back on time left Swindon at two a.m. So they (Betty and a neighbor) drove me to Swindon twenty miles east of Chippenham to catch the train. So here I am sitting in the West London Air Terminal waiting for the bus to take us to the airport twenty miles away. . . .

It was most delightful to see such happy friends. Dorothea's husband is a grand chap. My you will fall for him. They are so happy. Olive & Doug are very happy, Mr. Gliddon, who is 82, is as spry as ever and drives his car every day. What a man. He was so interested in everything last night. Mrs. G. doesn't hope to last until next Sept. and is quite upset at the thought of not seeing you. I assured her that she would. She thinks she will soon fail rapidly though admitted she never believed she would last this long.

There goes the announcer.

All my love
"Bill""

"Hotel Metropol Belgrade,
June 28th/58

My Dear Sweetheart,

Here I am set up in the Hotel Metropol, Belgrade. It is about 8 a.m. I'm just about ready for the day's activities, having had a shave and bath. There goes the telephone–Ziga is coming over to see me. I shall be very happy as I have seen no one yet whom I know well.

I arrived at Belgrade at 3:30 p.m. on the 27th. Mr. Marijan

Vivoda a young army captain, Vahia Koric, met me at the station (airport). We came to the hotel and settled in. Had tea and after a few hours' rest Vahid called for me and we took a leisurely stroll along one or two of the main streets of Belgrade, just to settle some of the food I had eaten during the past two days as everything I had eaten seemed to stay in my upper stomach for a lack of exercise. It is horrible to feel so stuffed. Sitting motionless in the plane for hours on end is no aid to digestion. However, this morning I feel a bet freer. I retired after a talk about the program with Vahid. . . .

For the next eight or ten days, I don't expect to be very free as I must fit into the arrangements which are always so necessary to keep things on schedule, but it is a bit of a bug-bear. . . .

It is pleasant to hear the peal of bells. They just started to chime, I suppose from some nearby church. From my hotel window, I can see a glimpse of water here and there over the roofs of three and four story buildings. The Sava or Danube cannot be far away. I see seven buildings under construction–two or three seem to be quite large and are already up to six and seven stories. Traffic is not heavy and a mixture of buses and small and few cars, horse-drawn vehicles, pedestrians. As the weather is warm, movement is leisurely. Men frequently stripped too the waist of their jackets with sleeves rolled up usually carrying something. Women and girls quite well dressed (very plain) also carrying bundles large and small. . . .

All my love, a big kiss for Bill.

Your Nurts"

"Metropol Hotel, Belgrade
July 2nd/58

My Dear Sweetheart,

I miss you terribly and would give anything if you were here –not long to wait now–twelve more days!

It has been a steady run of visitors calling at the hotel to see me or invitations out to see groups... Almost all officials are away now to Montenegro as the greatest celebrations in the history of this country will be held in the area of the rivers Piva, Tara, Sutjeska, in between which rivers is the high ground of the DURMITAR mountains. At this scene, Tito and his immediate forces, 19,000 men and women were practically surrounded by a force of 117,000 Germans, Italians and Ustasi & Bulgarians. From May 12th, 1943 to June 15th–the enemy tried to overcome and liquidate the Partisans but they made their escape by crossing the SUTJESKA river and then fanning out to the north. (Jones was in the country already when this occurred.)

Thousands are expected to go to that area by tomorrow morning, when the program will take over. Such as placing wreaths on war memorials, seeing Nassar, and visiting the scene of the river crossing. Then we (the visiting delegations) are to go to Dubrovnik for a day of bathing after which we shall be free. I shall then hie me to Ljubljana and Zagreb. Four five days at Ljubljana and two or three days at Zagreb. Then Ed Kardelj wants me to spend a day with him at Belgrade before I take off on the 15th. That should get me home on the 17th at the latest.

I have seen almost all old friends here in Belgrade and many new ones. Last night Deakin and John Henniker-Major arrived. I had supper with them and Vahid. Deakin is now head of one of the colleges as Oxford. . . .

All my love
Ever "Nurts""

It was Captain William Deakin who advised Churchill that he should consider looking into the loyalties of the Yugoslav Partisans which resulted in Jones' mission there.

Bill Jr. recalls one of his father's involvements: *"Right after the war he got together with one of the Partisans that he fought with, a Jewish Yugoslav–a brilliant brain and peace-loving man, and together with several others, formed a peace movement they called the International Forum for Peace. Conferences were held in different parts of the world, particularly in Europe and he went to these as often as possible. Delegates came from all over, including*

271

Africa.   This was a peaceful organization that later became incorporated, because of its similarity, into the United Nations. My Dad worked hard on this, though I was too young to really know just what he did."

People still remembered the man's exploits. In 1969, he was contacted by Pierre Berton to discuss a possible book.   An appointment was made but as Bill Jr. describes: *"Some emergency happened in Yugoslavia and Dad had to go.   He was in the diplomatic corps–a voluntary thing–but if called on, he went."* They never made a new appointment.

Bill Jr. recalls his father as having uncanny knowledge of the different factions in the west, aided and abetted by the American military. He knew all about the spy system and predicted exactly when Kennedy would be shot. His immediate comment was: "Shot by his own people." He seemed to have some inside knowledge about the Cuban missile crises in 1962. Everything was always so secretive and Bill Jr. and Helen only learned years later, that he really did know about these things though they never discovered his sources.

CHAPTER 51 – THE GRAND GARDEN PARTIES

The Joneses, invited a dozen Yugoslav friends for a barbeque on July 1, 1957. It was so much fun, the friends wondered if they could repeat the visit next year and bring some friends.

People began arriving from as far away as Toronto for the yearly event. Could they camp overnight? It became a weekend affair. People brought tents and trailers and eventually two 40-acre fields were filled with campers. A couple of rams and pigs were barbequed to help feed everyone, a stage was built, Yugoslavian dances were performed and songs sung. People swam in the river.

Bill Jones, master of ceremonies at the annual picnic at Belgrade Farms.
Photo courtesy of Bill Jones Jr.

The picnic developed a life of its own and Wellandport folks, not used to such huge influxes of cars, wondered what on earth those Yugoslavian communists were doing out at the Jones farm.

Came the day when police raided the picnic because they thought liquor was flowing too freely and the *Globe & Mail* made hay of the event. In a proper snit, Jonesy wrote his piece in reply defending events in Yugoslavia, the annual picnic and the liquor business.

Bill Jones Jr. recalls: *"Years ago, you didn't need a liquor permit and everybody brought their own. The police thought they had a case, but they didn't. Then the media made a big thing of it, but liquor was the reason, not anti-Canadian activities. Picnics were for people who were genuinely here as immigrants and interested in reconstructing their lives. Our immigration policy was to welcome them and Dad thought the cultural exchange a good thing. It was done with good intentions–but as it grew, there were security issues. People came who were dissidents and possibly there to cause unrest. We had to be aware that they might try to sabotage the event.*

"Many displaced persons from Yugoslavia, who were allowed to come here, had not been investigated because of our immigration system. They were hiding everywhere and were on the run. Some of them came to the picnics with the idea of disrupting them and causing friction. Occasionally fights broke out–maybe too much beer—though that didn't happen when Dad was alive. He held things together; he was a leading figure. After he was gone things were different and I didn't have the same ambitions towards it. I had to make a living.

"It wasn't just because of my father that 4,000 people came. Yugoslavs love to get together and barbeque on weekends but my father was certainly a drawing card and he enjoyed the weekends. It was a cultural thing. It's all part of his story."

It was such a newsworthy story, that Bill and Helen invited Marjorie McEnaney, a CBC journalist, to attend the next picnic. At the time she was part way through interviewing Bill about his war-

274

time activities for a radio program. She sent her regrets as a family visit intervened, and unfortunately the interviews were never completed.

The picnics continued for several years after Bill's death until Bill Jr. ended them due to the unstable political situation in Yugoslavia. Helen had become concerned to the point that she feared being there because of threats even though they had good security.

Several times, Bill heard a vehicle in their long lane at night and found someone just sitting there in the dark. Odd things happened. Things turned up missing.

They were particularly concerned when Marshall Tito made two-week stay in Canada. There were wide-spread protests. A delegation of 100 Serbs from all over Ontario demonstrated at Parliament Hill against Tito's communist regime as part of their desire for independence for Serbia and Croatia. A letter to Prime Minister Pierre Trudeau from the Royal Yugoslav Army Combatants Association said: "We realize that this protest and similar ones will fall up deaf ears, blind eyes and mute lips. But the spilled blood of beloved commander General (Draza) Mihailovich whose blood along with hundreds of thousands of our brothers soaked the width and breadth of Yugoslavia does not allow us to remain silent."

Different factions were working. In 1946, Mihailovich was convicted of war crimes in Belgrade, sentenced to be shot and his entire property confiscated. The sentence was carried out on July 18, 1946 in Lisiciji Potok, near the former Royal Palace, and he was buried in an unmarked grave.

The time came to end the picnics for good.

CHAPTER 52 - A REMARKABLE INVITATION

Bill extracted an envelope from his mailbox, exclaimed, "Embassy? Yugoslavia? Ottawa?"

Back in the kitchen, he and Helen found a letter on heavy, official note paper:

"EMBASSY of
The Socialist Federal Republic of
JUGOSLAVIA
In Ottawa

August 16, 1968

Major William Jones
Belgrade Farm, RR No. 2
Wellandport, Ontario

Dear Major Jones:

It gives me great pleasure to inform you that the President of the Socialist Federal Republic of Yugoslavia, Josip Broz Tito, has awarded you with the Yugoslav Decoration "Medal of Yugoslav Flag with Gold Wreath" for your very significant contribution to liberation struggle of the People of Yugoslavia in the Second World War and for your persistent, sincere and tireless efforts for development of friendly relations between people of Canada and Yugoslavia after the war.

Allow me, dear Major, to express to you my wholehearted congratulations and on this occasion also thank you for your noble activities.

Since the Canadian Government authorities concerned have

276

already approved your receiving the award, I would like to fulfill my pleasant duty and present you with this award. However, I would do it only after having talked with you and therefore, I shall be free to visit you towards the end of August or beginning of September.

To Mrs. Jones and you, my best regards,

Sincerely yours,
(signed) Dr. Tode Curuvija"

Bill and Helen were speechless, but he responded quite formally and sensibly:

"Dr. Tode Curuvija, Ambassador,
The Embassy of The Socialist Federal Republic of Yugoslavia
Ottawa

Dear Dr. Curuvija:

I am most grateful to you for your announcement of the award, "Medal of Yugoslav Flag with Golden Wreath," made to me by the President of the Socialist Federal Republic of Yugoslavia, Josip Broz Tito, accompanied by your personal congratulations and felicitations.

I assure you it is a great honour to me Mr. Ambassador, that my association with your countrymen during the 2nd World War should be so recognized. I have always considered the greatest experience of my life, excepting of course, my marriage, to be the year that I spent with the Yugoslav Partisans. I deemed that experience to be so profound and beneficial I was ever most grateful for having been privileged to be there. Any small part that I might have played was dwarfed to insignificance by the epic struggle made by your countrymen in their liberation. It has always been my cherished hope that the destinies of our peoples should run a common course in the betterment of human relations.

My wife Helen and my son Bill Jr. join me in all good wishes to you and your wife and family.

We anticipate your visit with much joy.

Sincerely,
"Bill Jones"

A few weeks later, the mailbox produced another envelope.

"Zagreb
September 9th, 1968
Predsjednik Sabora,
Major William Jones
Toronto.

Dear Sir:

This year is the twenty-fifth anniversary of the foundation of the Croatian Antifascist Council of National Liberation ZAVNOH. The date is an important landmark in the history of our people and will be commemorated at a special session of the Croatian Parliament on October 15, 1968.

On this occasion we remember the events and the people from the period of our struggle for freedom and democracy. We shall always remember that you were at the head of the first allied military mission with the Yugoslav People's Liberation Army, which arrived in this country on April 23rd, 1943, and that you personally attended the first meeting of our ZAVNOH.

It is with a feeling of deep gratitude that we cherish the memory of your stay with us and of the work that you then performed as a sincere friend of our people and a supporter of their armed struggle for national independence.

We know also that you have remained our friend until the present day and that you are continuing to develop friendship between our two peoples.

It is my great pleasure therefore to invite you to come to this country as our guest for the ZAVNOH anniversary celebrations, which will also give you an opportunity to refresh your wartime memories and to see again people and places that you remember from that time.

278

I would also like to use this opportunity to congratulate you most warmly on the high order conferred upon you by our President, Josip Broz Tito.

Hoping that we shall soon be able to welcome you among us again, I remain,

Yours faithfully,
(signed) "Jakov Blazevic"
Sabor Socijalisticke Republike Hrvatski"

A guest of the country! Well, they would certainly go! They remembered him 25 years later.

The Yugoslav Embassy in Ottawa issued the following press release on September 26, 1968:

"RE: Honouring of a Canadian, Major William Jones with the Yugoslav Decoration

The Canadian Veteran, member of the Imperial Black Watch, Major William Jones of Wellandport, Ontario, has been awarded the "Medal of Yugoslav Flag with Golden Wreath", by the President of the Socialist Federal Republic of Yugoslavia, Josip Broz Tito, on the occasion of the 25th anniversary of the founding of the Socialist Federal Republic of Yugoslavia.

This high honor is awarded to Major Jones as a mark of gratitude and recognition for his significant contribution to the liberation struggle of the people of Yugoslavia in the Second World War and his persistent, sincere and tireless efforts for the development of friendly relations between peoples of Canada and Yugoslavia after the war.

As the head of the First Allied Military Mission, Major William Jones, dropped by airplane on a moonlit night in the spring of 1943 in Yugoslavia and did admirable service in setting up contact between the Allied forces and the Yugoslav Partisans who had already for two years, in the heart of occupied Europe, far away from Allied Forces, with no one's help and recognition fought for the liberation of the country from Nazi Fascist occupiers.

. . . The ceremony of presentation will take place at the residence of the Yugoslav Ambassador, Dr. Tode Curuvija, 21 Blackburn Avenue, Ottawa, at 12:30 p.m., Monday, October 7, 1968. Following the ceremony, Major Jones, accompanied by his wife, will depart for Yugoslavia where he will attend the Jubilee Session of the Parliament of Socialist Republic of Croatia, one of the Yugoslav Republics. Twenty-five years ago, in the midst of a raging war, Major Jones attended the founding session of the Parliament."

A few days later he received a phone call and this confirmation from Bushnell TV Co. Limited/Channel 13/Channel 8:

"This will confirm our telephone conversation today about your appearance at our studio for a television interview when you are in Ottawa on Monday, October 7th.

I shall have a photographer at the Yugoslav Embassy for pictures of the decoration ceremony which will be incorporated with the interview when it is telecast. This will be on my program VENTURE, which is an hour-long magazine of the arts, science and current affairs, rather like the weekend supplement of a newspaper.

I shall expect you at CJOH-TV, 1500 Merivale Road, Ottawa 5 at 4:30 on Monday 7th. Our interview will be quite informal and unrehearsed, something about the decoration, and mostly about your experiences in Yugoslavia. It will last roughly 10 minutes. If by chance you have any pictures or slides of those days–which is unlikely–but if you have, we could use them—or film.

I look forward to meeting you next week.

Yours sincerely,
(Signed) "Ruth Johnson"

On Monday, October 7, 1968, Bill, Helen and Bill Jr. presented themselves at the Yugoslav Embassy in Ottawa where a formal reception was held. At 12:30 p.m., Dr. Ljubo Leontich, the Yugoslav Ambassador, announced that this was one of the greatest honors his country could bestow and it was awarded in gratitude for

280

the major's "impartial support and precious collaboration with the Yugoslav National Liberation Army as chief of the British military mission headquarters."

He presented Major William Morris Jones with this gold medal, the highest in this category, and citation which reads in part: "for your very significant contribution to liberation struggle of the People of Yugoslavia in the Second World War and for your persistent, sincere and timeless efforts for development of friendly relations between people of Canada and Yugoslavia after the war"."

Following the presentation Jones gave a thank you speech reiterating his admiration for the Yugoslav people and soon had his listeners wiping their tears. The kid from Digby, Nova Scotia had come a long way.

Designed by leading Yugoslav sculptor, August Inchich, the Medal of Yugoslav Flag with Gold Wreath has a bossed design of gold and silver with the Yugoslav flag in the middle from which radiate rays of gold and silver light.

Bill and Helen next hurried to the television interview, then caught the plane to Yugoslavia. Bill Jr. returned home with the medal and notes that his father never displayed it. He'd had enough of the horrors of war.

And if those newspaper articles didn't give Bill's neighbors plenty to talk about, they were undoubtedly awestruck that this somewhat unconventional farmer had accomplished all of this.

Bill and Helen visiting with Tito and his wife Jovanka at the Jubilee celebrations. (Note: Jovanka was a Partisan who held the rank of major in the Yugoslav People's Army.) This official photo was received by Jones from the "Office of the President of the Socialist Federal Republic of Yugoslavia with the compliments of the President's Office." Photo courtesy of Bill Jones Jr.

CHAPTER 53 – A MOST UNFORGETABLE MAN

On August 15, 1969, while working as hard as ever, Bill suddenly collapsed from a stroke

He was rushed to Dunnville hospital where he suffered three more strokes leaving him blind and paralyzed. Tenacious as ever, the "Lawrence of Yugoslavia", hung on for two long weeks, then went to his Maker on September 1, 1969.

Young Bill, 13 at the time, notes:

"The events leading to Dad's death are related to the injuries he sustained in World War I. He lost the left eye in the war from a piece of shrapnel and there was a lot of damage behind his right eye. When he had his stroke, the artery behind that eye had burst."

The funeral was held at the United Church in Wellandport and people arrived from far and wide. The Yugoslavian Ambassador to Canada gave a tribute:

"Dear Helen, dear young Bill, dear Canadian friends, at this sorrowful moment of farewell when we are putting to eternal rest Major William Jones, a thoughtful husband, gentle father, firm and persistent friend, allow me, as a representative of the Socialist Federal Republic of Yugoslavia to join you in this moment of grief and dolor, on behalf of the people of Yugoslavia. The news of the sudden death of Major Jones, the splendid Canadian veteran, member of the famous Imperial Black Watch, will echo sorrowfully in my country; for his personality and courage have been closely woven in the crucial days of the liberation struggle of the peoples of Yugoslavia.

"With a few moments of silence, with a tear in the eye, Yugoslav veterans will pause to pay tribute to this brave Canadian, first among the Allied officers to come to the mountains of Yugoslavia to fight shoulder to shoulder with Tito's Partisan Liberation Army against the fascist invaders. It was Major Jones who first boldly told the Western Allies the real and whole truth of the Yugoslav Partisans, of their glorious liberation struggle. It was Major Jones who thus opened the road towards better understanding, increased allied assistance and concerted joint struggle against the powers that had been trying to turn humanity back into the most obscure days of slavery. . . .

"Therefore, the legend of Major William Jones, holder of the Distinguished Conduct Medal and Bar, Order of Merit, Order of the Partisan Star, Order of the Yugoslav Flag with Golden Wreath, will live in my country as a legend of a towering honest man, who all his life stood upright. This legend of a warrior who yet was first and above all a man of peace, will live on and on and will serve as an inspiration to new generations. That is why Major William Jones will continue to live not only here with his wife Helen, his young son Bill and his friends in Canada, but also in far-away Yugoslavia, the country that he loved, the country which is so much indebted to him.

Thank you for all that you have done "Dear Bill". May you rest in peace and may your memory live forever."

Bill's old college mate, Dr. Frank Archibald commented: "There never was another quite like Bill Jones, the "Lawence of Yugoslavia."

The Yugoslav government requested the honor of erecting his grave marker at Riverside Cemetery which lies beside the Welland River in Wainfleet Township not far from Belgrade Farm.

Sadly the marker was later destroyed by vandals, the only one damaged at the time. Though no one was ever charged, Bill Jr. and his mother knew there were "other" factions from Yugoslavia in this country who might have perpetrated the desecration.

The monument was replaced by Canada's Department of Veterans' Affairs.

284

The William Jones grave marker placed by the Department of
Veterans' Affairs. Photo courtesy of Karen Rempel Arthur

Condolences poured in to Helen and young Bill and this
letter and accompanying tribute came from friends he had visited in
Portstratho, England in 1941.

A telling tribute from Nan and Chris Martin of Cornwall,
England, included Chris' personal tribute:

"A great character and a great man, and a very great friend of
mine over a long number of years. A man to lean on in emergency
and who had great strength mentally and physically. I can remember so many incidents I could almost write of them to fill a book.
He arrived in Kenogami P.Q. in 1924 unheralded but in a very short
time had made an impact on many, many lives which they will

remember for life. I can remember him entering the dining room of the King George Hotel, a powerful figure, not tall but thick shoulders and going like a C.P.R. train of those days full of steam and all eyes were turned on him, he was a magnetic personality.

In a few short weeks he had a "Cub" pack formed and in 1925 we had our first Scout and Cub camp at Lac St. Jean. Memories of this camp include Bill eating blueberry pie and pork and beans all off the same plate saying its gets mixed up anyway. Again throwing a handful of coffee into a can and making the finest coffee I have ever tasted. That was his way, he excelled in whatever he did. His was a dominant personality, you felt his presence and when he said something, you remembered it, such was his way. We circled Lac St. Jean, Quebec, by canoe in 1926 and what an experience this was, he taught me more in the week of camping than I ever knew was possible. I can think of him sitting over the front of the canoe getting shaved or 'dolled up' as he called it to have a civilized meal at Island House on the Lake, a house owned by Price Brothers for their employees, the next night we were almost eaten alive by the largest mosquitoes and black flies I have ever seen. I was nearly crazy but Bill imperturbable as usual swatting one and saying that's a big one Chris. He really was a wonderful companion. We visited the 'Péribonka' & the 'Mistassibi' Rivers and 'Pointe-Bleue' the Indian reservation and were made very welcome and Chief Carter of the Indian reserve and Bill had so much in common, the chief being an ex-army man.

Bill left Kenogami in 1926, I think and settled in Toronto. We did not see him again until 1929 when we were in that city and again in 1930.

In 1934, Nan and I returned to England and in 1939 we had a letter from Bill asking if I could help him get a job in the docks in Plymouth. I could not help, but that did not stop him and he badgered the authorities until they put him in Air Force uniform and he did some of his training at Torquay. In 1941 or '42 we met him at a little fishing village in Cornwall named Porthstratho and the next we hear of him was he had been seconded to the army and after some time had elapsed we heard he was with the resistance in Yugoslavia. What an exciting and interesting life he had. We both
286

hope very sincerely that someone can gather some of the threads of this wonderful life. The whole story can never be told but so much of it that is known would be worth recording and it must make all of us who have known him and come under his influence so proud to have had this great privilege of knowing a very great Canadian gentleman.

Some of the greatness of this man, Bill Jones, must surely have been his physical condition. I can see him now picking up a log from the lakeshore and carrying it up the beach which 2 or 3 normal men would have found difficult and how apparently tireless he was in a canoe, seemingly able to paddle on and on. We shall always remember him with great love and affection and if any of my words can be recorded as a tribute to a memory, I shall never forget. I shall be very proud to have been associated in some small way to A MOST UNFORGETABLE MAN."

Major William Jones has been memorialized, along with other courageous Canadians who fought in these terrible wars, at The Canadian Hall of Valour—Temple Du Courage located in Ottawa, Ontario.

EPILOGUE

A Strange Little Story

This strange little tale was related the author by Joe Maloney, now of Yarmouth, Nova Scotia, the downed airman whose story appears earlier in this book.

"On May 31, 2007 my wife and I were returning from a walk. There was a man in our front yard looking for information on Major Jones and he was told to see me. He had a priest`s collar and a Santa Claus beard, was well dressed and very polite. We invited him in and he gave us a contact address, phone number and email address in Bear River.

"I gave him what information I could easily reach and told him I would look for more. I wrote to him a short time later but he never answered.

"I checked with the local Catholic priest to see if he knew of him as I had concerns. One priest thought perhaps Father Innocent was a Russian Orthodox priest from St. John, New Brunswick. Father Innocent also gave me the address of Bethany Place, and Anglican house of prayer and hospitality in Digby, Nova Scotia and said he knew the major's sisters. Maloney contacted Bethany Place but they had never heard of him.

How very strange. Who was this stranger parading as a priest? One wonders.

One wonders just what secrets Major Jones took to his grave and those niggling questions will always remain.

William Morris Jones (1895 – 1969)
Photo courtesy of Bill Jones Jr.

NOTES FROM THE AUTHOR

Major William Jones died before his World War II exploits were declassified. Thus, two and two have been added together hopefully arriving at four. Yet there will always remain deep mystery about the man. There are gaps in his life that we know nothing of.

This is such a multi-facetted story made up of the bits and pieces of dozens of sources ranging from the internet, the Royal Black Watch Regiment in Montreal who kindly answered my request for information, the boxes and boxes of newspaper clippings, letters, speeches etc. carefully squirreled away by Helen Jones and supplied to me by Bill Jones Jr., an incomplete taped CBC radio interview of Bill Jones (Imagine, I could listen to his actual voice.) wherein he spoke of many events, conversations with Bill Jones Jr. and other individuals who knew him. Particular thanks go to Joe Maloney of Nova Scotia who spent hours on the phone telling me the story of the long walk to Drvar and his personal experiences with Bill Jones. His documents were invaluable.

After months of sorting, organizing, research, especially into the details of two world wars, note making and time-line development, the grand picture emerged of this most fascinating man.

I wish I had known him personally.

Made in the USA
Charleston, SC
25 November 2013